DON'T MIND IF I DO

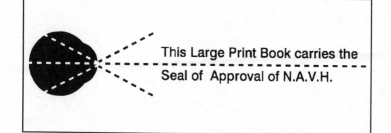

DON'T MIND IF I DO

GEORGE HAMILTON

AND WILLIAM STADIEM

THORNDIKE PRESS
A part of Gale, Cengage Learning

Detroit • New York • San Francisco • New Haven, Conn • Waterville, Maine • London

GALE
CENGAGE Learning™

LIBRARY OF CONGRESS CATALOGING-IN-PUBLICATION DATA

Hamilton, George, 1939–
 Don't mind if I do / by George Hamilton and William Stadiem.
  p. cm.
 ISBN-13: 978-1-4104-1083-2 (hardcover : alk. paper)
 ISBN-10: 1-4104-1083-8 (hardcover : alk. paper)
  1. Hamilton, George, 1939– 2. Motion picture actors and
actresses — United States — Biography. 3. Large type books.
 I. Stadiem, William. II. Title.
 PN2287.H178A3 2008b
 791.4302'8092 — dc22
 [B]
                                                                2008038118

Published in 2008 in arrangement with Simon & Schuster, Inc.

Printed in the United States of America
1 2 3 4 5 6 7 12 11 10 09 08

Remarkable challenges have made you
a remarkable man.
To my son Ashley, who has
made me proud.

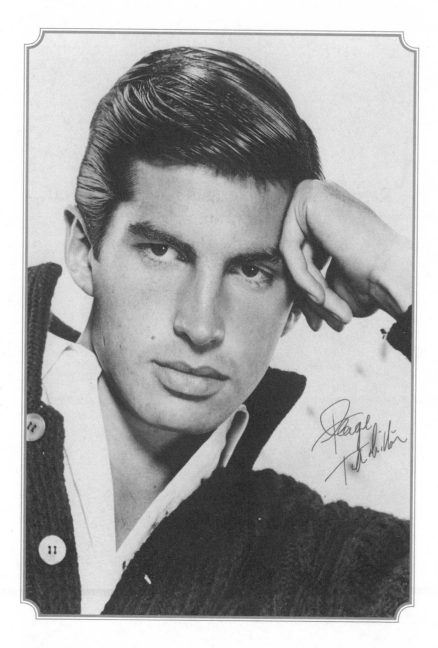

CONTENTS

January 14, 1958

Ben Thau
The Thalberg Building
MGM Studios
Culver City, California

Dear Ben,

Here is my follow up report on the test we did on George Hamilton. Mr. Hamilton is represented by agent Hy Sigal of the Mitchell Gertz Agency.

Mr. Hamilton is a sophisticated, self-assured young man of nineteen and certainly handsome enough to be a motion picture actor, but in my estimation possesses little else. His ability to act is marginal, but perhaps might improve with coaching. Mr. Hamilton attempted to sing a French song: "La Vie En Rose", but forgot the words. We did not offer him the opportunity to show us his dancing ability.

I question how devoted he is to the acting craft and not just on a lark. The head shots Mr. Hamilton presented have a 'dated look' better suited to the silent screen than today's post James Dean era, which leads me to believe that this young man has arrived in Hollywood thirty years too late. Frankly, his ideas of what our modern movie industry finds appealing forced me to stifle a laugh.

In summary, there is something there but I don't know what. I would advise that we not offer him a contract at this time. Of course, ultimately the decision is yours. If we were to use him at all I would suggest he could play a Latin, an Indian, a juvenile sidekick or possibly be featured in one of our period pieces. I would rule out comedies.

Sincerely,

Al

8

CHAPTER ONE
DESPERATE TIMES DEMAND
DESPERATE MEASURES

My life was a train wreck.

I had torn the rotator cuffs in my shoulders. This was a result of years of rehearsing for movies like *Zorro, the Gay Blade,* where twelve hours of fencing lessons one day, followed by twelve hours of bullwhip practice the next, had caused my shoulders to be stuck in the ten o'clock and two o'clock positions, in a sort of hideous, contorted version of Al Jolson in *Mammy.*

To make matters worse, I had blown out my knee in the Broadway musical *Chicago* when the young actress playing the dummy to my ventriloquist became too energetic and bounced so hard on my knee that I felt my right joint explode on the spot. The doctor later confirmed that part of the cartilage had shredded, making it temporarily impossible for me to walk. So much for the old razzle-dazzle. Even worse, not long afterward, in a bad parody of Errol Flynn in *Captain Blood,*

I had broken four ribs jumping aboard a friend's yacht. Plus, there was the little matter of my balance problem . . .

And that was the good news.

In the midst of my assorted agonies, my agent called me up. He seemed to call me only when three little old ladies in a nursing home needed entertainment. But this time, opportunity, big-time, he said, was pounding at my hospital door. My agent's chance of a lifetime was for me to be a contestant on *Dancing with the Stars,* the reality dance-off show pairing celebrities with professional dancers, recently imported from England by ABC. In its first season, in the summer of 2005, *Dancing* had been the number one show in the country, with more than fifteen million viewers.

My first response at hearing the offer was to laugh so hard that I nearly broke another rib. Well . . . well? the agent pressed me. Wasn't I thrilled? Wasn't I interested?

Sure, I thought. If we can find a dance where seizing up, screaming in pain, and dropping to my one decent knee was part of the routine.

"It's a great career move," the agent said, falling back on the ultimate showbiz cliché.

"The Bataan Death March had a better

chance of having a happy outcome," I replied.

"Millions of people will be watching," he said, giving me the hard sell.

"That could be a problem," I replied.

The agent sold and sold, puffing about how big the show had been in the UK and now here. What stars had been on the first season? I asked. He hemmed and hawed. Evander Holyfield, he said. The boxer. The champ. The guy whose ear Mike Tyson bit off. Trista Sutter. Who was that? I asked. Big star of *The Bachelor* reality show. Huge, he said. A star? Stars were different when I first started in the game. Who else? Kelly Monaco, the season's winner. Major soap opera star, major *Playboy* model. Who else? Rachel Hunter.

Rachel Hunter? Now, he was talking. Rachel, the supermodel, had been married to Rod Stewart, just like my ex, Alana, the supermodel. Rod and I, who on the surface seemed to have nothing in common, did share a seemingly identical taste in women. Before Alana, we had both been involved with Swedish bombshell Britt Ekland, and after Alana, we both dated the beauty Liz Treadwell. At least I always came first. In any event, in my Six Degrees of Rod Stewart game, the mention of Rachel Hunter made me feel that perhaps destiny was at work here.

"Good career move?" I sought the agent's assurance. It would be huge exposure, I mused. It was better than having folks continue to confuse me with Warren Beatty or, worse, forget me altogether. I had begun to get those people coming up to me and saying, "I know you. I know you."

And I would prod, "George Hamilton?"

"No, no, not him," they would reply. "What show'd you play on?" they would continue.

After I had rolled off half a dozen titles or so, they still had a blank look. Somehow the excitement disappeared when I had to give them clues.

At this point, I think it's important you know something about me. I have never been good at planning. You might say I hate plans. They take all the fun out of living. In my family, we liked to do the dumbest thing possible just to lessen the chances for success, and then work our way out of it. What is life without challenges? That's how we lived. So *Dancing with the Stars* was really no leap of faith. I knew I would heal. I knew I could pull it off. I didn't know exactly *how* right then, but I knew I could do it. "God watches after us," my mother had always assured us, and I believe that, too.

So I limped, hobbled, and dragged my disapproving body onto a plane and made my way from Florida, where I was recuperating, to Los Angeles — to Studio 46 in CBS Television City in Hollywood, with rehearsals already under way for a show that still had a few bugs to work out.

It was a scene of only slightly organized chaos. The costume designer was showing off sequin-bedecked numbers to doubting executives, while makeup artists were practicing their art on their reluctant celebrity captives. In the midst of all this, the network people were quarreling over musical arrangements. I could see they were all as ill prepared for what lay ahead as I was, and somehow this was consoling.

I met the other stars, my rivals for the mirror-ball trophy they gave the winner after eight weeks of dips and splits and twirls and whirls. There was no money involved, but stars were supposedly way beyond money. Publicity would be its own reward. This being network television, there was someone for every demographic, all here meeting and greeting, smiling, and trying to get a handle on one another: Oscar winner Tatum O'Neal; football legend Jerry Rice; Bond girl Tia Carrere; *Melrose Place* stunner Lisa

Rinna; sports anchor Kenny Mayne; news anchor Giselle Fernandez; rapper Master P; singer Drew Lachey; wrestler Stacy Keibler; and yours truly. I guess I was there to cater to the geezer demographic. At sixty-six, I was the oldest contestant by way too many decades. At my age, I wondered, shouldn't I have been at the Kennedy Center getting a medal instead of making a fool out of myself? Who did I think I was, a poster boy for AARP? On the other hand, it made me feel so young, while the Kennedy Center would make me feel like I was out to pasture.

One island of sanity in this sea of confusion was the host of the show, Tom Bergeron, the ex-host of *Hollywood Squares*. Ably assisted by cohost and E! reporter Samantha Harris, Tom was enormously capable and very funny. No one was better with a one-liner. He could always find something witty to say to cover someone's flub or to smooth out an embarrassing moment. This easy gift of his proved valuable time after time during the show.

My assigned partner was soon introduced to me. Her name was Edyta Sliwinska (pronounced EH-di-tuh), and she was so striking that I knew the only way I could upset this woman would be if I got between her and her mirror. For all her ravishing beauty,

Edyta still inspired confidence. After all, she had been partnered with Evander Holyfield the previous season and had stayed in the ring with him. She was tall and powerful. From the moment I met her I knew that I was in good hands. "Not to worry, little prince . . ." she fired off in an intoxicating Polish accent. While she had the sinuous body of a showgirl, she had the rock-solid personality of an ironworker. I quickly made a two-hour film in my head featuring Edyta driving a team of mules across the Polish countryside, while fighting off invading Mongol warriors, then — and only then — taking time to self-deliver her baby in the field.

For every complaint I had about my diminished performance capabilities, Edyta had a ready answer. "Because of my broken ribs, I have a little dip and twirl problem," I malingered.

"I can dip and twirl myself, no one will ever know the difference," she assured me with only the slightest touch of narcissism. Finally, a woman who's a self-starter! This was heaven. Mom was right. God is truly good.

For such a blockbuster, I was a little surprised by the show's skimpy operating budget. I guess I had been spoiled by my Hollywood studio days, when the red carpet was rolled out everywhere you turned. This was going to be strictly tourist class. No champagne and caviar on this trip — only the ubiquitous bottle of Evian water — if you were lucky enough to be tossed one.

Little did I know that the first part of the competition would be vying with other contestants for a rehearsal hall. Naturally, some halls were better than others. One had a leaky roof, another had been recently refitted and still had wet varnish on the floor, and most of them smelled like a Gold's Gym. They all seemed to have one feature in common: a wall of fame sporting framed eight-by-ten glossies of everyone from long-forgotten movie hoofers to the hottest new boy bands to the latest hip-hop gangstas. They were a visual reminder of how fleeting fame can be.

From one day to the next, we never knew where we were going, since these halls were rented for only a few hours each day. On more than one occasion we had to wind up our session quickly to make way for an incoming children's ballet class or the like. Eventually, the Arthur Murray Dance Studio in Beverly Hills came to my rescue by offering up their state-of-the-art facility. Did I mention that things have a way of working out for me?

The competitiveness in me was ratcheted up a notch when I spotted some of my competition. The clear favorite in my eyes was Drew Lachey, from the boy band 98 Degrees, which apparently did a lot of fancy Chuck Berry-ish moves. Plus, Drew had starred on Broadway in the musical *Rent*. Yeah, I starred in *Chicago,* but it cost me a knee. Drew was the brother and bandmate of Nick Lachey — the then husband of Jessica Simpson and half of the Robert Wagner and Natalie Wood of modern Hollywood coupledom. In short, Drew was big man on campus here in Television City. He ambled over to greet me. He had the tight, confident walk of a bulldog, with all the same assurance. Teamed up in the competition with a ravishing Filipino/Irish/Russian dancer named Cheryl Burke, he was thirty-seven years younger than I was, incredibly agile, with ripped muscles. I could barely believe it when in rehearsal he leaped catlike high above his partner's head and landed on both knees, skidding to a halt with a perfect smile on his face. I could only imagine the collateral damage I would cause if I tried a stunt like that. I needed a plan.

Of course, I knew the rudiments of dance. The deRhams' society-dancing class in New

York City where Mom had enrolled me, kicking and screaming, had taught me something. "Now, gentlemen," the elderly owner Willie deRham would intone in his bored voice, "grasp your young lady's right hand in your left hand and then close your hand as if you were wrapping it around a rose petal.

"No, no, Mr. Hamilton, your posture is all wrong. Hold your partner firmly. Lift your arms. Higher. Higher!" Instantly furious at me for not being able to capture the picture-perfect position he held in his mind, he decided I should instead dance with a piece of furniture. "I do not believe you are ready yet to dance with a young lady. So for the rest of your lesson your partner will be that chair." He pointed to a folding chair in the corner.

"Pick it up, Mr. Hamilton, now one . . . two . . . three . . . one . . . two . . . three . . . step, step, step . . . if you do this well, I may let you dance with a shotgun."

Years later, when I was a young man in Florida, one of my first jobs was giving lessons in a Palm Beach dance school. Before you think I somehow had an unfair advantage over the other candidates for the job, you should know that I survived in this brief employment only by staying one step ahead (literally) of my students. You see, I didn't really need to know how to dance. All I had to do was learn a new step each day and then teach it to my clients.

Each morning the head salesman/instructor would come in and remind us of our duties. "Remember, instructors," he would say, "these are married women, unmarried women, lonely women, desperate women, and mainly widows with lots of money with nowhere to go." Then he went on to explain that their idea of a social life was for all thirty couples from the school to go out together once a week, have a little veal piccata and a light wine, and then to start off with the same dance step in the same direction on the same downbeat. It was hideous.

"Now, Mr. Hamilton, today you will have Mrs. Bluestein, Mrs. Goldman, Mrs. Kelly, and Mrs. Coronio. Let me caution you, Mr. Hamilton, Mrs. Coronio is handicapped, so she will be in a wheelchair. Your job will be, on beat, to spin her wheelchair in the direction she wants to go. She will have the same feeling as if she were dancing, that's all she expects." Later, I did my best to accommodate by urging Mrs. Coronio to "put a little more snap in your wheelchair."

Also, during the lessons, we were advised to wear our watches with the face on the inside of our wrist so that near the close of our hour we could sneak a look at it and say,

19

"Oh, I'm so sorry, our time is about up. But if you were a lifetime member of our school, you wouldn't have to worry about time; you could dance for as long as you like." That's the way we sold lifetime memberships. But now I had much bigger problems than pitching lifetime memberships to willing widows. This time I had to *really* learn to dance and do it pronto.

The other theoretical leg up this geezer had was that my father had been a bandleader in the Benny Goodman/Tommy Dorsey era. I may not have known the dances, but I did know the music, from "Begin the Beguine" to "Chattanooga Choo Choo." Of course this was all useless now. The dance music they used on the show sounded straight from *American Idol,* and I had never heard any of it. To me, their jazzed-up versions barely resembled the classic dances they were supposed to accompany. I wanted music that could go with a more traditional fox-trot, tango, or cha-cha. I pleaded uncoolness, and my humility paid off; the producers allowed me to dispense with certain numbers they had picked for me in favor of a few of my own selections. Musical director Harold Wheeler went along.

Each day, Edyta and I would meet in the rehearsal hall to plan, and eventually execute, the great dance resurrection of yours truly. And each day Edyta would arrive right on schedule, wearing her usual warm-ups. It was what was underneath that was always a pleasant surprise. As the rehearsals progressed she wore less and less. Always the romantic — and in hopes I could charm her out of rehearsing for a couple of hours — I would stop off at the bakery on my way and pick up a lavish pastry. Anything to delay having to dance! Couldn't I just talk, or simply stand there and be adored? I quickly learned that thanks to her unbelievable metabolism and the incredible number of hours she spent dancing each day, Edyta could literally eat a horse (preferably a Polish Arabian) and not gain an ounce. My daily food delivery then burgeoned into huge potato dishes and whole loaves of bread, even a giant Polish sausage. You may think I was trying to seduce her. Actually, subconsciously I was probably hoping she would get too obese to dance and I could get out of the whole damn thing.

Soon, miraculously soon, Edyta began to deliver on her promise to make me look good despite my infirmities. She specialized in teaching dance to children. Even if this big old baby was not made to order for her skills, I was a prime candidate for her second specialty: camouflage. All I would have to do is move my arm to the side and Edyta would twirl like a dervish in any direction I wanted her to. She could also bend over backward and raise herself back up without help. If I simply placed my hand behind her back, it looked as if I was doing all the heavy lifting. Maybe there really was a way to snatch victory from the jaws of defeat, I began to believe. For fellow narcissists, this was like having great sex without messing up your hair.

Yet for all my emerging confidence, my mind kept planning escapes from the day of retribution that lay ahead. Some well-timed ipecac could make me imitate all the symptoms of a pandemic flu. That bay window in the rehearsal hall looked good — maybe if I ran crashing through it and somehow managed to survive, they would take pity on me and let me go. Or perhaps I could drive into a center divider and do sufficient injury to myself to escape the whole ordeal . . . I could see the headlines now: "George Hamilton, Oldest Contestant, Favored to Win 'Dancing with the Stars,' Dies of Punctured Lung from Broken Ribs Sustained While En Route to Big Win."

The Hamilton mind was at its best planning getaways — especially when faced with the prospect of humiliating yourself in front of an anticipated 25 million people in prime time (eight P.M. eastern time, seven central). Saddam Hussein, hiding in a hole in Iraq, wouldn't take those odds. Sometimes when you place your fate in the hands of destiny and your spirit calls, "Once more unto the breach, dear friends, once more; / or close the wall up with our English dead" (whatever that means), the god of wild abandon takes over. You totally let go and say, "What am I worried about? Forget about it. If everything goes south, I can always move to a small country (of twenty-five million or less) where they will never find me." Once you pass that point, a sudden sense of relief sweeps over you that resembles what the condemned prisoner must feel when he utters his final words: "Let's just get this over with." Then, and only then, do you experience real freedom from fear and get ready for the wild ride and out-of-body experience that lies ahead.

Another point you should know is that I've never been good at rehearsal. In my book, there's no substitute for the real thing. If I'm going to do something, I'm going to do it once and I'm going to do it right the first time. Evel Knievel taught me this lesson: If you're going to be a daredevil, don't practice too much. It's too dangerous.

Nevertheless, I did my best. Weeks of rehearsal, aided by my chiropractor and a sadistic sports doctor who made me do squats and lifts to strengthen my knee, sharpened my performance. But I never kidded myself. Drew Lachey, the boy-band icon who had far greater dancing skills than I could dream of, was going to win this — no question. All I wanted was not to be kicked off after my first dance.

Finally, in chilly January 2006, came the moment I had dreaded for so long, the moment of truth . . . or consequences. Edyta and I were number three in the lineup. You could hear the furious roar of hair dryers in the makeup room. Voices began to sound nervous while some contestants tried to feign nonchalance. "Oh yeah, I'm ready," Jerry Rice mentioned casually. "Sure, no sweat. I hurt a little bit, but I iced it." I could imagine him making that same statement at the beginning of a hundred pro football games where he was asked to play through the pain.

In quick order I'm called into the makeup room, where I go over and over my routine in my head. My chiropractor arrives to do a quick neck adjustment. I don all the accoutrements necessary to shore up my knee (leg brace, orthotics, support hose). For a moment I feel like a geriatric gladiator preparing to enter the arena. The finishing touches . . . well, maybe I could use another sip or two of Red Bull and a quick double shooter from Starbucks. Yes, that's better. That'll level the playing field with these twenty-year-olds. I'm ready. As I leave the makeup room, Randall, the costume designer, is rushing handkerchiefs to the female dancers, a few of whom are receiving the full-body-makeup treatment. If only I could linger a little. Too bad I have such a pressing appointment.

Then comes the announcement that we are going live in twenty-eight seconds. "What? What is that?" More Red Bull. A little face powder. Where's Edyta? There she is, completely ready and not a hair out of place. "And now, ladies and gentlemen . . . Mr. George Hamilton and his partner, Edyta Sliwinska dancing the cha-cha." The music starts. Edyta smiles at me and grabs my hand, and I start down the stairs with her, trying to summon all the spring of Fred Astaire in his prime. When I feel the warmth of the lights, I flash the smile I had learned to use to cover all my fears. Adrenaline, testosterone, whatever it is, begins kicking in, and I remember thinking to myself that no matter how bad I am, they can't kill me. I can barely hear the opening music for the drumbeat of excitement booming in my ears. Suddenly things are working that haven't worked before. My legs move with surprising assurance. My arms come up, no problem. I even manage to trail my arm behind me in that effete fashion the judges so favor. The dance that I expected to last an eternity was over in a flash. Last cha-cha in Hollywood? Maybe not.

The three judges were unexpectedly generous. "Geooorge! The master showman . . . so smooth, so debonair . . ." Bruno Tonioli effused. The Ferrara-born Bruno had been an Elton John video dancer and a judge on the British version of the show. Len Goodman, who ran a ballroom-dancing school in Kent, had also been a judge on the British show. Len was equally encouraging, though he cautioned that I should watch the frame; that was what dancing was all about. Carrie Ann Inaba, a Hawaiian singer and backup dancer who attended Barack Obama's prep school in Honolulu, almost seemed to be flirting with me. In the end, however, she confirmed Len's criticism, and gave me a 7 (out of 10) to Bruno's and Len's 8s. It stung, being judged like that by the woman who played Fook Yu in *Austin Powers in Gold-*

member. But, in the end, 23 was a pretty great score for a big faker like me.

Somehow, though, I felt that I looked a little plastic dancing with Edyta. No matter how clever we were with our moves, it was still pretty transparent that she was practically dancing her way into a coma while I was finishing without breaking a sweat. It was a cheat and everyone would know it. So I went into full damage control. Partly to come clean and partly to enlist sympathy, I told the world on camera in the interdance interview sequence that I was struggling against my various physical challenges.

Off camera, I told Edyta that the rules were about to change. I was never going to outperform the better dancers with my footwork. I would have to dazzle them with my showmanship. So from then on, I crafted an approximately two-minute mini-motion picture for every dance number we were in. Borrow from the great Fred Astaire? Don't mind if I do. A touch of Cary Grant? That's okay with me. How about a dash of Gene Kelly? Bruno, the effusive judge, called me the ultimate showman . . . the great trickster. Whatever it was, whomever I lifted from, the ends justified the means. As each week went by, others were voted off, but I remained in the race. Seabiscuit was round-ing the first lap and then the second and the third . . . the finish line was still far off, but if I didn't break down or throw a shoe, there was a chance, albeit a tiny one.

It was about this time that I met one of the most beautiful women I had ever seen, and I've seen a few. Stacy Keibler was a well-known lady wrestler who exploded the old stereotype to smithereens. Stacy was no fuzzy-lipped behemoth gladiator but a swan, a ballet dancer, a statuesque modern goddess with forty-two-inch legs, the greatest I had witnessed since I had costarred with Cyd Charisse back in the Pleistocene era. Judge Bruno called Stacy "a weapon of mass seduction." The first time I saw her lift one of her gorgeous gams above her partner's shoulder, the whole objective of my involvement in *Dancing with the Stars* shifted. It was as if the world had done a sudden bounce in its orbit, blowing houses and factories off their foundations. From then on I didn't care if I won or even showed well. All I wanted was Stacy.

It didn't hurt that at the time I met her, to save my failing knee, the chiropractor had suggested I see a doctor about getting steroids — you know, the performance-enhancing drugs that have damaged so many famous athletes' careers. This I did, and, aided by

DEPO Testosterone (aka 'roids), I felt like a twenty-year-old again. Snorting, flaring my nostrils, and pawing the ground, I was ready for action. The tight bodies and skimpy costumes of the female dancers began to work a new magic on me. It was as if my evil twin, Mr. Hyde, had taken over my body. I even imagined myself jealous of Stacy's dance partner, the happily married Tony Dovolani, when he had his arms around her.

As I began flirting outrageously with this gorgeous swan, the audience, whose call-in votes were as crucial to winning as the judges' scores, became more and more involved in my joke. They loved it when I convinced a local Beverly Hills jeweler, Yossi, to lend me a seventeen-carat diamond ring and I slipped it temptingly on Stacy's finger during her interview. I told her it was the Hamilton diamond and that it came with a curse, Mr. Hamilton. I enjoyed the hopeless pursuit, but I'm not sure Stacy's young actor boyfriend found the whole thing very amusing. Thank goodness he wasn't a wrestler, too.

This new diversion, obsession, or whatever it was, was, in the end, no real help to my original, nonamorous goal of staying on the show. Poor Edyta, who had done everything but carry me onstage, was now paying the price for teaming up with me. We quickly sank to one of the two couples eligible for elimination each week. There at the bottom, I found fellowship with Master P, a hip-hop star whose son, Lil' Romeo, had originally been scheduled to appear on the show but had dropped out, leaving Big Daddy to step up and in. Master P refused to rehearse at all and would wing it each performance, often with disastrous results. I loved the guy, the way misery loves company.

Commenting on his total scores, which ran from 8 to 14, he told me, "Aw, George, I don't care. I'm going home to my fifteen-million-dollar crib. How many people here you think have a fifteen-million-dollar crib?" On his weekly postdance interview, Master P rationalized poor performance by saying that it was all about his doing it for his "hood." I picked up on that and when I had my interview, I chimed in that I was also doing it for my hoods: Palm Beach and Beverly Hills. Master P quickly confirmed, "Me and George are doing it for our hoods." I was down with my homey. We became the best of buddies.

Eventually, though, no matter how Edyta propped me up, and no matter how many rabbits I pulled out of the hat, Edyta and I were eliminated from the contest. We had lasted a very respectable six weeks and placed fifth out of the ten original contestants. Not bad for a bandaged, kneecapped, and distractedly lecherous geezer. I can't say I was sorry. A montage of memories flashed across my mind, like the time the seamstress insisted I have butt pads sewn into my costume to add some booty, the way Lisa Rinna became obsessed with dancing and pulled her whole family in, and how Tatum O'Neal parlayed the show into a job on *Entertainment Tonight*. Edyta ended up marrying her dancer boyfriend, and Stacy never gave me more than an air kiss. So much for the supposedly irresistible charms of the aging roué. Sure, the Marlon Brando character in me from *On the Waterfront* would continue to bemoan that "I could've been a contender." This applied equally to *Dancing with the Stars* as to Stacy Keibler.

But thanks to the magic of testosterone, I had my summer of 1956 once more. My aches and pains vanished. I could be as age-inappropriate as Mick Jagger and get away with it. It was exhausting, but, jeez, it was great to be young again, to beat the clock, even if it was for only a few weeks. And better yet, I had spawned a whole set of younger fans, including cabdrivers, truck drivers, and students who now appreciated this rediscovered silver fox. They would shoot me the thumbs-up sign wherever I went. This happened for weeks, months after I left the show. Sometimes everybody would applaud when I entered a restaurant.

Performance snobs might say it was a little tacky, yet by risking everything I had learned a lot about myself . . . and I liked it. Funny how you can meet yourself in the damnedest places. The following year I heard that judge Len Goodman had told Jerry Springer he was no George Hamilton. As Master P would say, "Yo, dog, I'm down with that."

Chapter Two
Lovely While It Lasted

Despite what Louis B. Mayer may have thought, movie stars are born as well as made. For you to understand me, and for me to try to understand myself, if that's ever possible, it's important to know where I was born and what I was born into. The where was the small Southern town of Blytheville, Arkansas, which was as un-Hollywood a place as exists and serves to show that I've come a long way, baby.

My mother, Anne (aka "Teeny," a name I'll explain shortly), was incredibly beautiful, a real charmer, the ultimate Southern belle, irresistible to men, and able to pull rabbits out of hats. Her motto should have been: There's nothing incredible about miracles. She was a Virgo, organized and precise. For instance, she had an idealized picture in her mind of what a man should look like and was very particular about his dress, big on shoes and socks. If a man had the wrong shoes, strikes one, two, three — he was outta there. By the time I was born in 1939, Mom had scratched more men off her list than a major league baseball talent scout.

Then there was Bill, my half brother from Mom's first marriage to a Wall Streeter named Bill Potter in New York. Nine years older than I, Bill was the evil genius in our family, handsome as a god, clever as hell, talented, a born leader, our surrogate father when the real one wasn't there. But Bill was by no means your standard *Father Knows Best* sort of guy. Bill's idea of a fun kids' game was for him and his best friend to dress up in my mom's clothes, complete with heels and purse, and stand on the hassock in our living room pretending to be proper ladies waiting for the bus. The hassock was supposed to be the curb. When the pretend bus would arrive, they'd jump down with a lot of girlish *woo-hoos* and act out bustling aboard. Bill wanted me to come along and play the role of their kid. I told him I had a pressing engagement elsewhere.

Bill's boyhood obsession was the blond bombshell Betty Grable (of World War II pinup fame). You might think he had a crush on her. Wrong. He wanted to *be* her. He liked to compare his own legs with hers, which had been insured by Lloyds of London for a cool million dollars. (My mother had great gams, too.) Even before the "waiting for the bus" episode, I got the idea that Bill had some sexual identity issues when I stumbled onto a trunk full of dolls that he kept in the attic. The Davy Crockett and Charlie McCarthy dolls were okay, but I had difficulty coming to grips with the girl dolls with blond hair and wearing skirts. There were dozens of them. Jeez, I thought, he plays army with some pretty weird soldiers.

Then there was my brother David, thirteen months younger than I. I think they call that being Irish twins. But we were worlds apart in every way. I plunged into life and David tiptoed. But we worked well together in most matters. I just had to watch out for his terrible temper. When he was little, Mom slapped him across the face right in the middle of one of his tantrums. They might call that child abuse today, but I believe it did some good. It shocked him so much that he stopped ranting and raving and never went that berserk gain. David had this annoying way of pointing out the risks in everything we were doing. "Solutions, David, solutions," we told him. "We know what we're doing isn't smart." David probably should have been an actuary. He'd point out the dangers; we'd ignore them.

There was our father, George William Hamilton. New Englander. Son of the American Revolution. Dartmouth man. A Yankee stranger in a strange Southern land. Though a lot of issues came between us, not the least of which was Mom and Dad's divorce, I loved the guy. He was a dad from the old school — you were often afraid he'd punch your lights out. Under a hide that was tough as nails was even more hide that was tougher than nails. But as I said, I loved him.

Dad's great curse was that of having been a genuine "star" in the music business, leading a nationally famous orchestra, major compositions to his credit ("Betty Coed," "Wild Honey"), one of the founding members of ASCAP, brushes with radio and movie success. Mom had met him in Memphis in 1938, when he and his group, Spike Hamilton and his Barbary Coast Orchestra, were headlining at the Plantation Roof of the Peabody Hotel. That was as glamorous as it got in the big band days when bandleaders were the rock stars. Then the war came along, and instead of walking into another plum starring role as a military officer heading off to battle the Hun, he was rejected. Not by the studios but by the army. He was too old to serve.

A footnote about Dad. Mom was a dyed-in-the-wool romantic, with a totally idealized notion of what a man should be. I sincerely believe that if Dad had been successful in enlisting, and had headed off to war in the snappy uniform of the Army Air Corps (precursor of the Air Force), Mom would have adored him, they would never have divorced, and she would have been faithful to him until the day she died. But that's where the script and reality part company.

There was Grandfather Stevens, Dr. C. C. Stevens. We kids called him "Docky," for Doctor. He was one of two physicians in Blytheville. He was fun, he could play twenty different choruses of "Froggy Went a-Courtin'" on the piano, and he was one of the two most stable people I ever had the privilege of knowing. The other was his wife, our grandmother, Mildred Hubbard Stevens (called "Big"; Teeny was her "little girl"), who had aristocratic roots that wound back through the bluegrass of Kentucky to the tobacco fields of Virginia and to the titled nobility of Merry Old England. Southerners are big on genealogy, and Big had the right stuff.

Big also had a monopoly on power in the Stevens family. She and her well-placed brothers, Uncles George, Tom, Luther, and John, had accumulated a tidy little sum in business, all in our hometown. Big and Uncle George even owned the office building that housed the Sealtest Ice Cream Company. To us that was like owning the Empire State Building, with milk shakes thrown in. Big had all this money at her disposal and didn't have to answer to anyone in its dispensation. She used a lot of it spoiling Teeny, who got from Big just about everything she ever wanted.

Big and our dad, with their equally powerful personalities, were bound to lock horns, South versus North, our own family's Civil War. As the matriarch, Big felt it was her basic right to interfere with Teeny's marriage, while Dad, macho as he was, was used to having his own way. Teeny was right in the middle, and it was often like *Friday Night Fights,* with us kids cringing at ringside. Weighing only about ninety-eight pounds and slim as a reed, plus suffering from the early stages of tuberculosis, my grandmother was nevertheless a formidable opponent. Dad needed brass knuckles, and then some, to tangle with her.

I can't leave out Matilda, our cook, Mizz Five-by-Five, a name given her by bandleader Glenn Miller when he visited us. She was as wide as she was tall. Boy, could she cook, especially fried chicken and biscuits and sweet peach pie. She lived in a little house on the back of our property. She ruled David and me, but with plenty of patience, kindness, and love. Tildy could have worked only for a doctor, I suspect, because she had a nasty habit of getting into fistfights with the skinny little men she chose for boyfriends. If her swing didn't accomplish what she wanted, she kept a razor in her shoe to close the deal. That's when Tildy called in her employer, Dr. Stevens, for a little sewing practice. Between Teeny, Big, and Tildy, I got used to being around powerful women. In later life, as you will see, I couldn't settle for less.

Oh, yes, there's another member of the family I almost forgot to mention: me. I may have become a movie star, but in our little MGM by the Mississippi River, I was at best a supporting player in my family of stars. I guess I had the desire to star, or at least make a play for attention, for my role here seemed to be to keep everybody stirred up. I was incredibly imaginative, very restless, and not afraid of much. These were all good qualities for an actor and future man of the world, but they weren't that great in a family that, when not out adventuring or fighting with one another, just wanted a little peace.

Now that you've met the family, let me tell

you a little bit about Blytheville. Picture, if you will, an absolutely dead-flat vista, no hills, no mountains, no nothing, only miles and miles of rich, fertile land, the product of eons of flooding by the ever-widening and shrinking Mississippi River. This was the Cotton Kingdom: Mississippi, Louisiana, Tennessee, Arkansas, the states that possessed this most productive soil. Now picture in the center of all this lush acreage an incredibly small hamlet with one main street and about four other parallel streets, and that's all. You can add a few dozen homes and a handful of commercial buildings — movie theaters, a drugstore, a hospital, the usual. There were some nice Victorian houses, but despite all the cotton fields, this isn't grand plantation country. The big houses, the antebellum dynasties, were elsewhere along Ol' Man River. Blytheville was for the most part "just folks."

I was born on the eve of World War II. In Blytheville, adventure until then was defined as going for a soda at the fountain of Rothrock drugstore or taking in a double feature at one of the three movie theaters in town (Ritz, Roxy, Chickasawba). That all changed the day squadrons of bombers appeared in our skies, headed for a landing at the new Army Air Corps base a few miles away. It was 1942, and it was an invasion almost as tumultuous as when Union soldiers descended to reconstruct a rebellious South. This was an invasion of another kind, an invasion of youth, excitement, and new ideas, supported by a remarkable patriotic fervor the likes of which our country has never known since. Caught up in war spirit, Docky, Big, and Teeny generously offered to billet several officers from the base in the upstairs bedrooms of our ample home. These sharply dressed young aviators — majors, captains, and the like — were the pilots and bombardiers who had been aboard the squadrons of B-17s our family had marveled at coming in a few days earlier. We obediently surrendered our comfortable bedrooms and moved out onto the summer porch.

Mom's plan was that we would live with her parents temporarily while Dad finished up what he had to do in New York and rejoined us. We would then find our own place, so the inconvenience would be only temporary. There was a daily cheerful hubbub all around us and the clear sense of a noble cause. These airmen were receiving final training at Blytheville air base before being sent on to England to begin flying missions over occupied France. It was their last few weeks to sample the joys of being alive. In less than six months, most of them would be dead, shot out of the skies by Nazi antiaircraft guns or the agile Messerschmitt fighter planes that swarmed the slower-moving bombers. Such was the terrible attrition on air crews in the early stages of World War II.

Dad eventually rejoined us, but there had been enough time for Teeny to explore a number of romantic flirtations with the dashing boys who daily graced her presence. Mom, the eternal yet discreet romantic, tucked away her girlish notions in neatly tied packets of love letters she stored in the attic. I regret that I missed the opportunity to sneak a peek at those letters to see if any of them came from one of the officers billeted in my grandparents' home. Much later in life I asked Mom if any of her flirtations had been transformed into actual affairs, but she only giggled and never provided a satisfactory answer. Was I jealous? I don't think so. I had Big and Tildy to look after me. There was plenty of love to go around.

Contrast this wartime romance with the dismally drab reality of married life for Mom and Dad. Having been turned down by every branch of the service, Dad had eventually faced reality and returned to Mom and her hometown to take a job at the air base doing war work. Used to being a highly successful bandleader, a "star" with his own unique musical sound and his own radio show to boot, he was now a prosaic purchasing agent. Instead of living in well-appointed hotel suites where they could order room service, Mom and Dad now lived in a simple two-bedroom residence we called the Gray House where Mom did the cooking. Or tried to cook. Big, out of compassion, often sent over Tildy — head scarf, apron, and all — to prepare Mom's favorite meals of southern fried chicken or salmon croquettes with mashed potatoes, two tiny sweet pickles, and a few green peas, and, of course, cornbread. When we moved to New York, Beverly Hills, wherever, Mom would order this same meal, whether the restaurant was French, Italian, or Chinese, and especially if it was a swank joint like El Morocco that catered to your every whim. She loved home cooking, and so do I.

Encouraged by her patriotic girlfriends, Teeny attempted growing her own vegetables in a so-called victory garden. Actually, the newly sprouted vegetables had died so often and had to be replanted that defeat garden would have been a better name. When she figured out the cost of growing her garden, it came to about $30 a head of lettuce — a fact she neglected to mention to a very money-conscious Dad. I'm sure I get my own extravagance from Teeny, as a sort of lifelong rebellion against Dad's very Yankee and oppressive frugality. Nevertheless, I loved money, my own money. To that end, I took a lot of odd jobs, like being a pin spotter in the bowling alley and picking cotton in the hot fields. They didn't seem to enforce child labor laws in Blytheville, which was good for a little operator like myself.

Some aid and comfort came to Teeny when the wife of one of the base bomber pilots knocked on our door looking for work so she could be close to her husband. Her name was Kitty Strickland, and she was the first of a succession of nannies who were to influence our early lives. Mom made sure our nurses toed the line. She made up a little rule book for them, with such caution-provoking admonitions as, "If you ever use foul language in front of the children, you may leave immediately." "If you spit or have other obnoxious habits, you may leave immediately." Unfortunately, she had neglected to warn "never try to drown one of my children." As it turned out, Teeny walked into the bathroom only to find one nurse holding my head underwater in the tub, for a perilously long time, as I recall. Needless to say, that nurse was forced to leave immediately.

Such experiences made me love and value Teeny, all her absences notwithstanding.

Meanwhile Dad was having his own problems with his stepson, Bill. Dad was a man's man, who had had a tough, character-building upbringing in the rather dour environment of Newport, Vermont. He could also box. More than once he had punched out a rude or insulting patron at one of the venues he was playing after politely asking him, "Would you like to step outside?" Dad was intolerant of anything even remotely effete, effeminate, finicky, or fastidious — at the slightest sign he would warn you that you were going to end up a "toe dancer." We didn't really understand what that meant, but we knew in Dad's book it was something you didn't want to be, right alongside being a "slicker" or a "hustler," his other pet peeves. He must have despised his time in Hollywood. Dad's brief observations of Bill led him to believe that all he needed was to do some manly things like hunting and fishing. To his everlasting disappointment, Dad's heroic efforts to "make a man" out of Bill failed dismally. He tried to take Bill fishing, only to have the whole thing unravel as the result of a tiny chip that was missing from the lip of a Coke bottle. Bill refused to drink from the bottle, telling Dad he was concerned about swallowing glass.

Had he but known right then that he was in far more danger of being throttled by Dad than from any errant sliver of glass, he might have reconsidered. The lesson I learned was to drink any Coke that was offered to me. It seemed even sweeter back then.

Sitting around the radio at night to learn the latest war news was an obsession. After 1943, it became clear that America would win the war, it was only a matter of time. The legendary Glenn Miller, now in the service, stopped over in Blytheville to visit my dad. They had a chance to talk over old times. Glenn even asked Dad to get together with him in Chicago after the war. Glenn confessed he was a little worried about flying so much. He had recently witnessed a fatal crash, and it had bothered him. He said he had a bad feeling about flying. This was a couple of weeks before Glenn's plane disappeared, and he was never found. The other famous person who came to Blytheville during the war was Vice President Harry Truman. I was young, but the air base and its visitors and the big parties at the officers' club made Blytheville seem like the center of the universe to me.

As the world war wound down, the big bands were reviving. There was a lot to celebrate. Dad was more than happy to quit his purchasing agent job and become a star again. There was great excitement in being on the road. He took Teeny and us on some of his trips. One of my prime childhood memories is the smell of hotel rooms. What a scent it was, an amalgam of bourbon and Havanas and coffee and toast and the fine linen of the silver serving trolleys borne by waiters in starched white coats bringing the magic that was room service. It was the perfume of luxury, of wild extravagance, and it spoiled me forever. We began crisscrossing the Midwest and South, Dad's territory, like that of a traveling salesman, from the Palmer House in Chicago to the Cleveland in Cleveland to the Seelbach in Louisville and back to the Peabody in Memphis, where I had been conceived. I'll never forget those hotels.

My father's big song of his comeback period was "Lovely While It Lasted." One of the lyrics was, "Wasn't it a grand romance? We meet on the same street, but someone else is playing the game we played before." Teeny loved the song, though little did she know she would soon be singing it herself. So thrilled by the resurrection of Dad's career and self-esteem that she must have been blind to the downside of temptation, Teeny advised Dad to hire a girl singer to enhance the band's drawing power. I wonder if she knew she was picking her own poison. The vocalist Dad picked, June Howard, was a sexy lioness. Her pelvis met you a half hour before the rest of her. Dad couldn't resist. When June had the smarts, or poor taste, to ask Mom if she could call our father "Daddy," Teeny said a shiver went up her back. It was as clear as a sign in Times Square that they were having an affair.

Never the forgiving kind, Teeny confronted Dad when she caught him in flagrante with June at the Cleveland Hotel. Before walking out on him, she told him it was as if he had smeared mud across a beautiful painting. We were there with her and our nanny, Jewel. We had been looking forward to having a big time in the big city with Dad and Mom together, like a real family, like in the movies. We were so let down. How could Dad do this to Mom? To us? Still, I wonder if Mom wasn't a bit relieved that the marriage had ended. The compass of her security always pointed home to Blytheville, and that was where we were returning. One snowy night in 1944 we knocked on our grandparents' front door, and when it opened, we announced, "We're divorcing Daddy." The warmth and light that shone from that front door were unforgettable. Big, with arms extended widely, said, "Well, come on in," and hugged and held each of us.

There followed three idyllic years. I was free to be a child. Unlike brother Bill, who was nine years older and in a different loop in every possible way, my other brother David was my contemporary and my soul mate. Our world was our backyard at 1000 Main Street. That's where we would play every day until the setting sun forced us in. The peaked roof of our home, with all its turrets, served as Mount Everest, and we loved to sneak out the bathroom window to climb it. A flat-roofed outbuilding on our property doubled for the fort in *Beau Geste* and we guarded it jealously with our BB guns.

If that became dull, we'd climb up on the roof of Tildy's small house and fire BBs at our neighbor Johnny Loggin's water tank. The loud clang could be counted on to bring Johnny screaming out his back door, his own BB gun in hand, ready to make war. We even dug a small graveyard for dead birds and filled it with roadkill that we buried in shoe boxes and marked with little crosses made of tied ice cream sticks. When we could no longer find any dead birds in the street, we augmented the cemetery population by bagging live birds with our BB guns. Dad would have been proud of our he-manly exploits.

Sometimes I missed him a lot.

The neighbors down the street, the Mc-Cutcheons, owned two of the three movie theaters in town. Early on I made friends with their daughter Sally, who would invite me to go free to the movies. Even then I must have known that it's good to have friends in high places. In those days, your movie ticket (if you had to buy one) bought a lot. You'd see the previews, a short, a double feature (one was usually a Western), and a cartoon. If you hit the jackpot, you came when they were having a Cartoon Carnival. This provided an endless stream of Daffy Duck, Elmer Fudd, Donald Duck, and Bugs Bunny. In that more courteous era, the theater had a glassed-in crying room where moms with babies could enjoy the movie without disturbing everyone else. (I wish they had the same thing today for loud talkers and cell phone users.) I loved the movies, but it was beyond my wildest dreams to think I would be in them one day.

Like many children of my generation, I learned the basics of sex with another cute young neighbor, a year older than myself. I guess in my little six-year-old brain, she was a "hot-looking blonde," an "older woman," even. Perhaps it was that I was oversexed for my age or simply that my grandfather was a

50

doctor. Deciding I should begin my medical training early, I began playing doctor with this girl. We would meet in the family garage for regular examinations. I thought my brother David had a bad temper, but his was nothing like this little temptress's dad when he found out about it. I was humiliated for months to come.

I think of it now as "the last bomb" of World War II. This was the nearly simultaneous deaths of both my grandparents in 1947, just two years after the war had ended and all the flyboys had marched into their planes and taken off, leaving Blytheville's golden coach to become a pumpkin once again. The base was closed, much of the surplus equipment doused with gasoline and burned in a rush to conclude this unhappy time. Docky essentially died of exhaustion from a life too earnestly led. He had taken great care of everyone in the county except himself. Big, after a valiant fight, finally succumbed to tuberculosis. As the town mourned the loss of energy and excitement, we mourned the loss of our grandparents. I remember the funeral, the white chapel, Teeny in dark glasses, devastated.

Teeny and Bill had an answer to the grief: Let's do our best to avoid it. The house would be sold. We would be moving on. So after much packing, Mom and Bill tossed a coin in the driveway to decide whether to go to Palm Beach, Florida, or Hollywood, California. Bill had a sound business reason for wanting to go to Palm Beach. There had been a recent hurricane there, huge damage had been inflicted, and home prices would be low. Teeny had only one reason to choose Hollywood: To her, it was the most glamorous place on earth. In the thirties, she had taken a trip there and had never gotten over it. Teeny won the toss, and we were Hollywood bound.

CHAPTER THREE
GOING HOLLYWOOD

It was a sleek 1947 Buick Roadmaster, a real "wind splitter," that hummed and purred and ate up road faster than I could break one of David's toys. It should have run fast. After all, it was powered by the highest-octane fuel imaginable: our fantastic dreams of living "the Hollywood life" conjured up by watching endless Hollywood movies. Teeny fantasized about dating Clark Gable. Bill dreamed of meeting his alter ego Betty Grable. Bill's movie magazine education had taught him everything about Betty, including her height, weight, and bust dimensions, as well as the names and dates of all the movies she was ever in. Bill had become a walking fan magazine, a human encyclopedia of celebrity trivia, which was anything but trivial to him. He gave me my first real exposure to, and respect for, the power of fame. One thing was for certain: When we got to Hollywood, the last thing we would need was one of those "star maps."

As the car picked up speed and Bill, our designated driver, slipped the Buick into a nice groove, we began passing cars as if they were standing still. "I can't believe we did it," Bill applauded himself. He had been a big part of convincing Teeny to break the umbilical cord that had heretofore connected her to Blytheville.

"You're just going to love it," she reassured David and me. "There's nothing but sunshine, and we'll rent a house with a swimming pool."

Bill, now all of seventeen, was an excellent driver, steady, certain. God knows he had had enough practice by this time. When he was eleven years old, Bill started driving around town in our grandfather's old Model T Ford, propped up on a couple of telephone books so he could see over the dashboard, with wooden blocks tied to the bottoms of his shoes. When he was inevitably returned to the custody of Dr. Stevens for driving without a license, he would repentantly promise never to do it again, only to be caught on the road the following week. One of the big advantages to being a doctor in a small town was that the police showed undying respect for you, for only you could save them from mishaps in the line of fire.

Windows rolled down, wind wings tilted at just the right angle to catch the breeze, the Buick was our getaway car in our flight from the gloom of Blytheville and the loss of our grandparents and our father. Our road trip was all hopes and great expectations without any of the burdens of reality. It was a pattern my family was to follow over and over again in future years. When there was an unhappy conclusion to any chapter in our lives — a divorce, a death, even a fender bender — we would take off in our car (and later planes) and head for distant shores. I recommend it to everyone. Don't sit around and stew in your own juice, just hike on over to the other coast, dive into the ocean, get a perfect tan, and ask for a new deck of cards. There is no feeling of freedom quite as intoxicating as hitting the open road headed for God knows where. There's sort of a magnetic poles effect. You're repelled by what you already know and attracted by what you don't.

In the midst of our glee, I heard a moan coming from the backseat, where David, crushed between suitcases, was looking pale. "Can we stop for a minute?" he implored with a pained expression. "I have to go to the bathroom."

"Oh, for God's sake," Bill complained. "We're barely on the road and you already have to go to the bathroom. We'll never get to California at this rate."

"Can't you hold it for a little while?" Teeny asked hopefully.

"I already have," David answered.

I poked David in the stomach, the way you would poke a dead cat to see if he was really dead or just faking it. The groan he gave back confirmed he was not. We would pull over — filling station, roadside ditch, cornfield, whatever was available — then continue down the road for another few dozen miles until we'd have to stop again. It was going to be a long trip to California.

Do you remember those adventure movies from the thirties and forties where the hero was headed for the East Indies or some other remote place, and they'd show a line running from, say, New York City to the Cape Verde Islands and then around the cape of Africa, and then on to Ceylon? Well, the line between dots for our travel went straight to New Orleans, then to Texarkana, then across the great expanse of Texas to El Paso, through Taos and Phoenix, and on into Barstow, California, with a brief detour to Palm Springs. One thing about this trip that made it especially remarkable was that since Bill did the bulk of the driving (sometimes as much as ten hours at a crack), it was very easy to convince him to stop long enough to see every little wonder that was being hawked along fabled Route 66, the southernmost of the two transcontinental highways that linked the nation. The big advantage of taking this route was that you didn't have to cross any mountain ranges.

"Oh, ohh . . . ohh," I'd shout. "The sign says five miles off the highway there's the world's largest ball of tinfoil. Please, please, please, let's go see it." David would join me in an enthusiastic chorus, "Yes, please, please, please." It could have been a Civil War battle site, or a natural rock formation that looked like a bridge, it didn't matter, we were up for it. With Bill behind the wheel, no "wonder" was too silly for us to take in. Our childhood fantasies were running amok, exactly the way we guys wanted it.

For Teeny, it was a journey down memory lane. She had made this trip fourteen years before, in 1933, with the movie house owner Mrs. McCutcheon and her daughter Betty, whom Mrs. M was interested in getting into the movies. Betty looked like Joan Blondell. Being in "show business," sort of, at least at the exhibitor end, the McCutcheons had connections in Hollywood. Those connections led them to one of the top casting directors at MGM, the most glamorous of all the studios, home of Garbo, Gable, Tracy, Hepburn, Hamilton . . . but I'm getting ahead of myself. In any event, my mother almost got signed up to a contract at MGM decades before I ever did. Here's how.

After taking a quick look at Betty, the casting guy ruled her out for the movies. "Sorry," he said, "she looks too much like Joan Blondell." The McCutcheons had taken Teeny to the meeting with them. She was sitting quietly in the corner, though probably striking Greta Garbo poses. The casting director couldn't miss her. "Hey, you over there, would you be interested?" he asked. Of course Mom pretended not to be *wildly* interested. She answered, "I might."

"Well," he said, "you've got to cut your hair" — she had long hair, pinned up — "and I want you to show your freckles." He paused, then added, "You have a chance in the movies, a very good chance." He looked hard at Teeny, who had on a white linen suit. "But I can't tell how your figure is," he complained.

"Fine," Teeny said. Anything to be a star. She came back to MGM the next day with a loose, flowing dress and that's when the casting man "tried to get her in his lap," as Mom so colorfully put it. He was a hefty fellow, with that lap of his as big as an aircraft carrier, the way she described him to us. In his small office it wasn't easy to avoid falling into it. He told her that her having been married and having a child (Bill) would lessen her star appeal, but he would lie for her. Somehow this segued into his making the point that as long she had been married, it was a good idea for her to continue to have sex (meaning with him) to avoid getting rusty. After all, she wasn't a virgin anymore, so what was one more roll in the hay, especially with stardom as the carrot. Cutting to the chase, literally around the office, Teeny threw up the oldest defensive cliché: "I'm not that kind of girl." He told her it was never too late to change and continued his hot pursuit around the desk. Teeny ran faster than he did. He gave up and gave in and gave her a part, no concessions won.

My mother's prize was a tiny role as a Southern girl in a film with Robert Young, later of *Father Knows Best*. The setting was Paris (MGM's back lot could be anywhere you wanted). Teeny was supposed to say, "Would you-all drop little old me off at the Ritz?" They sent her to an MGM drama coach, who told her he didn't know what to do with her since she already had a genuine Southern accent. Also, she was supposed to be dressed in a long dress in the daytime with a dog under her arm. Teeny told the director, "I hate to tell you this, but in the first place a Southern girl never carries a dog under her arm or on a leash, and she never wears a long dress in the daytime, and she doesn't say 'you-all' singularly." Thanking her for the critique, the director came quickly to the bottom line: "You'd better say it the way it's written!" The drama instructor chimed in, "You'd better say it." Teeny wouldn't say it. You know that old saying, "I'd rather be right than president"? Well, Teeny would rather be right than in the movies. (I told you Teeny was a Virgo and very precise.) Thus ended the brief, happy movie career of Anne Stevens.

Back to our trip. On the way to New Orleans along a road that paralleled the river, we passed through Natchez, Mississippi. This was the real South, the grand South of myth and legend. There were manor houses, huge plantation homes that outdid anything ever pictured in Hollywood. Teeny could see herself in the arms of Rhett Butler. Bill could see himself sitting in a porch swing in one of those huge hooped skirts. As the unpaid help in the family, more and more gang-pressed to do wageless work for Bill and Teeny, I could see David and me picking the cotton, plucking the chickens, and singing mournful gospel songs.

We managed a stop in Galveston, Texas, just long enough to go to the beach and turn our lily-white skins into lobster suits. I don't know how Bill managed to avoid getting sunburned, but he didn't make things better by slathering Noxzema lotion on both David and me, which only served to hold in the heat and make things worse. When that didn't work, he poured vinegar all over us. This sent us howling in pain, and him howling with laughter. That was typical of our first aid: do something really stupid, followed by a bad outcome, followed by one-way laughter. How I became a sun addict after this, my awful first day at the beach, I'll never know.

Next, we stopped at the Adolphus Hotel in Dallas for a much needed luxury break. Ah, the delicious smell of a grand hotel, which evoked all the nice memories of traveling with Dad. I sometimes wished he could be riding with us. But I didn't want to spoil the party with heretical thoughts. Teeny was having too great a time.

Route 66 traversed just about every type of terrain: marshy swampland around New Orleans, wide treeless expanses across Texas, high desert in New Mexico, low desert in Arizona, and the most intimidating desert of all, that long stretch of nothing from Phoenix to Barstow. With temperatures sometimes reaching above 120 degrees, people advised that we wait until nightfall to make the run. Naturally we chose the day. Every car that crossed this last waterless stretch had a canvas water bag tied to the front grille. Ours was no exception.

That part of the trip was where I learned about the power of mirages. The shimmering heat waves coming off the highway created the appearance of a huge pool of water up ahead. Sometimes the illusion was even accompanied by phantom palm trees and people. The effect was so real that Bill hit the brakes, fearing we were about to enter the water. Of course, when you reached the spot that you could swear was water, it disappeared and you blew right through it. This was a useful lesson for a future actor and Hollywood deal maker. That promised profit participation at the back end of a movie deal was often just a mirage, and I quickly learned to get my money up front.

Inevitably, when we were tired of conversation or playing car games, we could sink into the wonderful humdrum of local radio. "Howdy, folks. This is Bob Skinner coming to you from clear channel WWKZ in Houston, Texas, brought to you by Big Boy Buick, where no down payment is too small to drive a Buick. The Big Boy slogan is, 'Hey, buddy, can you spare a dime?' Now, let me just slide over here and put on a platter titled, 'I don't want to die a miserable death in the desert because my mom and brother were too stupid to listen to good advice and drive at night,' as sung by the popular Texas quartet Death Never Takes a Holiday."

Somehow, we made it, and Palm Springs was our first taste of the California good life. Located in the middle of the desert a few hours from Hollywood, it was nestled against the foothills of an impressive snow-capped mountain range. Hollywood's elite played here. My first impression was: I wonder why. The town was small and dusty and not unlike the Indian reservations we had seen. Privacy was the answer. Stars could frolic here and nobody took names.

Nowhere was the privacy more complete than at the Palm Springs Racquet Club. Teeny knew the owner, Charles Farrell, a gentlemanly ex-actor who had created this gorgeous celebrity oasis. Renewing their acquaintance, Charlie generously invited us to stay over. In California for only a day, we were already hanging out at the pool in our bathing suits, sunning, enjoying a barbecue with the rich and famous at the very place that claimed to have invented the Bloody Mary, the drinking man's cure for the hangover. Maybe that's how I was able to transcend the excruciating sunburn of Galveston and become the once and future sun king. The glamorous Racquet Club could cure whatever ailed you.

Say, wasn't that Bob Hope in the pool? Bing . . . that's Bing, wish I could ask him to croon a few notes. And there's Dorothy Lamour in the lounge chair, where's her sarong? Bill's tongue was hanging out. He'd read all about this, but now he was living it. I would have been happier if Gene Autry or Roy Rogers had moseyed in, but Mom and Bill were riveted.

With her children occupied, Teeny went off to do her flirtatious networking. We watched her sitting at an umbrella table with Hoagy Carmichael (pianist, singer, movie star, he composed "Stardust" and "Georgia on My Mind"). They were having a drink and talking. He had been a bandleader in his early days and Teeny knew him from the Spike Hamilton era. By now he had made several movies describing his own on-screen persona as the "hound-dog-faced old musical philosopher noodling on the honky-tonk piano, saying to a tart with a heart of gold: 'He'll be back, honey. He's all man.'"

When Teeny returned to our room, she had Hoagy's autograph and gave it to Bill to start an autograph book. She told us she was joining Hoagy and a group of his friends for dinner later. Hoagy would be coming by to pick her up. She exhorted us to be on our best behavior when he arrived. I always had to laugh to myself when Mom asked something like that. There was no best behavior. You know the saying, "It is what it is"? Well, we were who we were. We weren't going to change and suddenly don halos.

Now, Mom was never, never, never on time for a date. Couldn't happen. Describing her makeup regimen, she used to say, "It takes time to paint a beautiful painting." Again, this was great training for my future romances with some very, very late movie stars, none later than Elizabeth Taylor, who seemed to take longer to do the masterpiece that was her face than Michelangelo took to do the Sistine Chapel.

In addition to the makeup marathon, Teeny would change her outfit two or three times before she would come out, so there was plenty of opportunity for David and me to polish our social skills. Hoagy, arriving right on time to pick up Teeny, received the unwelcome news that she'd "be a few minutes." I showed him where the whiskey and the ice were (we kept a bottle in the room for entertaining) so he could make a drink for himself. Hoagy saw a deck of cards on the little desk in our room and picked it up. He began humming to himself and playing solitaire. "Hey, son," he said, looking my way. "You know how to play poker?"

"No, sir," I replied. I was very polite. Don't forget I had just left the South.

"Come over here, I'll teach you," he said, shuffling the cards and dealing out a hand for himself and for me.

I really didn't know how to play. But I was a quick learner and luck was no stranger to me, so we were soon involved in a serious poker game. I asked Hoagy if he'd like to play for real money. This amused him. He asked if I had any money. I went over to my bag and pulled out the $25 I had saved from my job setting pins in the Blytheville bowling alley. "This'll get me started," I said. "My mom will cover the rest."

"Okay, son," he agreed with a bemused grin.

"My name's George," I said, "and I believe it's your ante." In a few minutes I had Hoagy down almost $100. That's when Mom came out announcing she was ready to go.

Hoagy could only implore her, "Can I have a minute to win my money back?" Time was not on his side. He lost everything. When we were done, I pushed him a ten spot from my pile of winnings. "Never take a man's last dollar. Always leave him with a grubstake." I remember hearing that in a Western I saw at the Roxy in Blytheville. What a player I thought I was, the genuine ace of spades. As they went out the door, I heard Hoagy say to Mom with all the charm he could muster, "You know, I'm getting tired of all these fancy restaurants. I'm a country boy from Bloomington, Indiana. Why don't we just head for a diner?" That was my first encounter with a star.

The three-hour trip the next day across the orange groves into Los Angeles was quiet, with lots of time to muse. We were all too tired to talk. Teeny had a lot of romantic ghosts chasing around in her head from her earlier adventures. There had been plenty of men in her life, but I guess she really had only two great loves. The first was a man named Bill Gerber from Memphis whom she met when she was young and impressionable. She described him, in rhapsodic tones, as someone who would make her knees shake and her teeth chatter when she got near him. Wouldn't you know then that Big, sweet but controlling as she was, would interfere with their love affair. Wrong background, wrong religion, I don't remember what, but Big stood square in the way.

Oceans of tears and much gnashing of teeth later, just before Teeny was to be married to Bill Potter at the Peabody in Memphis, which was Teeny's home away from home (Blytheville was only an hour away) and social headquarters, she ran into Bill Gerber. He asked to see her one more time. Big put her foot down. "You won't see him," she decreed, not before this wedding. "Oh, yes, I will," Teeny countered. For once she had stood up to Big, but only partially. After this one last romantic rendezvous with Bill Gerber, she dutifully returned and married Bill Potter. Then the man who had made her look like she was suffering from Saint Vitus' dance, shakes and all, faded into a sweet memory that she regaled us with time and again.

The other great love in Teeny's life and a name I heard all my childhood was Charles "Buddy" Rogers. Buddy was as all-American as you could get. Born in Olathe, Kansas, he had starred opposite Clara Bow in the 1927 Academy Award-winning film *Wings* and had earned a reputation as America's Boyfriend. He was also a skilled musician and bandleader, and a superb pilot who had taught young navy pilots how to fly during

World War II. In my mom's book he was a triple threat, since movie actor, bandleader, and pilot were at the top of her list of desirable male occupations.

They first met in Chicago in the early thirties when Teeny had convinced another beau, Al Ross, to take her to see Buddy's orchestra play at the famous College Inn. Al knew Buddy, so he asked him over to their table when Buddy finished the set. Buddy agreed to go out with them when he was through. Chicago in the Jazz Age was as much fun as New York. They went on an all-night jaunt of nightspots, finally emerging the next morning. Buddy commented how wonderful Teeny looked after being up all night. She didn't tell him she was repairing her makeup hourly. Buddy asked for her telephone number but didn't call. It hadn't worked out the first time, but Teeny had been bitten by the bug.

Next time she saw Buddy was on another jaunt to Chicago, at the 1933 World's Fair, where Buddy's orchestra was headlining. She was dating Frank Pilley, who headed Borden Milk. Teeny had a huge network of friends, and she was invited all over the country and fixed up with the most eligible bachelors in whatever town she was in. With her goal of reuniting with Buddy close in sight, she unashamedly steered Frank over to where Buddy and his band were playing. Buddy saw her again and got that old feeling, and *boom* — he called her and she had a date with him every single night for a month.

Buddy had a Cadillac convertible and a very thoughtful driver named Max, who would drive the two lovebirds out to Lake Michigan to take a stroll. They'd neck, as Teeny told us glowingly, "until our lips were chapped." Buddy was just "darling," to hear her tell it, and she fell madly in love with him. On occasion, Teeny would hear rumors about what Buddy was up to, and she'd say, "I would hear this about you." And he'd laugh. But then she read on all the front pages and heard on the radio that he was engaged to Mary Pickford, at that time the most famous actress on earth and twelve years older than Buddy. Teeny thought it was a joke, but it turned out to be true. It absolutely destroyed her. She couldn't believe it. Buddy told her he had to go and see his father about the marriage. She said she cried on Max's shoulder about how much she loved Buddy, but that was it.

Buddy appeared in Teeny's life once again during the war, when he flew an open-seated biplane into a nearby town with his pal Red Cramer and asked Teeny if she would drive down and see him. With Big's permission, Teeny went, accompanied by Betty Phillips, another close friend from Blytheville. No appearances of infidelity would be tolerated, not where America's Sweetheart, true Hollywood royalty, was concerned. Nothing happened, other than to keep Teeny's flame burning.

Mary Pickford was a tough act to follow, and she wasn't even offstage. But even Mary Pickford wasn't going to stop my mother, a woman who fervently believed in miracles. Now that Teeny was in California, she knew exactly where Buddy Rogers lived. Everybody did. Pickfair, the legendary home of Mary and her previous husband, the swashbuckling Douglas Fairbanks, was probably the most famous residence in America after the White House. The only question was when, and how, she would see him again.

During the war, General Douglas MacArthur had promised the Philippine people, "I shall return." Mom had made herself pretty much the same promise when she left Hollywood the first time. And now she was back. But this time she had abandoned her hope of becoming a movie star. It was too hard, too demanding, and the moral cost was too high. Sharing an insight with me culled from her earlier movie foray, she once told me that in 1930s Hollywood, with the casting couch system running full tilt, for a woman to become a star she would probably have had to sleep with an entire studio. Example: the casting director to get the role; the producers and director to keep the role; the camera, makeup, and lighting men to make sure you looked good; the film editor, so he didn't leave your best work on the cutting room floor; and so on and so on.

No, Mom was back this time for a refresher course in glamour. Instead of becoming a star, now Teeny thought she might just marry one. Hollywood was a big pond, full of big fish, and Mom was becoming a pretty good angler. Clad in Betty Grable "cutdowns" (a popular style of shoe — guess who convinced her to wear those), this time she was reinforced by the fertile imagination of brother Bill (now "of age" and firmly ensconced as the power behind the throne), not to mention the rest of her diminutive army. The reconquest of Hollywood had begun. But first we needed a place to live.

We discovered Archer Realty in the phone book. The proprietor, Frank Archer, was a friendly young man who took pity on us and found us temporary digs — a small apartment in Glendale, near the Rose Bowl. It couldn't have been temporary enough.

"This is what we drove two thousand miles for?" was our reaction. The two-bedroom before us smacked of a place where Ray Milland would have crashed during *The Lost Weekend*. It made Hollywood seem about as exciting as an eighty-year-old hooker. Bill was its worst critic. "We can't stay here," he exclaimed imperiously. Teeny calmed us all down and convinced us that we needed to stay put until other arrangements could be made.

The good Lord soon intervened, I suppose, because a day or two later I decided that the big Motorola radio in the building's entertainment room wasn't playing properly and that I would fix it. Not a good plan, I realize in retrospect, having had an almost unbroken string of past repair failures. At any rate, when I finished fixing the radio, there seemed to be about twenty-five extra parts. Attempting to get rid of these surplus pieces, I was discovered by the landlady, shrieking at the top of her lungs when she made me retrace my steps and saw what I had done.

We were invited to leave our hovel, and we decided we didn't need to be asked twice. We literally shamed Archer Realty into finding us something better. Our first real Hollywood home was small but charming. It was a rental house on a side street in the

Hollywood Hills called Flicker Way, just a few streets up from magical Sunset Boulevard. The area was known as Birdland because all the streets had avian names. The Beatles would spend time on Blue Jay Way and write a song about it.

No view before or after has ever surpassed it. In front of the modest ranch home with its sunken living room and huge sliding glass door was a steep drop-off. Just beyond that stretched a 180-degree panoramic view of Hollywood. At night it appeared as if a king's ransom in jewels had been strewn in front of us. The searchlights for El Capitan, the Pantages, or one of the other Hollywood grand old movie palaces helped add to the excitement. This was more like it.

Flicker Way became the staging area for Teeny's ambitious assault on the city. Mom made friends with a number of the Establishment, or Establishment-to-be, people, including Mary Laronetta, the StarKist Tuna heiress, and Lisa Farriday, a Central European stunner who was later to marry a major fortune and become a Palm Beach socialite. Soon Teeny was going off on yachts to Catalina and in Rolls-Royces to Palm Springs. She was now officially part of the Hollywood party scene.

Flicker Way was soon replaced by nearby

Sunset Plaza Drive. Here was a much more substantial home. Ultramodern in design, it also had a fantastic view. The Hollywood Hills weren't that developed then; aside from a few other homes on the street there was nothing but scrub-covered vacant hills and canyons. Teeny's social life began to include interesting movie types, like Sonny Tufts, an actor who had made a number of pictures for Paramount. A Yale grad from a prominent Boston family (as in Tufts University), he was beginning to develop a reputation as a Hollywood "bad boy," who would soon be sued by *two* women, each charging he bit her on the thigh. This was one near star who was not a role model for me.

One night Mom invited Sonny to dinner, and in a rush to get ready she asked me to help her stir the chicken salad. I was chewing some gum that accidentally dropped out of my mouth and tumbled into the bowl. I couldn't find it because it looked so much like the little chunks of dark meat Mom had cut up in there. So I just kept stirring, and Teeny, none the wiser, went ahead and served it to him. At the end of the meal Sonny said the flavor was good, though it was the "chewiest chicken salad" he'd ever tasted.

About this time, another bad boy caught

Teeny's eye, Clint Bagwell. He had a taste for liquor and he had a past. Clint was an ex-World War II fighter pilot from Georgia (good for Teeny) who had been shot down and now had a metal plate in his head (bad for Teeny). I think I may have told her it matched the hole in her head for going out with him. Clint possessed the rugged but dissipated good looks that Mom had come to adore. His idea of a good time was to take Teeny aerial joyriding. First he would do a few loop the loops in his plane, then he'd drop down close to the ground and find the nearest body of water, where he would skim the waves. At times, well fortified with Jack Daniel's, he barely avoided catching a wing tip and spinning in. Maybe Clint had remorse that he'd survived the war when so many others hadn't.

Certainly one of the most fascinating men to bow in and out of Mom's life during this period was another old soldier, General Jonathan "Skinny" Wainwright. At the time of his friendship with my mother, he was virtually a shattered man. Following the evacuation of General MacArthur and his family from the Philippines, General Wainwright had been made supreme commander and left to defend the islands against an overwhelming force of invading Japanese. After a number of heroic defensive battles, and to save unnecessary casualties, he and the rest of his command were forced to surrender. During occasional visits to our home, he told us war stories. As the highest-ranking American officer, instead of being shown any military courtesy by the Japanese, he had been bayoneted in the hip, confined to a crate, and fed crushed glass and gravel in his rice, which had thoroughly destroyed his health to that day. The general was very frail and walked with a cane. At age eight I preferred a fake Hollywood general. Where was Clark Gable or James Stewart?

Our next move was to 515 North Rodeo Drive in Beverly Hills. Although far from lavish by Beverly Hills standards, it reflected the family's growing sophistication. We had learned that although much of the movie business remained in Hollywood, the glamour and the glamorous people had all moved west to Beverly Hills or Bel Air. The transition to more prestigious environs seemed to inspire Bill, who began to emerge as an excellent clothes designer. More and more he was instrumental in upscaling Teeny's wardrobe. Unable to afford haute couture prices, Bill sketched, and then had a seamstress sew up, his imaginative designs. Mom was beginning to stop traffic when she went out, especially to legendary movie star watering holes like Mocambo, Ciro's, and the Cocoanut Grove. Long slinky gowns, full-length gloves, and hair pinned back in a chignon (Spanish style) became her trademark.

Meanwhile David and I were enrolled the Hawthorne School on North Rexford Drive in Beverly Hills. By this time we had acquired a driver to take us to school. You have to understand that this was Beverly Hills, so the cars that pulled up in front of school each morning were really something, brand-new Lincolns, Cadillacs, Bentleys, the best in rolling stock. Our driver was a wonderful black man named Tommy, and he drove us in his old, beat-up Studebaker, with more dents in it than the average Demolition Derby finalist. Arriving at school in this ruined hulk, right behind some mogul's kids getting out of a sleek limo, was mortifying. So David and I would scrunch down as far as we could in our seats, wait until the last second, and then pop open the door and dash out. No empathy whatsoever was forthcoming from either Bill or Teeny when we bemoaned our embarrassment. For all their high style, they had no time for snobby kids. To keep a foot in the real world, and to earn money of my own, which appealed to my deeply independent streak, I got a paper route. Both Teeny and Bill thought this was a great idea, even though I never saw Bill doing anything vaguely profitable. I guessed he was too artistic to worry about money.

The Hawthorne School offered me my first crack at acting. Inspired by the nearby La Brea Tar Pits, our school put on a pageant in which I portrayed a dinosaur, complete with huge papier-mâché face mask, while David was cast as part of the oozy tar pit.

One day after school, we saw Clark Gable walking by, smoking a cigarette. When he threw the butt away into the gutter, we dashed over and retrieved it. We brought it home and preserved it in an envelope labeled "Clark Gable's Cigarette." It was our own personal treasure, our version of the Hope diamond. Such were the perks of living and going to school in Beverly Hills. David and I may have actually gotten closer to Clark Gable than our mother did, her best-laid plans notwithstanding. Our maid had spoiled her first date with Clark Gable by telling him when he phoned, "Oh, Miz Anne's been waitin' by the phone all day for your call." I'm not sure the date ever happened.

Mother, as the beautiful new girl in town, did get to meet a lot of celebrities, while we kids were left with our Blytheville nanny,

Jewel, whom Mom had brought out to look after us. But nothing came of these "hot dates." Teeny wasn't impressed with Ronald Reagan. "Too wholesome," she complained, "but if I had known one day he'd be president, I might have reconsidered," she joked to me years later. Peter Lawford, on the other hand, was too fast for Teeny. Ever since I had beaten the great Hoagy Carmichael in poker, the bloom was off the rose of celebrity. Even at my tender age, I could see that these celebrities were no different from the rest of us, and all were a lot less cool than my own father.

Through Johnny Meyer, the right-hand man, the Mr. Fixit, of Howard Hughes, she met and dated the reclusive billionaire. She wasn't impressed with him either. "He was rude. He'll get up at an event and leave early just to get the press's attention. Vanity is not an attractive quality in a man." The bottom line was that none of these legends could compare to Teeny's icon, Buddy Rogers. I'm not sure she even saw Buddy at all. Bill, the gossip maven, later told us Buddy was totally preoccupied with the two children he and Mary had adopted during the war, and with his wife's increasing alcoholism. If Mom did see Buddy, she kept it a very dark secret. Gossip here was lethal, especially when

Hedda Hopper and Louella Parsons made it the national pastime. If Buddy had gotten caught stepping out on America's Sweetheart, fading though she may have been, it would have been curtains for him.

By 1949 the Hollywood idyll ended. Teeny was empty-handed both romantically and financially. She had gone through way too much of her inheritance. She was tapped out and actually worked for a while at a fancy dress shop called Marusha. But a salesgirl's wages weren't sufficient to keep us in the high style to which we had become accustomed, not on Rodeo Drive. So we drove back to the South, and its eternal swampy summertime, where the livin' was easy and, more important, cheap.

We didn't go to Blytheville, even though Teeny had three uncles there. One had a furniture store, the other was in hardware, and the third was the postmaster. Uncle George, the furniture man, was Teeny's trustee, and he tried his damnedest to teach her to live on interest, not principal. It was Uncle George who basically pulled the plug on Beverly Hills, but Teeny was dead set against returning to Blytheville and being under his conservative thumb.

George gave her just enough rope to get to Memphis, where we took up residence in the Parkview Hotel. It wasn't the Peabody, but it was gracious nonetheless, with verdant gardens and loads of Southern charm. It's a nursing home today. But as I was growing into adolescence, I began challenging the authority of my teenage surrogate father, Bill. To my mother, that was major insubordination. "If you keep being bad, I'm going to send you away," she threatened me. I called her bluff, and it changed my life.

CHAPTER FOUR
THE EDUCATION OF
GEORGE HAMILTON

Blytheville had disapproving Uncle George as well as too many sad memories, but Memphis was a primrose-lined memory lane of girlhood cotillions and dashing beaux and two marriages at the Peabody. Forget that they had failed; it was the romance of the process that mattered. Despite the nostalgia, the family's mood was edgy. Our apartment at the Parkview couldn't compare to the luxury of Rodeo Drive. Teeny found a job as a salesgirl at Laclede's dress shop, doing her best to follow Uncle George's admonition to live more practically. Just a few years before, she had been one of the store's top customers, spending copious amounts of Big's money. Now she was telling fat ladies with awful figures, "My dear, that looks absolutely gorgeous on you." She was not happy with the contrast.

Bill was left to rule the roost, playing Big Daddy, which he did with an iron fist.

David was enrolled in the nearby Snowden School. I was supposed to go, too, but that's when the wheels came off the cart for me. I don't remember the source of the blowup. I should have realized Bill was suffering from glamour withdrawal symptoms and was best left alone. Certainly I knew that as a general rule it was a bad idea to make him mad. Even though he wasn't a skillful fighter (slapping was more his forte), he was a lot bigger than I was and a lot stronger. I think in the heat of the moment I called him "Fatso." Vain as he was about being even a pound or two overweight, nothing I could possibly have said could been calculated to create more rage. His eyes glowing red, like in a horror movie, he grabbed me by an arm and a leg and spun me around in a circle, releasing me just when the g-force was at its greatest. I sailed in a great arc across the room and hit the wall with a thud. Things were getting dangerous for me, and I knew it was time for me to make my exit.

Thus when Mom began threatening to ship me to New York City to stay with Dad, her idea of the worst punishment on earth was my idea of a heavenly reward, not to mention an escape from Bill's unending wrath. "I've been bad," I confessed penitently. What a little actor I was. "I guess I have to go." Pretty please, I would have begged her. I hardly knew my father, but I really wanted to. He fascinated me, with his white tie and tailcoat, and the brilliant music he made. Plus he was in New York, which seemed the most fabulous place in the world in 1950. The great European cities had been bombed out or occupied to death during the war. This was New York's moment in the sun. So Teeny shipped me up north, which may have seemed to some Southerners like child abuse. In my conniving mind, I had pulled off a major score.

I moved in with my father and his singer-turned-wife, the beautiful, home-wrecking June Howard, and their young daughter, my half sister Sharon, in a quintessentially New York terraced apartment on East 57th Street near Sutton Place. Sadly, my father wasn't making music anymore. The big band era was pretty much over. Dad had fallen back on his Dartmouth Amos Tuck Business School degree and had gotten a great job as sales manager for the cosmetics firm Elizabeth Arden at 1 East 57th Street. If my father was impressive as a bandleader, he also was impressive as a brand leader.

Dad was my new best friend. He'd have me meet him after work for drinks, he martinis, me Cokes, at the King Cole Bar in the

St. Regis Hotel, under the famous Maxfield Parrish mural of the old king himself on his throne with two satanic jesters in red putting bad ideas in his head. He told me the Bloody Mary was invented here (a rival to the Palm Springs Racquet Club's own claim) and he would order one to give me a taste. How grown-up I felt.

Given that I was about to turn twelve, we would talk "man-to-man." Dad told me how important it was to be both a ladies' man and a man's man. He certainly was both, as borne out by his stories of his arty side as a left-handed concert violinist and his brawling side as a college boxer. He kept an old Stradivarius at the apartment, which he'd try to play for me. His range was limited, however, by a fight he'd had in Chicago that had severely injured his hand and had put him in the hospital.

I loved all Dad's stories of starting out on the jazz road, of playing the honky-tonks in Lubbock and Clearwater before getting to the big time of the Pump Room and the Starlight Roof. In those days if you wanted to play the society venues, you had to play for the Mob as well. Dad's agent was Jules Stein, later of MCA-Universal fame. His Dartmouth group, then known as Spike Hamilton and his Barbary Coast Orchestra, grew up to become George Hamilton and His Music Box Music, and an old-fashioned music box became his trademark. Dad told me how he created what he called the "Businessman's Walk," a seventy-eight-beats-per-minute rhythm, anything less than which my father was convinced would stop the clientele from drinking. Speed it up, boys, was his mantra.

I was so taken with the high style of Dad's orchestras and the other music men who were his friends, like Paul Whiteman and Gus Kahn, and the beautiful women they met on the road. How I wished Dad was still playing and traveling, for I would have loved to have gone with him. When I was a baby, when he and Mom took me on the road, they put my bassinet next to the bandstand. Dad told me how I screamed and cried when he played violin. I simply couldn't bring myself to hate him for cheating on my mother and breaking up our family; infidelity was an occupational hazard.

Besides, approaching my own hot-blooded adolescence, I could easily see the temptation posed to him by the lovely June Howard. She, too, had stopped working, having had some sort of nervous breakdown on the road (I hope not caused by my mother's Sherlock Holmesian pursuit of my father's adultery).

June often talked softly to herself, as if she were speaking to an angel on her shoulder. She seemed to stay around the apartment all the time, always wearing provocative, almost diaphanous dressing gowns.

One rainy day, when Dad was at work and Sharon was out with the babysitter, I was lying on the daybed in the living room where I had been sleeping. June, in an ice-blue peignoir, came over to join me. She didn't say anything. She just lay down beside me for a while, then mentioned something about "cuddling." If it was an offer, I could not refuse. So we cuddled, in the coziest way, though I could not help my preteen self from getting aroused. And what followed was as natural as the birds and bees neither of my parents had gotten around to telling me about. June was so sweet. She treated the whole thing as perfectly normal, never said anything breathless about how we had this huge secret and how could we keep it. There was nothing film noir about it, other than the hard fact that I had just betrayed my father and had sex with my stepmother. Not that there was anything maternal about June. I didn't feel any family tie to her. I was without guilt, even toward my father.

A child psychiatrist might have said I was getting revenge on him for what he did to my mother. But, thank goodness, they never took me to a child psychiatrist. I didn't have any buddies with whom to share the adventure of my being deflowered, though I'm not sure that I would have. One life lesson I had picked up from my parents was never to kiss and tell. A gentleman was always discreet, especially if he was fooling around in his own family. I still don't know why it happened other than that June was beautiful, she didn't feel like blood kin, and she made it nice and easy. It happened a few times, plus years later in California, after I had become a movie star, we had a *Same Time, Next Year* reunion and it was quite wonderful. I chalked it up as part of the whole sophisticated New York experience, my own sexual bar mitzvah.

Another part of my New York experience was attending a progressive school called Walt Whitman, where they seemed to concentrate more on teaching us Chinese than English. But before I could become a thoroughly modern Gothamite, I was yanked out of my wonderful new cocoon and sent to military school, which was my mother's backup punishment if sending me to Dad didn't work out. Perhaps Teeny somehow thought I was having too much fun in Manhattan with dear old Dad. Whatever it was, I soon found myself back in the heart of Dixie, in a place where fun was an alien concept.

The Gulfport Military Academy in Mississippi had all the amenities of a maximum-security prison. It was near Biloxi, on the Gulf of Mexico, and its motto was "We Turn Out Men." Military schools were to Dixie what Groton and Exeter were to Yankeeland. The idea was to get an inside track to West Point or Annapolis and become the next Robert E. Lee or Stonewall Jackson. I'm sure Teeny, who romanticized the military, was thrilled with the selection. We wore uniforms and drilled and marched and were trained as little leaders. Many of my classmates were the sons of big leaders; my roommate was the grandson of General Claire Chennault of Flying Tigers fame.

Needless to say, I hated the place. Half the kids were getting drunk on Hadacol, an alcoholic "tonic." The other half were lining up at the pay phones, calling their parents collect and begging them to let them come home. Gulfport seemed less like West Point than Stalag 17. The school was run by retired uniformed officers, mostly majors and colonels. I could only hope for their sake they were drinking men. I chose the Cavalry division as my sphere of training. Up to this point, my entire experience in equine matters was gleaned from a pony park on the corner of Beverly and La Cienega boulevards in L.A. (now a monstrous mall), where they would strap you to the saddle and slap your pony on the rump to make it trot. Gulfport would be a step up, at least for the riding.

I remember my first day in uniform, falling out in a riding ring, currycomb in hand, waiting patiently for the orders from the drawling Southern Sergeant Toomey.

"Gentlemen, this is a horse." He paused to make sure we got that.

Pointing to the horse's face, he added in stentorian tones, "This is the front end . . . you feed this end."

Next, walking behind his horse and pointing to its rear, he barked, "This is the back end . . . you clean up after this end."

The sergeant proceeded to the front of our formation. "I do not want you to confuse the two, because this will have dangerous consequences," he said. We leaned in to learn what they were. Sergeant Toomey pointed to a glass box containing some loose teeth, crushed hats, pants with hoof marks on them, and skulls with huge holes in them; we got the picture.

For a brief period I almost enjoyed my change of venue. But having my intelligence insulted daily, and screwing up so frequently that I practically lived with a nine-pound rifle and a forty-pound pack on my back, soon made me yearn for home. Accordingly, I appointed myself head of the Escape Committee. I found that if I could round up enough disgruntled cadets (that wasn't hard), we could pool our money and buy a train ticket. I'd write out instructions for the soon-to-be escapee and make sure he had civilian clothes. Our part of the plan worked perfectly; the first runaway cadets made it home without being caught. However, we hadn't counted on their parents bringing them back, which they always did.

I was next in line to try my escape when I was told there was a telephone call for me. It was Mom, calling to say she was getting married and would be moving to Boston. I made a promise to her on the spot that if she would let me come home right away, I would take care of her for the rest of my life. She said yes; I kept my word. Free at last! Or so I thought. By the way, soon after I left, Gulfport closed down. It is now a nursing home, like our Parkview apartments in Memphis. Is there a pattern here?

Boston was not the South, and it definitely wasn't California. The whole of Boston was created in the image and spirit of London, and was peopled by the oddest ducks you could imagine. I got the impression that aristocratic Boston had the same inbreeding problems as parts of the South. Centuries of marrying their own cousins had produced some interesting results. Sometimes this intermarriage created very quirky Dickensian characters with short necks, round bellies, large noses, and big ears. My new stepfather fit into this category.

As our car pulled up in front of 28 Chestnut Street, atop Beacon Hill, one of the city's premier addresses, Carleton Hunt stood at the top of the steps of his impressive five-story town house. He was dressed in a conservative three-piece gray suit. He was holding a pocket watch, which he put back into his vest pocket now that we had arrived. Time was apparently of the essence to him. Curiously out of place were the white cotton socks he wore inside his expensive Peal shoes. Usually this would have been the kiss of death for footwear-oriented Teeny, but I later found out that Carleton had an excuse, severe athlete's foot that would tolerate no dye.

Carleton Hunt was the proud product of many generations of Harvard men, a descendant of the famous Livingston family that had attended the birth of our nation, with the blood of naval heroes, Supreme

Court justices, and noble physicians running through his veins. Despite all the gilded roots, he was still a great disappointment to the eye. I was hoping he was the butler. As we prepared to alight from our car, Mom assured me that this was none other than Carleton himself. Right then, if I had had any say whatsoever, we would have started up the engine and motored away. But I didn't have a say.

Teeny had met Carleton on a brief visit to Boston to one of her Semple friends. He had asked her to marry him the very first night. Teeny considered this prospect but declined. Carleton insisted they have a blood test (a necessary prerequisite to getting married) before she left to return to Memphis, just in case she later changed her mind and accepted his proposal. It took the serious pushing of Teeny's coterie of friends as well as Bill's substantial influence to convince her to relent. There's nothing else going on in your life at this moment, they goaded her. Here's this rich aristocrat who's crazy about you. How can you refuse?

My reaction to our new home was, Wow, incredible! It was straight out of *Architectural Digest,* in a style designed for *Mayflower* descendants. As you entered the grand entrance hall, there was a polished colonial side table to the right of the door with a gleaming silver tray on it. In the tray were visiting cards. Above the table was an antique gold leaf mirror. The stairs were straight ahead and off to the right; through the doorway was the most beautiful living room you can imagine. Its walls were bedecked with solid gold leaf tea paper. Going toward the back of the brownstone, you encountered a well-stocked bar and sink. Then you pushed open two lovely glass doors to find the most wonderful private library: floor-to-ceiling bookshelves filled with gorgeous leather-bound books; red, blue, and dark green Moroccan leather book covers with decorated spines, silk endpapers, and — here's where it gets good — many of them signed by the Founding Fathers: John Hancock, Thomas Jefferson, John Adams, and the like.

Later I took one of these books to my new private day academy, the Prince School (for Yankee princes) for show-and-tell, and the teacher, followed by the principal, nearly fell over dead. They couldn't believe what they were holding. How many twelve-year-olds bring to school a book with a bound-in document signed by George Washington? At first they thought it had been stolen or was a forgery. I was well-known around the school after that.

A visit to all five floors, with their eye-popping treasures (including a room full of extraordinary railroad, maritime, and early New Orleans documents), soon showed me that Carleton Hunt, despite his deficiencies in countenance and physique, was the real deal: a true Brahmin blue blood. This was confirmed and enhanced when I learned that his father had donated a virtual treasure trove of pre-Revolutionary and Revolutionary War documents called the Livingston Papers to the Smithsonian.

All of us introduced ourselves. Tommy Hunt, Carleton's fourteen-year-old son, looked very much like a miniature of his father. Then there was the staff. Carleton had a rough Irishman who worked for him. "This is my man," he said, with no other explanation. We quickly settled into our luxurious new quarters and prepared for the wedding ceremony, which was to be held in the regal living room. This being Teeny's third wedding, Mom had decided to forgo the traditional white in favor of a simple pastel gown and a large hat. Carleton wore a cutaway and, I was glad to note, had temporarily retired his white socks. I wore my dress cadet's uniform, complete with sword belt and saber. It was a fine wedding. I think Bill was relieved. All of twenty-one, he had carried almost the entire burden of the family's well-being on his shoulders for years, and he secretly hoped that now that he had found us a safe harbor in Beacon Hill Boston, he could do something for himself.

Bill, who loved style and glamour — but not propriety — didn't stay around to make fun of the pomposity. He took off for Florida, which had always intrigued him, to go to Rollins College, a country club school with the best tennis team in the nation. Bill's roommate was Tony Perkins, the preppy son of the noted Broadway actor Osgood Perkins. Tony would go on to world renown as the star of Hitchcock's *Psycho*. He was also, like Bill, secretly gay, although Bill really wasn't keeping it much of a secret. It was just a subject no one was talking about in the early fifties, except in the pages of the scandal mag *Confidential,* and only if you were famous.

My brother David and I were inducted into the Prince School on the corner of Newbury and Exeter streets. I remember entering its hallowed arches and receiving my first taste of the stricter, more formal English education favored by Bostonians. Teachers carried pointers, which they didn't hesitate to wield with a resounding *crack* on your knuckles if you stepped out of line. I found it a very useful training aid; my grades steadily improved, so much so that I was offered a chance to matriculate at the even more rigorous Boston Latin School, to trade up. But I stayed put. For the moment.

I had learned to master my initial reserve when entering a new school. If I could locate a bully or other big-shot student, I would go right up to him and make myself known at the start. The consequences were much worse if you kept your head down and waited for him to pounce on you. That usually resulted in a sound beating. I tried to make him laugh. I once ate a drinking glass just to get a reaction. Another time I ate a disgusting concoction of catsup, mayonnaise, mustard, and every other vile thing I could get my hands on, just to get a laugh. It worked, and pretty soon I had everybody siding with me.

At home I had gotten to know Carleton and his son Tommy pretty well. Carleton didn't really work. He had inherited a seat on the Boston Stock Exchange. He had also inherited a "spendthrift" trust assuring him a comfortable life without labor. It was his custom to spend a few hours each day following the ups and downs of his investments. Then he'd return home for a modest lunch. Mom quickly entered the Boston social whirl and was absent much of the day, lunching or shopping, so I had ample time to talk man-to-man with Carleton. It was during one of these exchanges that I learned he was writing a book about his family. It was called *Who Cares!* Each page went something like this: "My family did such and such, and we're famous for this and that . . . who cares?" Honestly, when he described the premise of his book, I couldn't tell if he was serious or just pulling my leg. He didn't look like a kidder, so I had to take him at his word.

Tommy was often present but usually uninterested. Most of the time, he would sit with his feet propped up on the huge Stromberg-Carlson television set. The only times I witnessed him come alive was when he was playing a trick on his dad. Though not the initiators of the tricks themselves, David and I couldn't help but be tickled by them. The first I remember was a dribble glass Tommy had purchased from a nearby novelty store. Tommy would serve Carleton a glass of water. As Carleton drank the water, large amounts of fluid leaked out the hidden holes in the drinking glass, soaking his entire shirtfront. Carleton had absolutely no reaction, while we tried our best to avoid splitting a gut. An equally mean trick was a slice of rubber Swiss cheese prepared as a sandwich. No matter how hard Carleton tried to chew the cheese, it would not allow itself to be consumed, so finally he slipped it out from between the bread and put it on the side of his plate, again saying nothing, while continuing to munch away on the plain bread.

Tommy was beginning to consider investing in some incendiary inserts that would cause Carleton's cigar to explode, but we convinced him this would be going over the line. It seemed to me that Carleton was either the coolest character I had ever met or pathetically oblivious to what was going on around him. Perhaps all his years of heavy rye whiskey drinking had dulled some part of his brain, because I began to notice that after getting lightly toasted on whiskey, Carleton would pee in the sink next to the bar. I was aghast at this, especially when so many bathrooms were so close. On the other hand, it made me smile, since I was aware that the bartender at the party following the wedding had used that sink to store his ice. I wonder if anyone noticed the substitute for a dash of lime in their drink. It could have started a whole new trend.

The source of greatest friction between Mom and Carleton was, naturally, money.

To Teeny, the very first and most contemptible of the seven deadly sins was cheapness. She simply could not abide it. Unfortunately, if she had looked in Webster's for a definition of the word "cheap," she would probably have seen "Carleton Hunt." Carleton's less than loyal butler, whose main job, we quickly found out, was to be Carleton's drinking buddy and to pull him out of seedy burlesque joints in Scollay Square when he'd been "overserved," was quick to inform my mother that Carleton had loads of money and that he kept two different sets of account books, one that made him look poor that he showed Teeny, and then the real one that showed him to be a millionaire. This information was calculated not to please Mom.

Unhappy with the allowance Carleton was giving her, Teeny began to examine the pockets of his pants each night after he had retired. At the beginning there was plenty there, but soon enough, Mom would find only $4. There was the same $4 every night. It seemed that Carleton had caught on to her and would leave just what he was willing to lose. In fact, Teeny took only $2, feeling that community property applied even when rifling pockets. Teeny was waiting longer and longer before going up to bed in hopes that

Carleton would be asleep by the time she retired. Occasionally there was a note that said, "If you feel like it, wake me up." I felt kind of sorry for Carleton. "You're the only one who listens to me," he said and thanked me.

Teeny spent as much time as possible away from her new husband, much of it with her new best friend, Amber Howes, a wacky outsider who had also married a stuffy Brahmin and was as much a fish out of water here as Teeny. Amber admitted to Mom that she charged her husband for sex every night and insisted that the payment be in cash, on the bed table, in advance. Bill had first met Amber when he saw her and her daughter carrying a priceless Oriental carpet down Newbury Street. He invited them home, where Amber promptly stole all of Teeny's engraved crest stationery. Instead of making a big fuss about it, Teeny simply went to visit Amber and stole it back. It was the beginning of a great friendship.

Teeny's marriage limped along until just after Christmas of 1951. Teeny had become part of a Boston social group called the Gray Ladies. Each year they took on a charitable event. Teeny had read a letter to Santa Claus in the newspaper from a young boy say-ing something to the effect that he didn't want anything for himself, toys or such, just enough money to pay for his little sister's medicine and a toothbrush. Talk about pulling my mother's heartstrings. Teeny had deep compassion, especially for children. When she found out that there were scores of letters like this one in the Dead Letter Office, she brought them home, where all of us sorted them, looking for the neediest. She asked for donations from the Gray Ladies to answer the many letters. Time elapsed and there was no response. In an effort to cut the red tape, Teeny used Carleton's Filene's charge account and charged toys and shoes and whatever to it. When Carleton got the bill, all he said, "Oh, my God, oh, my God . . ." All the needy kids were happy that year, but we were homeless. Carleton had told Teeny, "I want to thank you for the most exciting year of my life, but I just can't afford you. Would you mind if we got a divorce?" Teeny agreed. We were out of there. The following morning's *Boston Globe* read, "Mrs. Santa Claus Leaves Boston."

Next stop was the Big Apple. Was I glad to see those skyscrapers again. We moved into the Alrae Hotel, off Park Avenue, now the luxe Hotel Plaza Athénée and one childhood residence of mine that didn't become a nursing home. Elegantly run today by my

German hotelier friend Bernard Lachner, I still think of it as my home and stay there every few months to remind myself of growing up in glamorous New York. I'm not sure how Teeny paid for it, maybe by loans from Uncle George back in Blytheville, but I doubt he gave her very much to live on in the Yankee Sodom. One way Teeny got by was by paying our new maid Willie Mae a princessly salary and then borrowing it back from her all week. I think Teeny put out an SOS to Bill who, fortunately for us, was tiring of Rollins College. In just the time it took to sell back his used textbooks at the campus bookstore (I bet they'd never been cracked), Bill hopped a train and returned to us. It was good to see him again.

Bill, our arbiter of taste, wanted no part of hotel living. Our first order of business under his command was to find an apartment in the best section of town. Money was no object. It was no object because we had none, so whether you were going to owe a little or a lot was inconsequential. We stopped looking when we found an apartment at 471 Park Avenue. It was five large, handsomely decorated rooms, overlooking wide, lush Park Avenue. It wasn't exactly what Uncle George had in mind when he admonished us to live a practical life.

A great address demands a top school, Bill decreed. So David and I were dispatched to Walt Whitman, the same progressive school I had attended when I had lived with Dad. I was still trying to figure out their curriculum: foreign languages no one used, science courses that involved folding paper to make little buildings, learning to play the recorder (the world's stupidest musical instrument), the triangle, and wood block.

Then a huge building fire forced us to flee our Park Avenue apartment. Leaping tongues of flame and huge billowing clouds of choking smoke sent us scurrying to the rooftop with our French poodle, Marquis.

Our next address was even better than our first. We occupied all four floors of a beautiful little brownstone at 116 East 64th Street. It even had its own elevator. New address, new school, of course. The formula was simple. We were enrolled in the nearby Browning School, a very preppy all-boys academy in the East 70s that claimed such illustrious alumni as numerous Rockefellers and Sulzbergers, the family that owned the *New York Times*. My classmates had surnames like MacArthur, as in General Douglas; Cointreau, as in Triple Sec Cointreau; Berghaus, as in the St. Louis Busch beer Berghauses; and so forth and so on. All of them were pedigreed, manicured, and set to go. Classes consisted of only eleven students each, so I soon knew all of them. Merely rubbing shoulders with them was elevating.

My best friend was Arthur MacArthur, son of the great general and an introverted, music-loving bookworm who was not at all a military type. Since Douglas MacArthur was from Little Rock and his wife from Tennessee, Arthur and I had a lot in common, two country boys in the big city. Arthur had had a difficult upbringing, having been dragged from military post to military post. As a result he didn't make friends easily. I was invited over to join him in play at his apartment. At least once a week, a driver would pick me up, and Arthur and I would have lunch at the Waldorf Towers Club. The general himself joined us on more than one occasion, but sometimes it was just the two little corporals, feeling very, very sophisticated.

Having been homeschooled in the Philippines during the war, Arthur had a vast knowledge of music and literature, including all the popular songs I had grown up with, and a fetish for Venus Velvet No. 2 pencils, which were the only things he would write with. I spent a good deal of time with Arthur and the general at their splendid home in the

Waldorf Towers, where people like the Duke and Duchess of Windsor and all the heads of state stayed when they came to New York. I learned a lot more history at the general's feet than I did at Browning.

Speaking of feet, while I was at Browning, Teeny enrolled me in the famous dancing classes of Mrs. deRham, who had been teaching the waltz and fox-trot to Gotham society for an eternity. She was the Arthur Murray of the *Social Register*. Arthur Mac-Arthur and I went together. Arthur often played the piano for the tango, which I would dance to. Nothing in my childhood has been as useful as deRhams'. Given Teeny's love of musicians and of music, I'm not sure why she never sent me for piano lessons or tried to get me to learn some other instrument, at least the violin. Maybe she was too distracted, or maybe I was.

About this time Frank Delaney entered Mom's life. She was told he was a free-spending, party-loving top lawyer (Marilyn Monroe was one of his clients). They had it partly right. He was a lawyer. I don't think Mom ever found a truly generous man in her entire life, certainly not to hear her tell it. Frank did Mom one big favor, though. He took David and me off her hands after school and during the summer by employing us at his law office. All I can say is that he must have been crazier than a bedbug, because he made David his switchboard operator and me his underage process server. David left the intercom key down on the switchboard, allowing an important client to hear Frank say, "Tell him I'm not here or that bastard will talk my ear off." By the same token, I was more than a little confused about what papers to serve on whom, so this teenage lawman infuriated quite a few people by inflicting undue process on them.

I could see that Frank wasn't too happy about how David and I were destroying his reputation, but he did do me one big favor. He told Mom that I was a "caged lion" and that she had to let me go. He probably could have said this about millions of young men my age who were passing through puberty, but it didn't hurt for Mom to hear it. It may have been the reason Mom let me go off to boarding school a few months later.

After leaving Frank Delaney's law office in complete chaos, I found a much more promising job working for a man named Sam Glauber in the downtown flower mart. He paid me $25 a week plus a 10 percent commission on what I sold in the shop. I had to clean the place and take care of the flowers. I never did get the knack of angle-cutting flower stems with the razor knife they gave me and had the wounds to prove it. I was also a complete failure arranging flowers. So I convinced Sam to let me sell flowers for him out of the shop on commission. I cut a new deal for $25 a week plus a 20 percent commission, plus I wouldn't come in that often.

With my official florist badge, I could gain access to every trade show in town, and when the Auto Show came to Madison Square Garden, I managed to pile up a tidy little sum hawking flowers to car manufacturers. Taking advantage of their natural competitiveness, I fibbed a bit and told Ford I had just written up a huge order for Chevrolet to supply flowers to them during the show. If Chevy's doing it, then we should do it, the Ford representative naturally concluded. I told the Ford guy that since they were featuring their new Country Squire station wagon, they needed lots of country foliage. The deal I made was for $500 a week for fresh flowers, most of which I picked up, barely used, from funerals and made a big profit. With this real order in hand, I went to Chevrolet and told them about the huge order Ford had just placed. They signed up too. In one day I made Sam $10,000. My $2,000 commission would be a great help in bankrolling my prep school education. Thanks to my ingenuity, I was able to take a very early retirement from the flower business.

Puberty comes with its own agenda, and right up there with "live to take another breath" was "locate girls." The flower business had introduced me to parties, cotillions, and the like. That's where the girls were. But if I was going to make that scene, I had to look right. I could always "borrow" Bill's tuxedo. However, if I were caught . . . well, the dialogue would go something like this, with Bill shrieking, "TEENY, tell George he *cannot* wear my things. That tuxedo belongs to *me*. I had it made especially for me and it cost a fortune. He'll ruin it." Now turning to me: "It looks *ridiculous* on you. Why would you even want to wear my clothes? Nobody looks at you anyway. TEENY, *tell him he is not to wear my things!*"

Sometimes I tried to challenge Bill. "I think you're wrong — I look great in your clothes."

Bill would then go doubly wild. "He's already ruined my expensive patent leather pumps, the formal ones with the red lining. He stole them from me, just stole them . . . and fool that he is left them outside in the bushes. They were rained on. Next day when I found them the toes were turned straight up, like footwear for Ali Baba and the forty thieves."

Instead of continuing to argue the matter, I selected Plan B. A little cash applied to the hand of a thrift store owner under the Third Avenue El and I was wearing the latest 1920s tuxedo. I always did look good in classics. Checking the pockets in these ancient duds was always a thrill. I found two unused movie tickets to the John Gilbert and Mae Murray silent screen epic *The Merry Widow*. Too bad I was thirty years too late.

Hormones raging and dressed to kill, my Browning pal Paul Fagan and I started making the rounds of the Manhattan debutante scene. Deb parties in my day were guarded like Fort Knox. Blatant crashing was almost guaranteed to earn you a flying lesson into the nearest alley propelled by at least two well-dressed gorillas. But Paul had a few connections, and we were both fairly good-looking guys with perfect manners, if you overlooked my Jerry Lewis haircut. Once we showed up to escort one girl, it was easy to arrange to escort another. Pretty soon we were showing up at parties in tony towns like Tuxedo Park, Southampton, Short Hills, even Newport. Sex was a natural by-product of being a good escort. Long make-out sessions with girls from Spence or Chapin who spoke through clenched jaws, a brief dalliance with a limo'd lovely from Long Island, a roll on the tennis court, skinny-dipping — I was up for it all. I subsisted on the eggs and bacon that was the standard late-night fare for these coming-out parties.

While I was wading into the social world, Mom was jumping into the deep end. "Café society" was a term recently coined by gossip czar Cholly Knickerbocker to describe a loose collection of celebrities, socialites, hangers-on, and hell-raisers who frequented the snazzy watering holes of the day. It was Teeny's cup of tea. Tired of the serious life with all the stiff-necked pretensions that had characterized her brief marriage to Carleton Hunt, she was ready to have fun again. In Mom's book that meant getting fashionably dressed, taking the arm of a "divinely attractive man" (her words), and making a grand entrance at John Perona's El Morocco, her favorite of a dozen glittering night spots.

Sometimes she'd take me with her on her dates (I'm sure they hated it, but no man denied a Teeny request), so I did see the show in which Mom starred as Queen of the Gotham Night. Here was the grand entrance: Teeny dressed like a million, on the arm of Frank Black, the conductor of the highly popular James Melton television symphony orchestra (Frank Delaney had exited the scene), came through the door of El Morocco, taking a left and walking down the few steps that led to the main room and the dance floor, passing the hatcheck girl holding the obligatory mink or chinchilla. "Isn't she precious?" Mom would invariably say, patting her on the cheek.

Drawn ever onward by the slow, seductive sound of a muted horn, Teeny entered the main room, where Alfredo and Carino, the deferential tuxedo-clad maître d's, were there to greet her. Teeny, sleek and sexy, paused just long enough for the crowd to take notice. Was she visiting royalty? A Broadway celebrity? With the maître d' and headwaiter in the lead, bowing and scraping, and the publicity man Henry O'Dormann and, later, Jim Mitchell falling in behind, Teeny began the grand march to a well-appointed zebra banquette. Its proximity to the dance floor confirmed for all, mouths agape in stunned silence, that this was indeed an A-list personage. The Chauncey Grey Orchestra, if they hadn't been certain they'd have been fired for doing so, would have put down their instruments and indulged themselves a long, admiring look.

Once Mom's party had been comfortably seated, everyone present, including all those handsome folks in suspended animation on the dance floor, could now exhale and the room could return to normal, with its pleasant cacophony of rattling plates, tinkling glasses, and happy chatter. My brothers and I were present, of course, but nobody paid any attention to us. It was a phenomenon I noticed over and over when I eventually became a celebrity in my own right. There was no competing with Teeny in the charisma game. She had it in spades. Mom loved to dance, and she loved the attention, but she hated the club food, dreaming instead of Tildy's salmon croquettes back in Blytheville.

New boyfriend, new home, new school — that was the usual order of things in our family. Our new digs were sensational, to put it mildly. We had moved to a gorgeous apartment at One Beekman Place, overlooking the East River, very close to where the United Nations Building was being constructed. For starters, our building had squash courts, a gym, an indoor swimming pool, even a grass lawn located behind the building that sloped down to the river. Our neighbors were people like Huntington Hartford, the A&P heir and the country's most extravagant playboy, and Mark Goodson, the *Price Is Right* game show king. Following a few brief forays into living on his own, which included a tiny apartment above the Gabor sisters (Zsa Zsa and Eva), and a trip to Europe aboard the *Ile de France* to visit his wealthy Potter relatives in the south of France, Bill rejoined us at One Beekman. How could he stay away from an address like this, New York's finest? Filled with all sorts of imperial visions from his trip to Europe, Bill set to work to remake our apartment into a showplace.

A few major pieces were purchased at auction. The rest were found in thrift shops, on the street, or in other unlikely locales. Bill could look at the leg of a chair being unloaded at five A.M. at a flea market sale and, before it hit the ground, discover a treasure. What an eye. The apartment came together nicely. Bill added his special touch of a velvet rope, the kind you see at movie theaters, in front of a small closet door in order to give the illusion that there was an entire separate wing that had been closed off for temporary renovation.

This was the ultimate party pad. Just as some people can mix a perfect martini, Mom and Bill could put together just the right mixture of people, a salon often drawn from society and show business, and make it click. Once a critical mass had been achieved, a guest nobody knew, drink in hand, would wander over to the piano and start playing, and the party was on. That's the way the best parties happened. No script. Just pack the room to overflowing with an interesting mix of people, add a little music, and let her rip.

If Mom didn't have something to wear, she'd ask our well-dressed maid, Willie Mae, to let her wear some cute little outfit she'd just bought from Lerners, which Bill would accessorize with some fabric remainders. Then Teeny would claim it as the latest designer creation, the new look from Christian Dior or such. If we ran out of liquor, Bill would send one of the guests out to buy more, naturally out of the guest's pocket. If Bill ran out of hors d'oeuvres, he'd dab a little dog food on some Ritz crackers with a slice of olive. "Oh, Teeny, nobody will ever know. After a few drinks you could serve them kitchen dust and they wouldn't care." There was only one unbreachable, unbreakable law: For God's sake keep the party going. All I knew is what I heard the next day. Truman Capote had been dancing around with a large plaster statue of Venus when he fell down a flight of stairs. It must have been some party, by the look of it the morning after. Bits of plaster of paris everywhere, ashtrays with mashed-out cigarette butts, thousands of empty glasses, a sea of crumbs crunching underfoot.

The fun for me ended soon enough when it became clear that as glamorous as it all was, as great a collection of life experiences as I was acquiring, if I wanted to have any real future in life I had to get serious about my education. Algebra One, what's that? Chemistry? All I knew is that's what I felt when I snuggled with a girl on the dance floor. Let's face it, I told myself, there were more holes in my education than in a bank teller who tried to draw his gun on Jesse James. So I pitched Mom on the merits of a boarding school education. "Let me take the train to Hackley, up the Hudson in Tarrytown, the top-rated boarding school nearest to Manhattan, and see what I can do," I suggested. She agreed.

I was impressed by what I saw. Hackley was what I imagined Harrow or Eton might be, right down to the ivy-covered walls. The admissions director was pleasant enough, if somewhat amused by the precociously enterprising young man he beheld. I was hoping I could make him take me seriously. After a few pleasantries, I bottom-lined my proposition for him. "You let my brother David and me come to Hackley, I'll have my dad send his two-hundred-dollars-a-month support check (a hundred for each of us) directly to you." I told him that we knew all about the Hackley honor system and we completely agreed with it. I also assured him we were good students and that we would take our homework very seriously. After a few minutes, he nodded his agreement and said he'd be happy to have us. Always one who hoped he could sweeten any deal he made, I asked him if we could keep the first month's payment to use for uniforms and supplies. He broke into a chuckle at my unmitigated brass and gave in, and David and I became sleep-away preppies.

Before you knew it, I was a member of the Glee Club and a smaller singing group called the Octet, a hall monitor, and secretary to the Board of Magistrates that enforced the school's honor code. I almost always had to recuse myself from voting on disciplinary rulings, as I was usually involved with the culprits in gambling and such. I also acted in school plays. There was very little time for studies. In New York, being sent "up the Hudson" usually meant that you were going to prison at Sing Sing. Being sentenced to Hackley struck many of my classmates in much the same way, but maybe everybody wants to escape from whatever school they're in. But this time, not me. I really enjoyed being on my own, out from under Bill's delicate but insistent thumb.

My best friend at Hackley was Herbert "Spike" Allen, whose father, Charles Allen, was the head of the powerful investment banking house of Allen & Company. The Allens had a country house in nearby Ardsley-on-Hudson, which Spike would invite me to on weekends. In the city, the Allens used to take Spike and me to Mamma Leone's in the theater district. It was like Sardi's then. All the great actors and actresses were there, Lunt and Fontanne and Ethel Merman and Mary Martin and John Raitt, and the Allens knew them all. It felt great being part of the club, a club where you got in either by talent or by the money to pay for the talent.

I remained enterprising and, given my success in the flower trade, became once again an "official florist," this time for the Hackley proms. Once I charged them for rare black orchids to fit a dance's *Black Orpheus* theme. Problem was that neither Sam Glauber nor anyone else had black orchids, so I got some supposedly indelible ink at Woolworth and dyed purple orchids black. Alas, the gym was hotter than Rio at Carnaval, and the black ink began melting all over the white dinner jackets and prom dresses. I had to talk fast not to be expelled. In summers I kept a foot in the business, picking up flowers at funerals and reselling them at weddings. There was a two-hour turnaround. If they died, I'd blame the heat.

Whatever academic shortcomings I had at Hackley, my life skills were being sharpened immeasurably. I could almost always get out of studying by claiming I was rehearsing for the Octet. As a hall monitor, I could choose to play poker with my classmates instead of supervising them. Because I was so good at gambling, I very seldom had to take my turn as a waiter in the chow hall. I would cancel a gambling debt if a loser would take my waiter duty for me. And because I was secretary to the Board of Magistrates, I could help out my buddies if they were hauled up on an infraction.

The other skill I sharpened during this time was making people laugh. I got so good at it they made me handle all the comedy bits when we performed in the Glee Club and Octet. One way or another show business was creeping into my life. On weekends off, I would resume escorting debutantes. I was now happily funded by my gambling resources. More and more I was appearing with Wendy Vanderbilt and other top-drawer debs, and people were beginning to ask, "Who is that kid?" I couldn't help but like the attention I was getting.

But time was running out on our New York adventures. Teeny had actually been entertaining the prospect of marrying Frank Black and settling down to a quiet domestic life. Frank insisted on the domestic part. Frank had plenty of fame and loads of money, and offered her all the love and security she could possibly want. Unfortunately, he had laid down a dictum that went something like this: If you hope to marry me, learn to stay home and don't let me catch you going to El Morocco without me. Ask a brook not to babble, a ball not to bounce, a bird not to fly . . . It ain't gonna happen, cap'n. Frank's rules and regs were just too boring for my madcap mother. When Frank would go to bed at eleven, my mother would sneak out for a "second night" at El Morocco. Alas, one night Frank got a second wind and went to El Morocco himself and saw my mother there having a wonderful time. At that point he called the whole thing off, and with it my mother's hopes of a happy Gotham home for her and her three sons.

There were other men, other rich men, but apparently none were father material. They always seemed to be high-rolling show-offs. One man used to give Teeny hundred-dollar bills to tip the ladies' room attendants. These were the kind of tips that Truman Capote's Holly Golightly survived on, but my mother was too much the Southern belle to take advantage of the situation. Still, she knew how to use her charm to get by.

Teeny took credit for inventing the doggy bag, which was unknown in those days. Even though Teeny didn't care for steak (loved those salmon croquettes), David and I were bloodhounds, so our mother would make the supreme sacrifice of ordering steak at Le Pavillon, Chambord, "21," you name it, take a desultory bite or two, and bring it home for her two-headed "Fido." Those rich dates and those *sacs de chien* kept our family well fed for years.

Christian Science saw Teeny through it all. She often said, "If we don't know where our next breath comes from, why should we worry about where our next dollar or our next meal will come from? God will see us through." She sincerely believed it, and we embraced her faith, because it seemed to work. I still met my father from time to time at the King Cole Bar. He had moved up to Riverdale to escape the stress of the city, but the commute and June's illness (she was institutionalized for a time) made things even worse. I didn't see much of my stepmother, and there were no family reunions involving Dad and Teeny. New York could be a small town, but it was also huge enough for them to lead lives that didn't intersect. However stressed she was, Teeny made our lives glamorous, giving us birthday parties at El Morocco, taking us for ice cream at the Stork Club. We were at the red-hot center of the world, with a red-hot mama putting on the greatest show on earth, for about a dime. I still don't know how she did it, but there was always this book on her nightstand, Adam Dickey's *God's Law of Adjustment*. That title was the story of our lives, and little did we know what the next chapter would entail, other than the fact that it would be a cliffhanger.

CHAPTER FIVE
FOUR FOR THE ROAD

The year was 1955 and I had just come home to Manhattan for summer vacation from Hackley. We were still living at One Beekman Place. There was a terrible racket in our first-floor apartment, and when I opened the door I found my mother entertaining the entire cast of the hit musical *The Boy Friend,* including Julie Andrews, who was making her Broadway debut. They were singing around the piano, drinking, being frightfully witty, as only New York "theahtah" people could be. Show business was not only in my blood; it was forever ringing in my ears. I'll never forget the first *Boy Friend* song I heard coming through the door: "I could be happy with you / If you could be happy with me / I'd be contented to live anywhere / What would I care / As long as you were there?" The lyrics, from this show about English swells on the Riviera in the Roaring Twenties, have stuck in my mind, for they foreshadowed the uprooting of my family that was about to happen.

One of Mom's best friends in attendance that evening was Hope Hampton, the city's quintessential first-nighter. Hope had been a silent film actress, an opera singer who married well, and a clotheshorse who was known as the Duchess of Park Avenue. She was constantly photographed in her Norell gowns, Harry Winston jewels, and full-length chinchilla coats. Years later, when she spotted a girl in jeans at the opera, she declared, "Glamour is dead!" and never set foot in the Met again.

Teeny, who was around forty-five at the time, was very different from Hope, who was a sophisticated version of Mae West. Hope owned her town house on Park; Mom rented. And when the party died down the night of my homecoming, she sat me down and informed me we weren't going to be renting at One Beekman anymore. Of course I was disappointed, but we had always had great addresses in New York. When were we leaving? I asked her. Next week, she said, shockingly. Where were we moving? She had no idea, but out of town. Way out. We were off to look for America. I hated the idea of leaving New York. My mother had weaned me on sophistication. Bill, now twenty-five, who was dabbling in the unspeakably glamorous-seeming world of modeling, had gotten me my first magazine layout the year before, at fifteen, for *Look*. It was my first taste of fame, and I liked it without quite figuring how to sustain it. But whatever it would take, it could happen only in Manhattan, and here we were leaving this glittering paradise for God knows what.

Teeny did have a task for me. She gave me $1,300 and dispatched me to buy a getaway car for us, preferably a Lincoln Continental, her favorite. She also showed me a AAA TripTik map of the United States with a zig-zag marker line going sort of north by south-west. My mother had decided it was time for her to get married again. Her plan was to make another epic cross-country road trip, like our journey to California when Big and Docky died. The goal now was to visit all her old boyfriends, the ones she had passed up, thinking that perhaps she'd been too rash. She had decided she wanted a good father for me and my two brothers, and she was going to hit the road to find her man.

There were actually a number of my mother's many creditors at the *Boy Friend* party, though these were the sort of men who would tend to get lost among the flamboyant show people. There was the manager of the neighborhood Gristedes market, the dentist, the tailor, the dry cleaner, the pharmacist, the support staff whose patience enabled us to live as glamorously as we did. They loved my mother and cut her a lot of slack, because she made their lives exciting and introduced them to people they would otherwise only read about in the gossip columns. My mother was entirely indifferent to money. One of the key tenets of her faith was that we would somehow be divinely supported. We might be broke, but we would never be poor, looked over but never overlooked. That was what faith was all about, and it had miraculously always worked for her. Now we were going to take our faith on the road, one more time.

The next day I carried my wad of cash to J. S. Inskip, the luxury car dealer to the rich and famous, and found a Lincoln Continental. It was pea green. I called brother Bill, the art director of the family, before I plunked down the cash. Pea green? Never, Bill vowed. Blue, navy blue. A Continental had to be blue or it wasn't a Continental. But it was all they had, so I took it anyway. (We would paint it later on.) The Inskips may have found it a bit odd selling a car to a teenager who couldn't drive, but money talked. They delivered the Lincoln to One

127

Beekman, where Mom was packing up the furniture to be auctioned. She wasn't sentimental about things like that. She believed in traveling light, no encumbrances.

One woman came to see the furniture before the auction. The way Bill reeled off the fabricated provenance of everything so entranced the woman that she bought it all, for about $7,500, and the auction was not necessary. As we had paid only a fraction of that for it, that was quite a windfall. It was thanks to the brilliant eye of Bill, who could have been *the* decorator, the Billy Baldwin of his generation, if he had been more driven and focused. The saddest part of leaving was saying farewell to our maid Willie Mae, whose clothes and whose loans of her salary had gotten Teeny through many a tight spot. She was family to us, and we all cried. Years later I found Willie Mae at a hotel on the Avenue of the Americas. We laughed and cried. She was happy because she had a normal job that enabled her to support her son Junebug, not one that required her to give her money back to her boss. Still, she missed the excitement.

Mother was the last of the true romantics. She had a type: dashing, patrician, courageous, gallant, athletic, aesthetic, or, in two words, Buddy Rogers. The money wasn't the point for her at all. But it wouldn't hurt. Like my mother, Bill, the Svengali of our family, wasn't particularly interested in money; he was interested only in the glamour that money could buy. Of course the glamour Bill had in mind cost a fortune, hence this road trip to find a man who would make my mother happy and make my brother's impossible dreams come true. Bill didn't want to turn my mother into merely his cash cow; he wanted her to be a queen. What a wildly unrealistic family I came from, but I had no idea at the time, only a bubbly disequilibrium. The whole thing was like a rolling French court. My mother was Marie Antoinette; Bill was Cardinal Richelieu; I was a lowly courtier; and David, now thirteen, was an even more lowly court handyman.

Bill and Mom created an aura or force field of excitement that drew people to them, and that same force field would eventually create the excitement about me that enabled me to become a movie star. They insisted that I, like they, always be on. For instance, at three in the morning Bill might wake me up and say, "Betty Nell Holland from Blytheville just dropped by. Come say hello." I'd try to beg off, but he wouldn't let me. This would go on every night, and I got very little sleep. The road trip would be a vacation for me, away from Mom and Bill's perpetual party. Thank goodness the car was huge, for it had to contain my mother; myself; Bill; David; our poodle, Marquis; plus our bags. Bill was the designated driver. David got carsick every hundred miles. Marquis had his own needs.

Our first destination was Washington, D.C., to visit "the General," an air force luminary named Bill Hall, who had been Teeny's beau at Mrs. Semple's when he was the star center on the West Point football team. This was the guy she had dumped for Bill Potter because the frumpy way Bill Hall looked wearing his father's civilian clothes shattered Teeny's fantasy of him in his dress grays. Teeny had visited the General once before some years back. That time she had stayed at the estate of Evalyn Walsh McLean, one of the world's leading heiresses and former owner of the Hope diamond. Teeny was about to marry Carleton Hunt, but for some reason wanted to see Hall first, the way she had wanted to see Bill Gerber in Memphis before marrying Bill Potter. Such were Teeny's mating rituals. She told me that she and the General lay in each other's arms crying all night, but dutiful Mom decided to follow through on her plans, which, as best-laid plans tend to do, went astray. Now she was ready for the General, who was still very old West Point, tall and commanding. Unfortunately, he had just been betrothed right before we arrived. "He wasn't the wrong person," my mother noted, always philosophical, never despairing. "It was the wrong time." It was like a Cole Porter song.

Next stop was St. Louis, where we stayed with a very prominent Dr. Hansel and his family in the elegantly bucolic suburb of Kirkwood, where the Budweiser-owning Busches lived. We had no idea which boyfriend my mother was there to see. She just went off to follow her romantic dream, knowing we were in good hands. Dr. Hansel seemed to want to turn me into some kind of outdoorsman. We went fishing, picked strawberries in the woods, rode horses at the clubby Otis Brown Stables, made fresh peach ice cream. At night Dr. Hansel would polish off an entire bottle of wine and pass out. After a few days Teeny returned, empty-handed. "He was perfection when I knew him," she said. "But not now." That was all she told us, and we knew not to press her on a sad subject.

Then we went to Memphis. Teeny was always something of a reigning princess in this queen city of the cotton kingdom; there were lots of lost loves here. First in line was a man named Billy Condon, a tobacco heir known locally as the Snuff King. Mother billeted us with a grand family, the Berry Brookses. Virginia Brooks was one of Teeny's best friends from Blytheville and Memphis. She could trace her genealogy to Charlemagne. The Brookses lived in an estate called Epping Forest Manor. Mr. Brooks was a big-game hunter, a pilot, an explorer. Too bad for Teeny he was married. He tried to make a sportsman out of me, taking me hunting every day. We even shot foxes at night. But I was deeply confused as to who my role model should be. Ashley Wilkes? George Patton? Ernest Hemingway? Should I have been reading *Country Life, Stars and Stripes,* or *Field and Stream?* Einstein and *The American Scholar* were not in my mother's mix, but oddly enough, Tommy Dorsey and *Billboard* were. Suffice it to say, my teenage head was spinning with conflicting options. I sure could have used a real and permanent father figure.

My mother's hunting was less successful than my own. The Snuff King wasn't up to snuff, and the other plantation types who had worshipped her when she had held court at the Cotton Carnival simply didn't measure up to her beau ideal of adolescent perfection that she had somehow never gotten over. Even as she got older, Teeny remained terribly nitpicky, especially about clothes and grooming. I'm sure that's why I became such a fastidious dresser, to try to measure up to Teeny's impossible standards, not to mention Bill's style dictates. Even before I started dating, I learned firsthand how fickle beautiful women could be.

We next went north to Columbus, Ohio, where some once golden boy had "let himself go," which was one of Teeny's most frequently invoked dismissals. "He's not his best" was another. We went to Boston, Washington, Texas, south by southwest. Many towns we didn't even stay in. Mom would leave us in the car, go out and have dinner, emerge with a frown, and off we'd go. Eventually she wouldn't even do dinner. She'd have the gent wait somewhere and tell him we were in a Cadillac, so he wouldn't know it was us when we drove on by. Sometimes she'd have Bill drive around the block several times just to be sure. Bill was an even tougher critic than our mother. "You can't be serious," he'd exclaim with disgust. "He's so tacky." And that would be that. At one point he tried to convince Teeny to tell her candidates to stand on the porch while we did a drive-by, but only if they had hair and teeth. She was too kind for that.

Eventually, the divergence between Teeny's dreams and reality expanded to Grand Canyon proportions. The generals, the sports heroes, the yachtsmen — none of them turned out as my mother remembered them. "He's not at his best" became "Drive, Bill," the subtext always, "What could I have been thinking?" We were down in Laredo, Texas, when, with Bill's advice and consent, Teeny decided to scrap her entire plan. America was for the birds. Old boyfriends were like Douglas MacArthur's old soldiers. They may not have died, but they surely faded away. What next?

With her husband-hunting odyssey a failed venture and our backs to the wall, our undaunted mother pulled one of her famous rabbits out of the hat. At our lowest ebb, she received an invitation from Amber Howes, her eccentric Boston chum, to come visit at the seaside villa Amber had rented down Mexico way, in the fabled seaside village of Acapulco. The siren call of mariachis and mambos and, perhaps, machismo was too loud for Teeny to resist. Acapulco was a dream destination in those days, before the big hotels and the Carlos 'n Charlie's chains took over. It was more like Tahiti, or Bora-Bora, or the Seychelles, a place to escape, and reeking of romance. Maybe it wasn't an ideal target for a mother with three boys and a poodle, but where romance was concerned, nothing stood in my mother's way.

You might have gathered from an earlier mention that Amber was a character. But she was more than that. She was one of the funniest and most outrageous people I've ever met. The downside of all her fun and frolic was that she was not to be trusted. When Amber came over to our Beacon Hill house with her daughters, and one of the girls needed to use the bathroom, she'd tell them not to bother, just pee in the fireplace. Remember Carleton Hunt and the sink? What was it about Bostonians and their toilet habits? There were plenty of bathrooms around but very few takers. As you can well imagine, in stuffy Boston, Amber was frequently snubbed because of her unorthodox ways. That was a mistake because Amber knew how to get even. She would find an excuse to visit the person who had offended her. Then she'd make sure she was standing on the very finest rug they owned, usually a priceless family heirloom. Amber knew how to make herself vomit anytime she wanted to, and all of a sudden she would gush forth all over their prized possessions, sometimes hitting a love seat or other treasure for bonus points.

Although any invitation from Amber should have been automatically suspect, Mom had grown weary of retracing her past and was yearning for distant shores and new romantic vistas. Acapulco seemed like the most romantic place in the world. To hear Amber tell it, you could sleep outdoors every night and live off bananas you picked from a tree and fish you pulled out of the sea. It was the Garden of Eden with tequila. We were hooked on the idea.

Before we crossed the border, Teeny went to AAA and got another TripTik. It had pages and pages of roads highlighted in red marker. We crossed into Mexico at Laredo, Texas, where we stopped to get tourist papers and Mexican auto insurance. We were told by an officer at the border that we would be taking the road along the mountainous spine of the country all the way to Mexico City, which was high in the mountains itself. From Mexico City we would then descend to Acapulco and sea level. We were also told about a stretch of highway along Mexican Highway 85 that went from the town of Tamazunchale to Zimapán, where the road rose ten thousand feet in sixty miles. This was a very dangerous stretch where, the officer pronounced gravely as David nervously took notes, many tourists had died, and due to the fog that settled over it in early morning and late afternoon, it was important to time our trip for the middle of the day. As we pulled away from our helpful adviser, Bill mumbled, "What was all that about fog?" David was too busy writing to answer him.

The trip up the mountainous road started out easily enough; it was hours before we began to learn that there were a few tricks to driving in Mexico, including the one-lane bridges. The idea here was for both cars approaching the bridge from opposite sides to stop at the signs that said "Alto." Then the car that had made the stop first had priority and could cross the bridge. In practice, the Mexican drivers simply honked as they approached the bridge, and whoever honked first proceeded across. Trouble was, who could really tell who honked first? Near misses, and worse, were frequent. Soon it felt like we were on the roof of the world. There were no guardrails along the highway, and since there were often drop-offs of several thousand feet, you really had to be careful not to drift off the road. Apparently, more than a few people had, because on some of the worst bends we saw dozens of little white crosses marking the spots where travelers had been killed.

Naturally we arrived at the deadliest dangerous stretch of road, the one the officer had warned us about, at precisely the wrong time of day, early morning. David had been frantically trying to warn us from the notes he had taken, but no one was listening. "Bill, remember they told us not to take this stretch in the early morning or late afternoon? I have it right here. Well, I'm checking my watch and it's eight A.M. That's early morning."

"Details," Bill replied with haughty disregard. "Caution" was not a word in my family's dictionary. Instead of waiting for the fog to burn off, we just barreled right on into it. David, in resignation, sat back in his seat, a little paler and a lot less comfortable. The fog was one thing; remaining on the road when you couldn't see it was another. But ultimately, even more frightening, was the fact that none of us understood the implications of having "overdrive" on our car.

Overdrive was like an extra gear. Its purpose was to provide enhanced fuel efficiency. Overdrive was meant to be engaged only when traveling at high speeds on a flat highway, certainly not in mountainous terrain where it would actually prevent you from gearing down and using your engine's own torque to control your speed. The long and the short of it was that Bill was burning the brake pads at an alarming rate. Soon there were no brakes at all, and Bill was yelling, "Oh, my God, the brakes aren't working!" He promptly demonstrated that fact by pushing the brake pedal to the floor several times with absolutely no reduction in speed. This was like tapping out "we're going to die" on telegraph keys, and it caused us all to sit bolt upright in our seats. It wasn't all that different from the times as kids in the Hollywood hills we'd tie our skates to the bottom of an orange crate and come whizzing down the steep hills praying for some shrubs or bushes to crash into. Except this was arid Mexico, short on bushes and shrubs, plus we were way too far above the tree line for any vegetation.

Bill was so terrified that I was afraid he might just throw up his hands in desperation and that would be it for us. We'd be one more little white cross along the roadside. That's when Teeny showed her mettle. "Just keep going," she insisted to Bill, with a commander's firmness in her voice. That worked as a plan, though only temporarily. We were picking up almost uncontrollable speed. Then, before disaster could strike, the road leveled out and we were suddenly headed up again in a sort of horrible roller-coaster effect.

"What do I do now?" Bill asked as the car began to slow dramatically on the upgrade. "Just keep going," Mom shouted, now in an even firmer voice. Unfortunately, at this point, Bill came somewhat unglued from the pressure and caused the car to stumble and choke just as we were going up a steep grade. If it had been possible to make a bad situation worse, this was it. We were now rolling backward down the road, with no brakes, a sheer drop-off to one side, a hard-rock mountainside to the other.

By now, Bill's requests for instructions had mutated into a disturbing scream. "Cut it into the mountain!" Mom insisted.

"Yes, cut it into the mountain," David and I chimed in. It was a good life lesson for me: When faced with two desperately bad choices (and heaven knows I've been there), always take the one that at least promises you some hope of walking away from it. As we continued to roll backward, Bill finally came to life and began to crank the steering wheel vigorously. Slowly, but surely, the back end of our car came around. We were now away from the road's edge and the drop-off into oblivion. Instead we rolled toward another kind of oblivion, the massive rock cliff on the inside of the road. But God was looking after us, as Teeny always promised he would. Some loose dirt and rubble cushioned our stop in a very theatrical cloud of dust. It was a Hollywood ending, too. We were all safe. Bill promptly passed out.

A truck stopped to offer help, but the driver quickly saw that our brake pads were shot; he had no way to fix them. Bill began to revive, but he was shaking so badly that someone from the small crowd surrounding us stepped out and injected him by syringe with a substance that caused him to curl up in a fetal position and drift off to La-La-Land. Say what you will about Mexico's drug problem, but this was one time when all I could think was, *Ay, que bueno!*

Time passed, and when a nice German couple in a Mercedes-Benz came by, Mom decided that I should go into the next town and get help. With only a Spanish phrase book in my pocket and no real fluency in the language, I agreed to accompany the German couple to the next town, the hamlet of Zimapán. Along the way, I did my best to master the Spanish for "my brakes don't work" (*Los frenos no trabajan*). I quickly learned another lesson about traveling in Mexico. These very friendly and helpful people are reluctant to let you know that they don't understand your language, so they frequently answer your questions, such as, "Have you got a mechanic here?" and "Will he back soon?" with a resounding *"Sí,"* when they have absolutely no concept of what you have asked them. As a consequence, I wasted a lot of time waiting for a mechanic who never showed up. Eventually I gave up and hopped a garbage truck back to where the car had broken down.

Halfway back to the scene of our near-death experience, I saw what looked like another one: our Lincoln Continental zooming around the mountain curves like a bat out of hell. I was certain that I was going to see my entire family destroyed before my eyes. As this hellish apparition got closer, I realized, from the large sombrero and Emiliano Zapata mustache of the driver, that this wasn't Bill at all. Teeny must have charmed this daredevil driver to take the car on into Zimapán. The family was in a Model T a few bends back. They had stopped to let David relieve himself in a roadside slit trench, and for some reason it was their Mexican driver (not Mom, who was distracted, or Bill, who was still passed out, or David, who was busy) who saw me on top of the garbage truck and waved the truck down. I've always wondered what would have happened if we had not rejoined one another at this juncture. Perhaps I could have wangled a seven-year contract at Churubusco Studios in Mexico City instead of at MGM in Hollywood.

Following a brief delay in Zimapán, where we finally located a mechanic to repair the brakes, we were on the road again to Mexico City. Teeny had taken over the driving, feeling that Bill had gotten us through the rough part and should take some time to rest his shattered nerves. Mexico City was gorgeous, and there were several outstanding hotels from which to choose, the Reforma, the Bamer, and the Regis (the latter was destroyed in the huge 1985 earthquake). Too bad that none of these was within our financial reach. Instead, we made our temporary abode an unprepossessing little hole-in-the-wall, whose name I forget, and hung out at Sanborn's restaurant, where they served American food, until Uncle George could wire us money for something more substantial. When we managed to run out of even enough money to visit the restaurant, we subsisted on popcorn and avocados.

From starvation to conspicuous consumption was a natural leap for my family. With the funds we received from Uncle George, we moved into more comfortable quarters at the Hotel Regis, but before we could blow all our money on hotel rooms, trinkets, and fun, we received news that one of the maids who served our floor had parrot fever, which was wildly contagious, and we would have to be quarantined. Thus ensued a period of free living at the hotel's expense. In addition, as recompense for our inconvenience, we were guests of the hotel for all our meals. As it turned out, the maid had mumps and had concealed it by wearing a scarf around her head while she worked. We were lucky enough to live for free and not get sick, either.

After a week or so we were released from our enforced captivity, and Mom and Bill began to get out and enjoy the Mexican social scene. Bill probably would have been better off if he'd remained quarantined, because returning drunk from a bar one evening, he had the poor judgment to relieve himself on the side of a monument to a Mexican national hero. He was promptly arrested and taken to jail. In the middle of the night, we received a phone call from Bill telling us of his plight and instructing me to sell his solid-gold watch for enough money to bail him out. He told me not to be a fool about it, but to get at least $100, to write down the name and phone number of the person buying it so he could buy it back, and to take the money to the jail. Funny how clearly Bill was thinking now. Why, I wondered, wasn't he thinking that clearly when he decided to pee on the statue in the first place?

Bill ordered me to hurry, because at midnight all the prisoners would be transported to a real prison. I did as I was told and found Bill and a few other gringos shouting obscenities at the Mexican guards, who fortunately could not understand a word of what they were saying. After this, we all agreed it was a good time to get out of town. The trip down to Acapulco was uneventful. We had been warned not to travel the roads around the city after dark because banditos were not just a romantic part of the past but active at setting up road blocks and robbing tourists. We had visions of *The Treasure of the Sierra Madre,* when actor Alfonso Bedoya and his gang are posing as police. Resentful of being asked to show his police badge, Bedoya says, "Badges . . . We don' need no stinkin' badges!" Fortunately, we had learned our lesson about ignoring warnings in Mexico, so we did as we were told.

Acapulco was everything we hoped it would be. Much of the town was built into the side of a cliff overlooking the world's bluest and most beautiful bay, with gray whales frolicking in the distance. Sinatra's song "Come Fly with Me" immortalized Acapulco in the public's imagination as one of the ultimate venues of the jet set. But that song came out in 1963, which was a very good year for the resort, as Elvis made *Fun in Acapulco* then as well. In 1955, when we arrived, Acapulco was still a sleepy, underbuilt tropical hideaway. The only stars who came here regularly were he-men and fishermen John Wayne and Johnny Weissmuller, to take advantage of the unparalleled deep-sea fishing.

We arrived at Amber's rented home. As promised, it was attractive, roomy, with a lovely wide porch accented with tropical hanging hammocks. Best of all it, it had a beautiful view of the ocean. However, there was a small problem in paradise. After driving several thousand miles and nearly losing our lives on Mexico's mountainous roads, we were coolly informed by Amber that we had come at a bad time, that she already had houseguests and couldn't have more, and that if we liked we could sleep overnight on the porch until we could find a place to stay. We were stunned, to say the least. I thought to myself, maybe she found out that it was us who had stolen back the crest stationery she had stolen from us.

Amber was outrageous; we knew that going in. Her own mother had gotten fed up with her the very day we arrived and had decided to take a bus back to the States. Amber had called the Mexican National Police, the Federales, and told them her mother was a thief who had stolen some valuable jewelry. The police stopped her bus en route to the border and dragged her off, nearly giving her a coronary in the process. After some pretty unpleasant treatment, they eventually returned her to Acapulco and Amber in cuffs. Amber really knew how to play rough.

At length, we did find a small, comfortable, affordable hotel, El Faro, which was right across the street from El Mirador, the stunning hillside hotel masterpiece. Mirador's outside dining area overlooked a marvelous natural feature, a split in the rocks where the tide came in. La Quebrada, as it was called, was the site of a spectacle that rivaled anything ever seen in the Roman arenas. Young and, might I add, courageous divers would scale the towering cliff above the split in the rocks, and after praying at a shrine, wait for an incoming wave, then make the most breathtaking dives you could possibly imagine — headfirst, straight down, the equivalent of a ten-story building. It was a scene that never failed to impress even the most jaded tourist.

Teeny enjoyed herself in Acapulco by partying all night. By day she would squander what little money she had on wild clothes like bolero skirts and a rare but unhousebreakable black Lhasa apso named Nietzsche to keep company with our poodle, Marquis, who had broken a leg that the local vet set with a cardboard splint that never let it heal. Marquis became understandably nasty, but Teeny treasured him like one of her boys and took both dogs everywhere. Meanwhile, I met a lovely Mexican girl about my age named Rosario Valle Vasquez. She seemed endlessly desirable to me, with her pretty features, golden skin, and lovely long black hair. I learned a little about Mexican courtship practice. In the beginning, when I first dated her, I was accompanied by a host of family members who would chaperone us, but as time went by and they got to know me better, the chaperones began to dwindle away. The absence of chaperones made me nervous. I was tempted by the lovely Rosario, but I did not fancy having a Mexican shotgun wedding at my tender age.

By now, Amber Howes had come back into our good graces and we were all celebrating what we knew were our final few days in Acapulco. It was a typical Acapulco bash at the very hot Boom Boom Room, Latin band playing, everyone downing tequila, shot after shot after shot. And Amber was up to one of her earthy tricks again. At our table was a very proper Philadelphia Main Liner, clad in Bermuda shorts, madras shirt, and penny loafers, who was also pretty well potted by this time. Most people danced barefoot, and he was no exception, having slipped off his loafers and left them under his chair.

I don't know what it was about him that Amber didn't like; maybe his pretentiousness reminded her of what she hated most about Boston and her husband. At any rate, while the Main Liner was busy dancing, Amber slipped under the table and peed in both of his loafers. Although everyone was shocked when they realized what Amber was doing, they were also fascinated to see what the proper young man would do when he returned to the table.

After the dance, he came back. The whole table held its collective breath when he began to slip his shoes back on. You could practically hear the squish. All I can say is that he must have been related to Carleton Hunt, because just as Carleton had evidenced no reaction with the dribble glass and rubber cheese, this gent did not bat an eyelash. He just went on his merry way for the rest of the evening as if wearing pee-flooded shoes was the most natural thing in the world.

Teeny soon realized that no man in this

seaside Sybaris was father material, and, after a few decadent months, she packed us into the Continental for the long drive back to New York City. She planned to live on more of those inheritance payments from Uncle George in Blytheville, at least until love walked in. Teeny was in major denial about the precarious state of our finances, but coupled with this was the intensity of her spirituality, which she conveyed to us as well. Even if no Sir Galahad came to our financial rescue, God would be our sugar daddy. The divine would always take care of us, and that belief was what made me feel secure. But I still hated to be leaving. By this time, I had gotten hooked on Acapulco, just as I had been hooked on Manhattan. "Never cry for anything that doesn't love you back" was a lesson Mom drummed into me. Home was wherever we hung our hats, which turned out to be everywhere on earth. The main idea was to get up and go, and live, live, live. There were no sad farewells for the Hamiltons. Besides, Mother assured us we'd be back, and Mother was never wrong.

"Okay, here's the plan. You take half the loot and we'll split up. Colt, you and the boys ride east. Frank and the rest of us will head west. We'll all meet up again at the hideout in two weeks." That was the obligatory scene in every outlaw Western in my day, and not too different from our real-life situation leaving Mexico. Nobody wanted to drive those monstrous mountains again. So we hired a steely-nerved driver to take the car, its luggage, and one of our dogs back to the border. I went along to keep him honest. Meanwhile, Mom, Bill, and David piled onto a train with our other dog. We agreed to join up again at the border in Nuevo Laredo.

All went well. The rendezvous was completed and the driver was paid. We peeled out of Mexico, thanking our lucky stars to be in one piece, and laid tracks for New York City. We were rolling along, cruising down the highway, making great time, when somewhere outside Terre Haute, Indiana, we heard a fearful noise that sounded like a cry from all the banshees in hell. Little did we know, the hired driver (he of the steely nerves) had been driving the car without motor oil. The engine was now bone-dry. Without warning, the big Lincoln V-12 seized up and came to a gear-crunching halt. When we looked under the hood, for what reason I cannot state, since we hadn't the foggiest idea of what should be located there, all I could think of was that somebody should have taken pity on the poor smoldering, sputtering mess and put it out of its misery with a well-placed .45 round through the engine block. There was a motel nearby. We dragged our luggage over to it.

It was nice to know people and Teeny knew them all. Fortunately, one of them was a car dealer with a repair shop in Columbus, Ohio, who agreed to have our car towed to his place to be fixed. One caveat, though: He warned us not to expect to drive the car for several weeks. Next morning we were roadside, sticking out our thumbs in the old hobo salute. Mom was bedecked in her most alluring Mexican outfit. I was wearing peasant pants and a small sombrero. Not a good choice, I might add, for touring the byways of Middle America. You could hear the chortles, snorts, and guffaws of passing motorists. Hmm, I wondered, could we possibly have been away so long that we were now strangers in our own land?

As Dr. Stevens liked to say, "There's more than one way to skin a cat." Accordingly, Mom hid us behind a tree. Then, doing her best imitation of Claudette Colbert in the hitchhiking scene from *It Happened One Night,* she tried to entice someone to stop. The results were meager — a smile here, a wave there. Mercifully, at long last, someone did stop.

"Would you like a ride?" the nice-looking,

dark-haired man asked politely. At a glance, he didn't look like an ax murderer sizing up his next victims, so we all came out from behind the tree, and Mom asked, "How many of my children and how much of my luggage and how many of my dogs can you fit in your car?"

He answered, "Oh, Lord, lady, I don't know!" Mom made up his mind for him by packing in as many of us in his car as it would hold. The good samaritan wound up transporting Mom, David, the two dogs, and a trunk full of luggage. Bill and I were able to hop a ride on a milk truck. I was just glad to be rolling again, but Bill dismissed our seedy conveyance with a sneer. "Oh, the inelegance of it all!"

If Bill wasn't happy with his present mode of transportation, he was even less cheered by what followed. Mom had only enough money left to send her three boys home by bus. We agreed we'd all meet back at the Alrae, the same residential hotel we'd stayed at when we first came to New York. When I think about it, this was really quite a noble act on my mother's part. She was choosing to remain aboard the *Titanic* while making certain her children had a place in the life-boat, and all this while holding two dogs! I'll admit I heaved a sigh of relief as I waved good-bye to Mom and the memory of our recent misadventures, pounded my jacket into a serviceable pillow, and fell asleep almost before the Greyhound pulled away from the station.

Teeny, I was to learn later, went to the train station, where she encountered an old flame who happened to be taking the same train and was happy to lend her the difference between what she had and the price of a ticket. Since he had a sleeping compartment, and had done her a big favor, naturally he had ideas of their rekindling the flame. Teeny had no such intention. After sharing a pleasant drink with him in the bar car, she politely inquired, "Now tell me, which of my dogs would you like to take to your compartment? The Lhasa that's not housebroken or the French poodle that's housebroken but mean?"

Unhappy with both prospects, Mr. Chivalry answered sheepishly, "I'll take the mean poodle." He took Marquis to his compartment with him. That night Teeny taped a note on his door with her address and phone number. It read, "Hope you enjoyed the poodle. Please call me in New York and I'll be happy to pay you what I owe you." Next morning her old flame sent back the dog by the porter with his own message: "Thanks a lot."

By a little magic, Mom beat us home. By the time we arrived, she had established temporary quarters at the Alrae, and we heard music and laughter coming from her room. "How did you do that?" we asked in amazement. "You left after we did, and you're here already with a party going!"

"I taught you everything *you* know," she answered, arching an eyebrow for emphasis, "but I didn't say I taught you everything *I* know."

CHAPTER SIX
BY THE BEAUTIFUL SEA

Our next home was 860 Fifth Avenue, a five-room apartment that overlooked Central Park and provided the closest thing that New York had to trees, sunshine, and fresh air. We welcomed this bucolic change. Teeny and Bill were trying to make the best of their return, but their lives had been severely interrupted. It wasn't easy picking up loose ends in busy Manhattan. There was simply too much going on too fast. Besides, big interruptions, such as Mexico had been, afforded a spectacular opportunity for a big change.

The spark that ignited that change was a simple fragment of a sentence. Teeny was walking through the building's lobby when she overheard the doorman speaking to the building manager. The key snippet was ". . . came for Mr. Jesse Spalding."

"What was that you said?" Mom stopped to ask the doorman.

"Oh, some mail came for Mr. Spalding. I was just going to ask the manager if we had a forwarding address."

"Mr. Spalding lives here?" Teeny inquired.

"Yes, ma'am, right up until a week ago," the doorman added.

Mom turned to the manager and asked, "And do you have his forwarding address?"

"Yes, Mrs. Hunt, he has an address in Palm Beach, Florida," the obliging manager replied. Jesse was an old flame of the "keeper" type, and Mom's ears perked up when she heard his name. She had met him many years before on a trip to Miami and to her he was "drop-dead handsome" and very romantic. Mom once explained it to me this way: There are some people you meet and something powerful happens, and one way or another, for good or bad, you know you have to see them again just to get them out of your system. (I think you know by now that Mom had a flair for overstatement.)

"I can't believe he lived here in the same building and I missed him," she moaned. That was one mistake she wouldn't let stand. It didn't take much to convince Bill to join her in a jaunt to Palm Beach. That was where he'd wanted to go in the first place when he lost that bet in the driveway in Blytheville. So it was decided right then and there that when David and I returned to Hackley, Teeny and Bill would leave New York and check out the landscape in Florida. Such is the dime on which a life can turn.

With some reluctance and a lot of fast talking, Hackley agreed to readmit David and me after what seemed an excessive hiatus from learning. Rather than convincing myself I should now buckle down and concentrate on my studies, I came to the opposite conclusion. I reasoned that in reality life was a popularity contest, and the prize didn't go to the best and the brightest but instead to the one with the nerve to stick out his neck, to poke his head out of the crowd. If you had brass enough, and you used all the talents you'd been given at birth, you were bound to succeed, or at least annoy the hell out of everybody: If that didn't work, you had to be willing to place all your chips on black or red and let it ride. That way you would either succeed fantastically or fail miserably. I have never felt comfortable anywhere in between.

So I resolved to be in everything. My prime activities again were the Glee Club and the Octet. Warren Hunke, the school's musical director, was a really fine musician who taught us, in four-part harmony, a wide array of melodies of the collegiate genre, the stuff of the Yale Whiffenpoofs as well as barbershop quartets and beer hall ditties. I think he could see that I was never going to dedicate myself to being a great student, so he offered me the alternative challenge of performing before live audiences.

The Hackley Octet was the distillation of the best singers from the much larger Hackley Glee Club. I was no great shakes as a singer. I just listened to the guy next to me and parroted what he did; if he hit a bad note, I hit a bad note. What sold me to Mr. Hunke and ultimately the audiences that attended our performances was my comedic flair. While the rest of the Octet was doing their best to sing like automatons, I would lose my place in the song, wander around, drop my sheet music, and fall down while trying to pick it up, whatever it took to get a laugh. And it worked.

With these bits perfected, Professor Hunke decided to take our act on the road to, of all places, girls' colleges. You can only imagine the joy that filled my heart when I heard those wonderful words: "girls' colleges." There was a lot to be said for the curriculum I chose for myself. Chasing girls, hanging out at Mamma Leone's with my preppy buddies Bert Hand, Herb Allen, and Bobbie

Vincent, faking track by hiding in the woods and joining the runners on the last lap, appearing with the Octet on Ted Mack's *Amateur Hour,* becoming school poet laureate. I was enjoying myself so much that I hardly noticed it was spring break. David suggested we go see the family in Palm Beach. In their phone calls, Teeny and Bill had gushed incessantly about how wonderful it was and how much fun they were having.

When a Hackley professor named Richard Hudson told us he was headed for Key West, we asked if we could tag along as far as Palm Beach. He said he was happy to have the company and even agreed to pick us up for the return trip to school. Our journey south was uneventful enough, but I couldn't forget, or stop feeling guilty about, what I had done to Mr. Hudson's prized play only a few weeks before. Mr. Hudson was our English teacher, and he had written a play as his doctoral thesis and spent literally years polishing it. He had at long last decided to put on this very special play with his English students cast in the various roles. I had been selected to play the lead role.

Mr. Hudson's opus was a somber play about a boy who had left Russia and was now trying to make his life in the United States. I recall it as a verbose and morose little production that featured the introspective main character tromping about the stage with a heavy knapsack on his back while making equally weighty pronouncements. Frankly, it had bored the hell out of me, though I would never rain on my teacher's big parade by telling him.

Everything went well at the rehearsal. However, on the night of the performance, before a packed house of Hackley students and their parents, I went completely blank. For the life of me I could not remember my next line. The other actors in the scene with me kept waiting and waiting and waiting, but nothing came out. I could see the terror building in their faces. That's when I decided to fake my lines by pretending to be speaking Russian. My pseudo Russian sounded pretty good and it solved my immediate problem, even though it made no sense whatsoever. Unfortunately, it didn't do anything for the other actors, who were waiting for me to give them their cues.

With all the grace under pressure I could muster, I elected to improvise further. I began signing. You know, what they do for deaf people and, being the kind guy I am, I encouraged my fellow actors to "sign" me back. This at least gave them something to do other than just stare at me in sheer horror. Poor Mr. Hudson, hearing the building laughter and noticing that his beloved play had suddenly gone horribly wrong, began hauling down the curtain, which fell across my shoulders as I frantically continued to sign. Surprisingly, everyone kept laughing and applauding. Somehow I had managed to transform serious drama into light farce.

When Mr. Hudson came backstage after my performance, he turned to me. "Mr. Hamilton, tonight I gave you the opportunity of a lifetime. Words cannot begin to express the alarm I felt when I realized you were departing from the lines. I'm sure you are aware I have spent many years working on my play and carefully planning every step leading up to tonight. I want to thank you, Mr. Hamilton. In your skillful hands my play worked far better as a comedy. I suggest you give some thought to going to Hollywood to be an actor. I will write you a personal recommendation."

Mr. Hudson was a stand-up guy and I liked him for it. I've always wondered how generous I would have been if I had spent all that time working on a play only to have it treated in such a freewheeling fashion. But honest to goodness, I had no choice. When I say that words failed me, that's exactly what they did.

We pulled into Palm Beach in the early morning. I could see what Mom and Bill were raving about. This really was a special place. As we toured down the estate section, I was impressed by how grand the lifestyle was here. I checked the address I was given. Their house would be here somewhere on North County Road. These houses weren't quite as grand as the palaces we'd seen coming in, but they weren't shabby, by any means. I asked Mr. Hudson to slow down; we were getting close. Hold it, there it was, a tiny wooden house painted bright red. I poked David in the ribs and pointed to it. He looked back at me with a frown that amplified my concern.

"Is this it?" Mr. Hudson asked.

"No, no," I automatically responded. "It's a little farther down." I made him continue down the road until I saw a house that looked sufficiently imposing. "That's it."

David picked up on what I was doing and agreed. "Yes, that's it. You can let us out here." The professor shot the place an admiring look and drove off. David and I quickly toted our bags back to the little red two-room house. Unfortunately, the shack Teeny and Bill had rented would not have served even as a decent toolshed for one of the grand Palm Beach mansions. After I had recovered from the shock that we were to live in the tiniest house on the island, we rang the bell, were greeted warmly, and set to work exploring our new digs, which didn't take long since there were only two tiny rooms plus a Lilliputian galley kitchen and a bathroom with a shower you had to hunch over to enter.

"I'm impressed," I said, with my nose about a mile in the air. Ironic, wasn't it, that I was now the house snob when it was Bill who usually occupied that role. (Could I be turning into Bill? That was a scary thought.) Having gone to Florida's ultimate country club college, Bill was fully acquainted with America's ultimate country club city, the "last resort" for the country's, as well as many of the world's, rich and social. Even though it looked a lot like Beverly Hills — palm trees and bougainvillea and Spanish confectionery architecture — and shared many luxe attributes, Beverly Hills was mostly about Hollywood, and Palm Beach was mostly about world domination and the elegantly spent leisure time that came therefrom. Palm Beach was short on movie stars. The only denizens who had any real connection with Hollywood were tycoon Joseph Kennedy, who had owned RKO, and Dina Merrill, regal daughter of reigning dowager

Post Toasties heiress Marjorie Merriweather Post, who was trying to become the next Grace Kelly.

But what Palm Beach lacked for Bill in celluloid glitz, it more than made up for in decorative elegance. There were probably more fine antiques here than in all the palaces of Europe combined, since the palaces had been bought out by the Yankee plutocrats and their acquisitions-mad multiple spouses. It was decorator's heaven, and Bill didn't have much trouble talking Teeny into giving it a shot. Bill and Mom were having the time of their lives and were rarely home. Palm Beach was a seasonal resort that partied like mad for about five months (the "Season") and then went into hibernation. Sometime in April, Worth Avenue, the main drag of glamorous shopping even then, closed down completely and the store owners and employees drifted back north.

Bill was dating a princess (Princess God Knows Who from God Knows Where) who wanted to leave her husband and child to marry him. Not exactly the marrying kind, Bill tried to cool her ardor by constantly reminding her that she'd lose her title if she persisted in this crazy plan. The princess remained steadfast in her willingness to throw all caution to the wind. Bill told Mom that had he been able to become a prince by marrying her, he might have taken her up on it. Bill would have been superb with a title.

Teeny was dating Noel Seeburg, the jukebox king, and the music never stopped. They were stepping out to all the great local restaurants and nightspots, world-famous watering holes for the rich, such as Nando's, the Colony, and Taboo, all of which she adored. Best of all, unlike her ex, Frank Black in New York City, Noel enjoyed going out almost as much as Mom did. I tried to follow all their social comings and goings (parties, charity balls, private clubs), but it was making my head spin. "I'll sort it all out at the beach," I said to myself. So I threw on my trunks, grabbed a beach towel, and the baby-oil-and-iodine concoction that passed for suntan lotion, and headed for the sun and surf.

Just as an alcoholic needs alcohol, or a gambling addict needs action, my inner child yearned to be oceanside. You can imagine how excited I was to be in Palm Beach. It was glorious. I had seen other beaches (Santa Monica, Coney Island, Galveston, Acapulco), but they were nothing like this. Soft, powdery, white sand, a nearly cloudless blue sky, and a teal green ocean with absolutely no temperature shock when you plunged in. This must have been what Mecca was like for Muslims. *Allahu Akbar,* there was no doubt about it.

And that sun, oh, that glorious sun! Once I had gone through the red nose, red cheeks, and red shoulders phase, my color had metamorphosed into a handsome cinnamon brown. My legs were so tanned, in fact, that I adopted the island's tradition of wearing loafers with no socks. After a few days of ritualized sunning, I noticed that the girls were beginning to react to me. It was subtle at first — a nod here, a turned head there, a wink from a cutie passing by — but something was definitely beginning to happen. I had experienced another epiphany: Suntanning was going to be to me what the phone booth, funny blue suit, and cape were to Superman. Without a tan I was just another paleface in the crowd. With one, I could do some pretty amazing things.

On this spring holiday I met Merle Tuck, a very attractive, very sporty young lady, who sped around in a cute little MG sports car. Newly licensed, she was happy to drive me everywhere, which usually included days on a wide stretch of beach just north of the Kennedy compound (soon to become JFK's Winter White House) and nights socializing at one of the frequent poolside parties. The limbo had become wildly popular, and clad in bathing suits or Bermuda shorts, we'd dance the night away to a throbbing island beat.

During the tremendous swirl of social activity I enjoyed that spring break, I found myself attracted to more than just the endless sunshine and party atmosphere. Palm Beach girls were really something! I can best describe them as a combination of the natural chic you find in Eastern girls, together with a healthy, wholesome beauty that I can only credit to loads of Florida sunshine, orange juice, and fresh air. It was painful to leave paradise, but return to school we must. I kept my fingers crossed that time and circumstances would bring me here again.

You know the feeling when you're going with someone but constantly thinking of someone else? Well, that's how I felt when I returned to Hackley to finish out the year. I couldn't wait for time to elapse so I could return to the beauty and promise of Palm Beach. Of course I probably bored all my pals to death recounting my tales of paradise lost, but they were patient enough to listen. Meanwhile, I wrote a few letters to Merle to keep up with the Palm Beach goings-on. The big news for me at Hackley was that I was elected president of the Glee Club, which was one of the most prominent positions on campus. As my junior year came to a close, I was relieved to find that despite my dreadful neglect of my studies, I had at least managed to score all gentleman's Cs.

In our final counseling before taking off for the summer, the school advised David and me that in their opinion it would be better if we were to attend separate schools. They backed it up by adding they were renewing only a partial scholarship for one of us. Their reasoning, I believe, was that due to the many inconsistencies in our prior education, we both had a great deal of catching up to do. I think they believed that David might possibly make the necessary effort, but they were convinced, and quite rightly so, that I wouldn't. The two of us thought it over for about five seconds and solved the whole issue by neither of us ever returning to the school.

By summer I was back in Palm Beach and loving it, even in its dead season. We had now moved up a few notches in the residence department. Wise old Bill had convinced Teeny not to rent anymore but to take her last $7,500 and use $5,000 of it as a down payment on a fully furnished house at 1469 North Ocean Boulevard, which was the Fifth Avenue of this resort. This adorable three-bedroom minimansion had a lot of Spanish revival charm and was situated on the last bend before you reached the Palm Beach Inlet (the end of the island). The house backed up on the same beach Merle and I had explored during spring break, one of the widest and loveliest in the area.

Our choice of schools was an easy one. There was Graham-Eckes, an on-island private school for kids whose families had a gazillion dollars. Then there was the public high school across the Intracoastal Waterway in West Palm Beach, for kids whose families didn't have a gazillion anything. Since my family fit squarely in the second category, it was decided that David's junior year and my senior year would be played out in a bebop, sock hop, ducktail, ponytail, poodle skirt, motorcycle jacket heaven called Palm Beach High, *American Graffiti* with a tan.

Almost immediately I got into trouble. We had been taught to drive, at much risk to life and limb of all concerned, by a wonderfully generous and brave friend of Mom's named Helene Fortescue Reynolds, who had once been married to the Reynolds Aluminum heir. A world traveler, she was often away for long periods. When she left this time, she tossed us the keys to her pink 1956 Thunderbird convertible, which we used to get to school. Once we had overcome our natural aversion to pink, we agreed we had a very cool ride.

In an amazingly short time I went from being a snooty little Eastern prep school boy to a freewheeling rock-and-roll high schooler. And leave it to me to find the fast crowd. It must be my constant desire to fit in, but before you could count to three, I was drag racing at streetlights and siphoning gas out of tractors parked on country club golf courses (we called the siphon a "Georgia credit card") to help pay for all the gasoline I was burning up.

It was during one of these drag races that the police pulled me over and told me they'd clocked me going 90 in a 25 mph zone. They called it reckless driving and said I would surely lose my license. They were completely right, of course; I did lose my license for six months. However, the experience wasn't all bad because I met an amazing guy named Sean Flynn, the son of the famous actor Errol Flynn, who was coming up before the same judge for his third offense of speeding on his motorcycle. They took Sean's license away, too. We laughed at our mutual predicament and made a pact that we would date only girls who had cars and that we'd give each other rides. From the looks of Sean, who was even more of an Adonis than his dad, I figured it was a pretty safe bet he'd be riding first.

Sean's mother was the French showgirl/ actress Lili Damita. Lili had married Errol in 1935 when he was a nobody, just before he hit it big with *Captain Blood*. The year they split, 1942, Errol was charged with (and later acquitted of) the statutory rape of two teenage girls, and he was off and running. Lili had taken Sean, who was a year younger than I, to live in the "healthier" (than Hollywood) environment of Palm Beach. Big mistake.

Sean had a deeply complex psychology. He was an unwanted baby, whom Lili stuck Errol with as a revenge pregnancy, for they rarely saw each other. Lili hated Errol, and Sean was ambivalent, because on one hand Errol was the most unfit parent on earth, but on the other he was the most hypnotic. Errol's idea of fatherhood was to take Sean to El Morocco and buy him a hooker. Not a bad idea, to a horny teenager. Sean's tales of high seas adventures in the Mediterranean and Caribbean on Errol's yacht, the *Zaca*, filled me with adolescent envy. I wished my father were Errol Flynn. What boy wouldn't? I also wished my real father, no slouch himself, was around.

It wasn't because she had a car, or because her dad was the owner of Cocrane Buick, but when I first laid eyes on Elizabeth Cocrane, I wanted to let them linger there forever. She had luscious blond hair, the kind you see in shampoo commercials, and her silky smooth skin was stretched tight over her beautiful face and well-defined jawline. To make matters even better, she had a very romantic little cleft in her chin. A bell rang in my head that said that if I were going to be Mr. Cool at school, this had to be my princess. I think it was my willingness to make a fool of myself to win her affection that did the trick. Liz lived on the island, too, so we spent hours after school in each other's company, romancing and reading poetry, with only an occasional break for me to copy her homework.

Palm Beach High School had an amazingly advanced theater arts program ably helmed by a man named Frank Leahy. I was tapped for the starring role in *Brigadoon* (the part Gene Kelly played in the movie). If I was surprised by how my tan attracted girls, I was absolutely bowled over by the aphrodisiacal effect of a romantic starring role. Girls' eyes now verily danced when they fell upon me. There are no crushes like a teenage girl's crushes, and being the focus of them was intoxicating. The high-water mark was when I was presented with the Best Actor in Florida award after a competition at the University of Florida, in Gainesville. Directed by Mr. Leahy, we performed a scene from *Aria da Capo* by Edna St. Vincent Millay. I felt like the Laurence Olivier of the tropics. Slowly a realization began to dawn on me that maybe, just maybe, I *did* have a calling. Like the song from Disney's *Pinocchio,* "Hi-diddly-dee, an actor's life for me . . ."

Teeny had her own drama going. She had rekindled the passion in her old flame Jesse Spalding, whose presence in Palm Beach was what had lured her down here to begin with. They had finally connected, and Jesse was now getting serious. One afternoon when Teeny was sunning poolside, wearing no makeup and an old bathing suit that sagged from lack of elasticity, Jesse had just appeared. In a brief conversation with him, Mom discovered that he had total recall of every moment they had ever spent together, and he told her he had an important question to ask her. Teeny begged his indulgence, excused herself to comb her hair, don makeup, and put on a new bathing suit, whereupon she returned to Jesse and said, "Now, what was it you wanted to ask me?"

174

They were married and honeymooned in New York City. I have always had this theory that anyone can hide his or her faults and fake it for at least six months or possibly a year. That's why long engagements were so important to older generations. It gave the intendeds plenty of time to screw up. It didn't take even six days for Jesse to do just that. While staying at a Manhattan hotel on their honeymoon, Jesse had a few too many and started acting up. It was late at night. With both of them undressing to go to bed, Teeny decided she had had enough. She convinced Jesse, who always slept in the raw, as he called it, to check on his shoes, which he had left in the hallway to be shined by the porter. Once he had sauntered out in his birthday suit, Teeny locked the door solidly behind him and proceeded to go to bed.

For Jesse, this was a predicament. But with the ingenuity that only drunks can show, Jesse found a towel in the hotel's linen closet and wrapped it around himself. Emboldened by his success so far, Jesse now screwed up enough courage to knock on the door of the room beside theirs. This was a stroke of luck for Jesse, because the man who answered the door was a fellow drunk, who, after lending Jesse a pair of shorts to wear and having a drink with him, saw nothing wrong with Jesse's plan to step out on the six-story ledge and try to inch his way over to the window to the room where Teeny was now fast asleep. It would have been possible if the ledge had been continuous, but it wasn't. So with the aid of a towel held at one end by Jesse's new friend, he managed to step across the yawning space in front of him and over to the ledge in front of Mom's window. But wouldn't you know it, the window was locked.

By now, a crowd of late-nighters had gathered below. All eyes looked upward. Was this troubled soul about to end his earthly days? "Oooh, I want to watch this!" they buzzed. The police and fire department soon arrived. After bashing in doors, many of them the wrong ones, they decided to lower a rope to Jesse from the roof. A couple of things were now beginning to turn in Jesse's favor. The cool night air, and the realization that what he had done might have fatal consequences, had caused his alcohol-soaked brain to sober somewhat. Also, Jesse was if nothing else very athletic by nature. (A life of tennis playing will do that.) So, with an embarrassed grin worthy of Jack Nicholson, Jesse shimmied all the way down six floors to the street.

Mid-descent, while hanging from a rope

and wearing only his borrowed boxer shorts, Jesse was snapped by a legion of newspaper photographers. His little stunt made the wire services. The next morning, on the front page of the *New York Post,* as well as a host of other papers around the country and the world, there was Jesse hanging it all out. Teeny made light of it. "Thanks to all the publicity," she said, "when I came home at least I didn't have to answer a lot of boring questions from people wanting to know how was my honeymoon."

I was faring much better on the home front, where Liz and I were spending frequent romantic evenings under the stars. One night when we were exploring our mutual passion at the abandoned Dodge estate, we decided to conclude events with a skinny-dipping session. The whole world had seen Burt Lancaster and Deborah Kerr in *From Here to Eternity.* That scene of them rolling in the surf had made a big impression on me. Apparently it had made a big impression on others as well. Stark naked, we ran right into another pair of skinny-dippers. One of them was Jack Kennedy, at that time a senator from Massachusetts. His companion, I found out later, was Flo Smith, the lovely ex-model wife of Eisenhower's ambassador to Cuba, Earle "E.T." Smith. The handsome senator gave me the biggest I-won't-tell-if-you-won't grin and we all went on our merry ways. Years later, when we were properly introduced, he took me aside and reminisced about the incident. He hadn't forgotten one deliciously naughty second of it. The man had total recall.

My circle of buddies was also expanding. Pepe Fanjul, soon to be a sugar baron, and Fernando de la Riva, a ladies' man in the best Porfirio Rubirosa tradition, were two of my friends from the wealthy Cuban community who had fled Cuba ahead of Castro's revolution. Together with rich Venezuelans, they added a new charm and zest to an already sophisticated town. Yet my most fascinating pal was the enigmatic Sean Flynn. Sean and I took an overnight boat to Havana together to drink and debauch at the Nacional and Montmartre, in the Batista-Meyer Lansky glory days, our own fifties Latino version of *Animal House*. Neither of us had seen anything so extravagant, the armies of naked showgirls, the music, the rum, the cigars. No one was carded. Who cared? Plus I was with Errol Flynn's son. The red carpet was rolled out. I could see how valuable that Hollywood pedigree could be. The acting was one thing; the lifestyle was out of this world.

Sean, who had appeared on his father's television show, was a true party animal and lady killer. He was intent on following in his father's footsteps and would star in a few years in *The Son of Captain Blood,* where his handsome looks captured everyone's attention. I have every confidence he would have succeeded as a major actor, probably even eclipsing the accomplishments of his dad, had the adventurer in him not prevailed over the actor. On a photojournalist mission to Cambodia during the Vietnam War, he disappeared and his body has never been found. It was presumed that he died at the hands of the Communist rebels. Every life lost is a waste, I know, but the loss of Sean had a profound and long-lasting effect on me.

About this time Teeny was having renewed problems with Jesse. I don't think it was Jesse's fault, really. He was a nice enough guy and a passably good stepfather. He took David and me out on his boat, showed us some of the intricacies of deep-sea fishing while intoxicated, and taught us how to clean your catch after a couple of stiff shots. Jesse's downfall was the constant financial pressure under which we lived. We were conditioned to it; he was not. Jesse was a poor man from a rich family. Something of a bad boy and a ne'er-do-well, he had been cut off financially by his wealthy mother, Mrs. Elliot Maxwell. Of course, Teeny had no idea at the time of her marriage this was the case. I think Jesse himself thought that he had been romancing an heiress, not a pauperess. Whatever the case, they were star-crossed from the beginning. I think of it this way. If you took a surface-dwelling fish down to, say, one thousand feet below sea level, he'd probably implode from the pressure. By the same token, if you took a terribly spoiled rich man and put him in an atmosphere where he constantly had to wonder where his next meal would come from, he was almost certain to buckle under that pressure. That was what happened to Jesse. David and I, who were way beyond our years in pressure handling, found ourselves constantly reassuring Jesse that everything was going to be all right. Of course, it didn't help that good old stepdad was bringing home drunken mariachi bands to serenade Teeny after the bars closed at three A.M., or that he would come home so loaded that he walked around in big circles, falling down several times before reaching the door. I'm afraid we shattered poor Jesse, so I don't think it was cruel when Teeny decided Jesse wasn't really going to be part of the solution to her problems, but rather was himself part of the problem. They were divorced soon after.

With my high school graduation approaching, I realized that I needed to make some plans about what I wanted to do with my life. I would have loved to become a doctor like my grandfather, but the prospect of ten or more years of college, med school, internships, and more did not speak to the gypsy in my young soul. The call of the studio soundstages must have been echoing in my subconscious, for the immediate summer months ahead would lead me onto my collision course with the destiny of stardom.

CHAPTER SEVEN
BECOMING MYSELF

Whatever germinating passion I had for going to Hollywood had less to do with my adventures on the Palm Beach High stage than with my adventures in the Hamptons in the summer of 1957, which I will always remember as my Summer of Love. As decades go, they didn't get much less erotic than the fifties. It was the buttoned-down, buttoned-up Eisenhower era. People wore Davy Crockett coonskin caps. Khrushchev was threatening to bury us, and a lot of people, believing him, were building fallout shelters. The big social story of the times was Grace Kelly becoming Princess of Monaco, though living in Palm Beach and seeing my own brother turning down princesses made royalty somewhat less alien to me. The other big news was Elvis Presley, but being from Memphis, I was no more overwhelmed about the future king than I was about the new princess. He seemed like a regular

Southern guy, just with a lot more rhythm than most. It was an era of suburbia — lots of martinis but little sex, at least that anyone talked about.

I had just finished my senior year at Palm Beach High School, one course short of graduation. I would have to go back for a semester to finish. I hadn't thought about college, didn't want to. In those days there wasn't the admissions madness that came to be with the baby boomers. I was preboom, and I just assumed that if I wanted to go to college all I had to do was head to Gainesville and show up, unless I could somehow finesse a scholarship to Rollins. Dartmouth? Out of the question. Too cold, too hard. Besides, my father had died, at fifty-six, of a sudden heart attack in my senior year, and I was too upset by this premature loss to do the rah-rah alumnus thing.

I was traveling with my class to see the school choir band play in a competition in New Orleans when I found out the awful news. I had been chasing after a girl in the band. She played one instrument; I was about to play another. I think my father would have been proud of me. Teeny called to tell me about Dad. She was just recovering from a gallbladder operation and wasn't able to go to the funeral, though I'm not sure she would have gone even if she were well. I told her I *had* to go.

I jumped on the first bus back to Palm Beach and rode all night, in a numb daze. From there I got some money and caught a plane to New York, flying with local debs Wendy Vanderbilt and Sandra Topping, who were very comforting to me. Not so my father's family. I went straight to my father's apartment, but it was sealed off. He had died in his sleep. Dad had split from June Howard and was living all alone. At the apartment I met up with one of my father's brothers. "Why are you here?" my uncle asked me, with suspicion and hostility. He was a tough Vermont Yankee. I told him I wanted my father's beloved solid gold pen-and-pencil set, his ring, his cuff links, and especially his violin. The uncle turned me down flat, saying everything had been bequeathed to Dartmouth. "Don't count on me," he warned me, shutting down any possibility of my own Yankee ingenuity appearing on his fenced-off premises. It was a painful but valuable life lesson: Never count on anyone for anything. I spent the night at the Alrae. It was a sad homecoming.

The next day I went to the funeral at Frank Campbell's on Madison Avenue. There was a large gathering, though I knew almost nobody. My father looked terrible in his open casket, in a drab blue suit. June had put a toy violin in his hand. Dad would have hated it. The piped-in music was "I'll Be Seeing You," a song that has never left my mind. I thought to myself that if Dad had been able to keep playing his music, he would still be alive. Big business and all those martini lunches may have done him in; he could not get the artist in himself united with the businessman. This too was a great lesson to me: Do what makes you happy.

I thought of the time we had spent together, watching boxing matches on television and wrestling, the two Georges laughing at Gorgeous George. We had never talked about feelings. That wasn't masculine, and my father, for all his sweet music, was terminally masculine. Men shared time, not emotions. I recalled some of the things he had taught me, about going up and introducing myself to strangers and never being shy. If you were quiet, you scared people, he told me. Look people in the eye, he said. And smile, my mother would add. Never let anyone think you're judging them. I wasn't judging Dad, but I couldn't stop lamenting how awful he looked in that casket. To paraphrase W. C. Fields's own epitaph, I'd rather Dad had been in Philadelphia, playing the Bellevue-Stratford.

One of the mourners, a woman in black, was crying inconsolably, sobbing so loudly I wanted to comfort her, but the funeral director held me back. He explained that she was a professional mourner, a regular at Campbell's. She had no idea who Dad was. Years later I found Dad's Tiffany pen and pencil at an auction and bought them. He had splendid handwriting. I've never stopped missing him and wanting to live up to the ideal he represented.

I was looking for some sort of escape the summer after high school, and I found it, as I so often did, through a friend of my mother's. Jerry Riker owned a chain of commercial hotels in New York. He had been encouraging me to become a hotelier and said he could get me into the Cornell School of Hotel Administration, which was the West Point of room service. Given my love of hotels, it wouldn't have been a bad career choice, especially for a boy who had no idea what he wanted to do when, and if, he grew up. Bill was still begging the question as he approached thirty, so what was my rush? One of the properties in which Jerry had an interest was the Westhampton Beach and Tennis Club. He offered me a job as a sort of cabana boy. It sounded good to me. I liked the beach, I liked working, and it provided free lodging.

Right away, though, I saw that Southampton and East Hampton were where the social action was. Westhampton was full of flashy cloak-and-suiters from the rag trade on Seventh Avenue. They arrived with big cigars and mercenary floor models, with whom I didn't stand a chance. I was the hired help. Yet if I went farther out on the island to the preserves of the *Social Register,* I found I could reinvent myself as a Palm Beach millionaire playboy, with the aid of a good tan and my bespoke English thrift shop finds. I would tell people that these duds, with their slightly frayed high starched collars and slightly tatty linings, "had belonged to my grandfather." In this territory of pedigree, vintage played very well.

I even wore thirties spectator shoes, bought also from the thrift shops, but there was nothing effete about them. I liked the look of F. Scott Fitzgerald and Fred Astaire, and that's what they wore. It was all a Gatsby ploy to get girls. It was interesting how once I discovered girls, the art and utility of clothes just came to me. I got the biggest thrill out of dressing up. Clothes made the man, but they "made" the women as well. And they made friends. Those two Russian

187

aristo-playboys Oleg Cassini, who would go on to dress Jackie Kennedy at the White House and who had been married to Gene Tierney, and his brother Igor, "Ghighi" to me, who wrote the Cholly Knickerbocker society gossip column for the Hearst papers and to some was the most powerful voice in New York, both noticed my attire. Their compliments led to conversations and on to friendships.

I remained broke, but never poor. A well-dressed man could go only so far on the kindness of strangers. Being able to pick up a few tabs was essential. So I became something of a rumrunner, in the honored Joe Kennedy tradition. I used some of my old flower contacts to buy cases of whiskey for $10 apiece and sell them for $50 to after-hours tipplers when the Beach Club bar had closed. I was thus not only stylish but also flush. More and more, the idea of Cornell hotel school was getting under my skin. Maybe hospitality was my true métier.

Then I met Betty. Betty Benson was nine years older than I was and about a century more sophisticated. She looked like a young Rosalind Russell, but more model-like, angular, with a hint of Audrey Hepburn and all the effortless elegance that implied. She may have been from somewhere in the wilds of the South, but she shared that vague provenance with Capote's Holly Golightly, whom she was often said to have inspired. For all Betty's outward delicacy, she was a real dame. She had the mouth of a stevedore and the moves of a snake charmer. She was also married to Sam Spiegel, one of the most powerful, successful, high-living, and outrageous producers in the history of Hollywood. But I didn't know that when I met her. She was just Betty, Betty Boop, like in the cartoons, and she was a force of nature.

I first encountered the hurricane that was Betty on a terribly stormy night that summer. I was alone, having a drink at a roadhouse called Gene's on the Bay, when off the bay in a little motorboat came these two glamorous drowned rats, male and female. The female was drenched to the bone in a superclingy Pucci shirt and pink pants and sandals; the aging male wore polo shirt, khakis, and Topsiders. I couldn't take my eyes off her, particularly since the wet effect was maximum sexy. She must have seen me staring at her. Her green eyes locked with mine. Her opening line was, "Hi, sailor. Whose little boy are you?" I instantly wanted to be hers.

Betty was already fairly drunk. She introduced herself and her friend John and said they had come over to meet some friends for dinner and got caught in the flash storm. They were stuck in the pitch-black, roiling bay for hours, and neither could swim, but somehow they made it. Their friends never showed, and they decided to invite me back to the guy's house for our own party. John and his wife were Betty's friends. She complimented me on my thrift shop clothes, from my silk ascot to my linen pants, which she told me fit perfectly, to my Italian loafers. They put on some jazz records. John had a trumpet and began to play along. I had had so many rum punches at this point that when I noticed a set of drums, I was uninhibited enough to begin banging away. They were even drunker, because they praised me as if I were Gene Krupa. I spent the whole weekend there.

Betty had come to New York when she was eighteen, dying to see the world. She had plenty to escape from. Her parents split when she was a baby, her mother taking her to Virginia from her Daytona Beach birthplace. Then her father came to Virginia and kidnapped her when she was six. She endured an awful custody trial, where she chose Mom over Dad and never saw him again. After these rocky beginnings, Betty's amazing success could be a paradigm for ambitious Southerners. She moved into the

Barbizon, "for wayward girls," as Betty put it.

Betty, who was a lithe five foot seven and a half inches (every fraction counted) and all of ninety-nine pounds, made her first stop the Conover modeling agency, which preceded Eileen Ford as the premier mannequin broker in the city. She was signed up by Conover's wife, Candy Jones, the world's first supermodel (Candy was six four) who rivaled Betty Grable as the GIs' favorite pinup girl during World War II. Conover turned out to be bisexual and Candy became a self-proclaimed expert on the paranormal. So Betty quickly got used to people who were "out there," in contrast to her Main Street roots, but that was what she was fleeing from. Betty hit a fiscal sweet spot right away, being signed up as NBC's "color girl," on whom the network did all its testing for its nascent color broadcasting.

They gave her a rainbow of outfits to wear and let her keep them all, hence her instant chic. Plus she was earning $100 an hour, when the best models like Suzy Parker and her sister Dorian Leigh were getting only $75. She moved out of the Barbizon and rented an apartment on the chicest block of the city, 52nd Street between First Avenue and the East River, down from the queen of co-ops, the River House, and steps away from Greta Garbo. Soon she was stolen away from Conover by Huntington Hartford, who had started his own agency to collect the beauties he was addicted to. Hartford was so obsessed with women that one time he chased a girl for about ten blocks in New York, only to find when she turned around that she was his wife.

Unlike her neighbor Garbo, the last thing Betty wanted was to be alone. Betty, who viewed New York as a small town of the rich and famous, met everyone who was anyone. Her life was remarkably similar to my mother's: dating rich men, hanging out at the Stork and El Morocco. But unlike my mother, who had these adolescent romantic notions of aviators and war heroes and bandleaders, Betty was more realpolitik about her liaisons.

She met all the great writers in New York, Capote, Tennessee Williams, Gore Vidal, all of whom were crazy about her. But the reigning women in town — Marlene Dietrich and Slim Hayward (wife of superagent Leland) — took to her as well. She went in every direction: fag hag, soul sister, but usually object of desire. She was pursued by such married moguls as William Paley and Jock Whitney, who were each wed to a famous Cushing sister (Babe and Betsey, respectively), supposedly the fairest in the land. But the one they all wanted was Betty Benson. She had a serious affair with impresario Mike Todd between wives Joan Blondell and Elizabeth Taylor.

There was only one other movie producer who could be a suitable encore for Betty, and that was Sam Spiegel, who had produced Oscar winners *The African Queen, On the Waterfront,* and *The Bridge on the River Kwai* and would win even more for *Lawrence of Arabia.* The Polish-born Spiegel who, like most movie producers worth their salt, had done several jail terms and had been deported once, using the name S. P. Eagle for years to camouflage his transgressions. Spiegel lived larger than any other man in the film business, especially where harems of starlets, models, and deluxe call girls were concerned. He was a modern pasha. Even Huntington Hartford deferred to him. So when Betty belatedly told me she was his wife, I couldn't have been more intimidated.

Betty and Sam had wed not long before she and I met, just as *Kwai* was about to open in 1957. She had spent the year before with him in Ceylon, where he was shooting the film, with countless R & R excursions to London and Paris and Venice and Hong Kong. Betty's life was impossibly and intimidatingly glamorous. What in the world did she want from me? But she had that Southern charm and ability to make you feel right at home, and as beautiful as she was and as much as she had seen, there wasn't a pretentious bone in her serpentine body. She loved to have fun, and she thought I was fun. And what about Sam? They were, as the French would say, "sophisticated" about their relationship. Don't ask, don't tell. He was three decades older than she, and he was habituated to harems. But Betty, whom Sam called "Betty-Boo," was no vestal virgin, either. As Betty once said, "I had a lot of charms on my bracelet."

Part of Betty's charm was that she had no agenda other than having a wild and wonderful time. She had no interest in becoming an actress, even less in being a socialite, or getting her name in Ghighi Cassini's column. On the surface she was without ambition. Then again, if you were married to Sam Spiegel, you didn't *need* ambition. He had all the ambition in the world, and all the success. Betty was thus completely relaxed, in her madcap way, and I learned a lot from her about how to just go with the flow, which was pretty much my nature anyhow.

Spiegel was away for the summer, putting deals together and arranging the filming at Shepperton Studios in London of his new movie, which would start shooting the following year. *Suddenly, Last Summer* was a Gore Vidal adaptation of a Tennessee Williams play starring Elizabeth Taylor, Katharine Hepburn, and Montgomery Clift. That it was about cannibalism was lost on me. What struck me was the A-list of it all.

I so wanted to reciprocate Betty's hospitality, to treat her like a contemporary I was courting. But she wasn't and I couldn't. What do you give the woman who has everything? What do you give Mrs. Sam Spiegel, Lady Hollywood? I was so broke I couldn't send her a case of champagne or vintage wines. I couldn't afford nice flowers or perfume. All I could afford was a case of Dubble Bubble bubble gum. I saw her chewing it once; that's where I got the idea. A case of Dom Pérignon wouldn't have made her happier. If it made me seem like a kid, it made her *feel* like a kid, and she loved it.

It wasn't all hearts and flowers. Our usual trysting spot was the Commodore Hotel, near Grand Central. Like Dustin Hoffman in the 1967 production of *The Graduate,* I would check in and wait for my Mrs. Robinson to arrive. When she did, I'd usually order a pizza to be delivered. She could get the caviar from Sam. One night we got into an awful fight over something, or nothing, and Betty threw the pizza at me, splattering the wall and smashing a lamp. We were so loud the house detective came and threw us out. I had never felt so humiliated, not to mention the fear of possibly turning up in Earl Wilson's gossip column the next day and then getting rubbed out by the hit men I was sure Sam had in his employ. I told Betty, as we were standing out in the noise of Madison Avenue, that her behavior had never left me feeling so humiliated in my life. She burst out laughing. I'm the girl, she said. I'm the one who's supposed to be humiliated. She had a point. We both had a big laugh, kissed, and went for a makeup pizza.

All along Betty was telling me that I had all the makings of a Hollywood star. If she liked me, *they* would like me. I had the right stuff. She exhorted me to go west and pursue it, and given that she was married to the giant of the business, I couldn't help but take her encouragement with more than just a grain of salt. Just being with Betty made me feel like pretty hot stuff, but it also made me sad, because I had the biggest crush on her. Our fling could go only so far. Sam Spiegel's "sophistication" notwithstanding,

Betty never said, "Oh, I'll introduce you to my husband and he'll make you a star." That was in movies but not real life. And if I took Betty's advice to pursue becoming an actor, Sam Spiegel, if he ever found out about us, would surely end my career before it began. Betty laughed off my paranoia. She said Sam couldn't care less.

I grew up fast that summer. I would have been delighted to keep seeing Betty, but Sam was returning and summer was ending. Some other boys who worked at the Beach Club were planning to drive cross-country to Los Angeles to see how true the American dream of California actually was. Betty pushed me to go with them. I left, but Betty and I became friends for life. I would never get over her, and that experience did a lot to spoil things with Liz Cocrane, my Palm Beach sweetheart. With Betty I had grown up overnight. I had seen Paris; I couldn't go back to the farm of Palm Beach. At least not until I had taken my shot, my incredibly long shot, at Hollywood.

Driving across country with my two buddies, Bob Lynn and Lou Spooner, both from Boston, was a road trip that put me back in my place as an eighteen-year-old party boy in search of a fraternity. We had a '49 Ford. I had no idea how to change gears, so I kept the car in first until we hit New Orleans and I realized there was a problem. We ultimately broke down in the burning hellhole of Gila Bend, Arizona, and were stranded for a few wretched days until we got the Ford patched up. When we finally rolled into Beverly Hills, a cop, noticing our battered jalopy's Massachusetts license plates, pulled us over and was about to arrest us. Nobody walked in Beverly Hills, and nobody drove old cars, except the help. I pulled myself together and indignantly told the officer, "I went to school here, sir," dropping the name of Hawthorne and maybe Buddy Rogers as well. The cop backed off. It was another lesson I had learned from my father: Put your foot down. Let people know who you are, in the most charming way, of course.

My buddies wanted to get a motel room and get drunk. They had no interest in film careers, or any careers for that matter, wanting only to buy time before going back to school, back to reality. I figured I would eventually return to Florida and get my diploma. But I had been here in California before and I knew that the reality of Los Angeles was its very unreality, which I prepared to embrace. Playing the company commander, I decided to get us some decent lodgings. I called our old realtor Frank

Archer, who remembered my mother from our stay in the late forties. I filled him in on Teeny, told him about Jesse Spalding. Frank found us a little bungalow near Sunset and Wetherly and vouched for us to the owner. Talk about going out on a limb, but Frank would do anything for Teeny, as most men would. Bob paid the first month's rent, Lou paid the last, and I promised to be good for the second. That was wishful thinking; I had all of $90 at that point.

That summer I had met the gossip columnist Sheilah Graham, who had been a guest at the Westhampton Bath and Tennis Club. Sheilah was nearly as powerful as Hedda and Louella. She had been an English chorus girl and she could write. Her best seller *Beloved Infidel,* about her romance with F. Scott Fitzgerald, would soon be made into a film starring Gregory Peck and Deborah Kerr. "You should be an actor," she had said to me, out of nowhere at the club, and I was deeply flattered. She, like Betty, thought I had something, though I'm not sure what. Encouragement like that kept me going.

I got the names of some agents and some photographers to take head shots, which were like passports in making the rounds. One of the photographers, who had the indelible name of Melbourne Spurr, offered to take four shots of me for $90. I bargained him down to $80 so I could eat for a while. At first we tried shooting with me wearing a ten-gallon hat, but it made me look like a midnight cowboy. So I urged him to go classic, and the result was a slicked-hair, sepia series that made me look like a young John Barrymore. So here I was, John Barrymore in a James Dean world. Dean was dead, but all the young actors wanted to be him, or Marlon Brando. There was a huge generation gap between the rebels and the established stars like Cary Grant, James Stewart, and Rock Hudson. The rebellion hadn't actually started yet, but the seeds were being planted. But I simply wasn't a ripped T-shirt guy. I was the son of a bandleader, so I had to be what I was. I would have to market myself as a piece of counterprogramming rather than a piece of counterculture. I thus took my very thirties head shots and started pounding the pavements. I had no car. My roommates shared the Ford until it broke down permanently.

First I had to eat. Our old maid Tildy in Arkansas had told me as a boy how the slaves could survive on something called hoecake, the recipe for which was flour, water, bacon drippings, and lemonade. We picked the lemons from the trees in our yard, a testimony to the Garden of Eden aspect of L.A. life. The hoecake was disgusting. Being hungry in Eden was no treat. Being bloated and citric was even worse. Then I met the actor Nick Adams, a Ukrainian from Pennsylvania who had come out to Hollywood as cold as I had and had made it, appearing with James Dean in *Rebel Without a Cause* and just starting his own television series called *The Rebel*. Rebels were in.

Nick took me to his gym, Vic Tanney's on Hollywood Boulevard, where I met Robert Conrad, another self-starter from Chicago, who had just landed his first series, *Hawaiian Eye,* and would go on to the huge hit *The Wild Wild West*. It was good to meet "real" people who were actually making it. Nick and Bobby were living proof that dreams in Hollywood could come true.

Nick was so nice to us, telling us which restaurants were actor-friendly, meaning they would let us run tabs until our ships came in. He also knew which hostesses would let actors eat for free. This was a *Michelin* of survival. There was one kind hostess at a place called the Knife and Fork, to whom I turned for aid and comfort when we were starving on Thanksgiving. "There's a turkey in the freezer," she said sweetly. "It's yours."

I went back into the freezer and picked up a huge thirty-five-pound bird and hid it under my raincoat. But on my way out, who should come in but the owner, stationing himself between me and the door and chatting with the cashier. I didn't dare walk past him. I looked like a pregnant man with this bulge under my raincoat. Hollywood was full of weirdos, but I was pushing it here. So I ordered a cup of coffee at the counter and bided my time. And bided and bided . . . The owner didn't move, and the turkey began defrosting. Soon a puddle was forming at my feet. This pregnant man looked like he was either peeing or breaking water. Then, even worse, the long turkey neck defrosted and fell off into my lap, between my legs. When the owner finally walked away, I high-tailed it out the door, leaving a huge flood at the counter behind me. Talk about giving thanks. We cooked that bird and lived on it for weeks.

By December, my buddies had had enough. They packed up and went back east, leaving me with turkey leftovers and a whole house to pay for. Luckily I finally landed an agent, a fellow named Hy Sieger, who was a junior associate at the Mitchell Gertz Agency, famous in Hollywood for having sold an actor who had been dead for two years to a movie, then replacing him at the last minute, saying he was not available. Hy was willing to take me on, send me out, and feed me as well, or let his mother do it. I became an honorary Jew, stuffing myself with kreplach and gribenes, and occasionally camping out on the floor under Mama Sieger's kitchen table. She spoke mostly Yiddish, and I learned the language from her. Oddly enough, there was another agent in the office, a handsome stud named David Resnick, who would go on to marry Betty Benson decades later, after Sam Spiegel went on to his Kwai in the sky.

Hy soon found a "go" film with a young director who liked my Barrymore look, although he didn't want to use it. The man was Denis Sanders, a UCLA film grad who had already won an Oscar for a short film he had made as his master's thesis. Impressive, I thought. Even more impressive was his upcoming film, *Crime and Punishment, USA,* in which he wanted me to play a contempo Raskolnikov. Wow! Here I was playing Dostoyevsky for an Oscar winner. Denis liked me, but the Barrymore would have to go. He saw his project as a tragedy for the beat generation, and what he saw in me was Tony Perkins, not the Great Profile. I would have to muss up my hair, discard the starched collar. I would have to play bongo drums, for

203

heaven's sake. But who was I to complain, a guy who was stealing turkeys to eat? It was not only a paying job, it was a starring role, a home run my first time at bat. Denis would go on in a few years to discover Robert Redford for his film *War Hunt*. He had an eye.

And I had a job! Hallelujah! I would be playing the lead, a law student who murders a pawnbroker to get money to save his sister from the clutches of a rich older man and has to cover it all up. Hitchcock meets Dostoyevsky. Plus the cast was prestigious: Mary Murphy, who had starred in *The Wild One* with Brando; Marian Seldes, the distinguished stage actress; Frank Silvera, the great black character actor who played the detective who stalks me. I had arrived. There were lots of bragging rights on this one. How easy it seemed.

I can't remember the shoot at all, except it was very verité, taking place in Venice, by the beach, outside at a lot of drive-ins and car lots and factories. After all, this was Beat Dostoyevsky, not Czar Dostoyevsky. One rehearsal, however, was unforgettable, because it almost got me killed. I was at Mary Murphy's apartment on Beverly Drive, doing some "line readings," so to speak. She was very sexy, and I was very excited by her. And I assumed the whole idea of being in pictures was to have flings with your gorgeous costars. Suddenly, Mary blurted out one line that wasn't in the script, "It's him!" Him was her lover, as well as agent, the very formidable Kurt Frings, who came smashing through the door. Kurt, a former professional boxer, was as scary as his heavy German accent. He was the son of a cardinal from Cologne, but he had taken to the ring before becoming one of the most powerful agents in the business, handling Elizabeth Taylor and Audrey Hepburn, among many others. Kurt was a brawler who took meetings in steam rooms and subsisted on a lot of steak tartare and steins of beer. In other words, Attila the Hun.

The only thing that saved me from Kurt Frings's wrath was that he was supposedly blissfully married. His wife, Ketti, had just won the Pulitzer Prize for her Broadway adaptation of *Look Homeward, Angel*. Just a few weeks before our run-in, Ketti had been on the cover of the *Los Angeles Times* as its Woman of the Year. Kurt, who had an agent's keen sense of publicity, saw that getting his own picture on a *Times* cover for eviscerating the new lead of *Crime and Punishment, USA* would destroy his marriage and create trouble he wanted no part of. He thus let me off the hook. I kept it completely professional with Mary from then on.

The film was completed in early 1958 without further incident. I figured I would just sit back and let the star-making machinery take its course. But nothing happened. Month after month, the release of the movie kept getting pushed back and pushed back. It was *Waiting for Godot* or, rather, Waiting for the Dough, of which there was none. I had gotten paid virtually nothing for my debut, actor's scale, which weighed about a feather. The idea was that this starring role would lead to others. Momentum, baby. No such luck. My agent found me nothing, unable to alchemize my part into the ineffable "heat" and "buzz" that would get me another one. Hy Sieger wasn't that kind of "power" agent. He wasn't Kurt Frings or Swifty Lazar. But his mother fed me and he was loyal and I was grateful, a rare quality in a business where the easiest scapegoat for your failure is your agent.

All I could do was lower my sights to television, which was definitely B-list in those days, if not lower. I had a contact in the casting office at Screen Gems Television named Buster Vogel, and I used my last savings to buy him a bottle of Jack Daniel's to bribe him into getting me something. He put the bottle in his desk drawer and promised me good news if I called him on Monday. I did, and he did have a job for me, a bit part on the *Rin Tin Tin* television series. Bowwow. I donned the dreaded cowboy hat and played the title role in an episode called "Misfit Marshal." Kiss Barrymore good-bye forever.

Buster then got me an even more insignificant moment on *The Donna Reed Show* and another oater called *Cimaron City*. Best of a bad lot was a bit on *The Veil*, a *Twilight Zone*-ish anthology of horror shows hosted by Boris Karloff. Instead of playing cowboys, this time I played an Indian. Meeting Frankenstein was a thrill that mitigated the ignominy of my situation. That was something to write home about. Boris himself honored me with a bit of useful advice: "Never let your jacket gap away from your neck. It's the mark of the bad politician and the bad actor."

It had been Hollywood or bust, and in one year, I had had both. I had entered the Dante's Inferno of celebrity and had a taste, but now I was ready to abandon hope. It looked as if *Crime and Punishment, USA* was going to be stillborn, never to be released. Maybe in Russia. My hopes were fading fast. The only way I could top *Crime and Punishment, USA* was to get Sartre's *Being and Nothingness*. That's how Hollywood can make you feel when the phone doesn't ring. But then, in the fall of my year of waiting, it rang, but not from Hollywood. Venezuela was calling, in the person of a man I had met in Palm Beach named Oscar Molinari Herrera.

Oscar, who had come to Florida from Cuba, was a member of the family that would give us the designer Carolina Herrera, who would also become a friend. Molinari was the Italian half of the family. In the midfifties, the superrich of Cuba — land, sugar, and tobacco barons and their entourages — had begun pouring into Florida fleeing the ever-looming specter of communism. Oscar was a true Renaissance man: a poet, a painter, a great writer, and, with his trademark white linen suits and dark tan, an unbelievable ladies' man. Oscar represented all the style and glamour I would later attempt to emulate in Hollywood.

He had followed my career through my family in Palm Beach and was mightily impressed. He had no idea what the sordid reality was. I looked good on paper. Oscar was thrilled, as almost everyone is, to know what he erroneously thought was a real movie star. When Oscar sent me an invitation to visit him in Caracas right in the middle of my new career's dry spell, I jumped at it. I was joined by another pal from Palm Beach, Orator "Orty" Woodward. Orty, though not the golden-tongued speaker his name implied, was more cautious than my brother David and a good man to know in a pinch.

Oscar arrived late to meet us at the Caracas airport. His white suit was soaked in blood, and he told us that he had been in an accident on his way to pick us up. His beautiful companion had been injured and he had taken her to the hospital. What an old-school gentleman. Suddenly we were surrounded by a mob of reporters, all shouting at me. One of them asked in broken English how I felt about starring in a movie about the life of Simón Bolívar. I had no idea what he was talking about. Oscar whispered that he had told them I was going to play the part of El Libertador. "You're an actor. They love actors. They don't know you yet, and I've just helped your image." The next day I was on the front pages of all the papers as the man who was to play the great liberator of South America, the George Washington of Venezuela. Everywhere we went you'd have thought that Bolívar himself had been resurrected because the crowds went wild.

Caracas in 1958 was the most elegant place I'd ever seen. I hadn't been to Europe yet, but everyone said Caracas was more fun than Rome and the girls were even more beautiful than in Paris. Yes, the rich were richer and the poor were poorer here, but I didn't get to meet any poor people, just tycoons and beauty queens. Spain itself was a dead zone under Generalissimo Franco, but Caracas partied the way Madrid was supposed to, dinner at midnight, dancing till dawn, sleeping until noon, just in time for tanning in the midday sun. Palm Beach was a mausoleum by comparison, and Acapulco was a little beach shack.

While I was playing my role as Hollywood luminary, I got the brilliant idea to become a bullfighter, mainly because I saw that the bullfighters got the most spectacular women. This was a time when Ava Gardner herself had thrown over Sinatra for Dominguin, the king of the ring, so I thought I was onto something. I was actually pursuing the Ava Gardner of Venezuela, a Miss World named Susana Duijm, an exotic goddess who was half Dutch and half Indian (subcontinent). Susana held me at bay and egged me on to attend bullfighter classes at the Salón de Torero. The day I had my first bull, she promised, was the day I could have her.

What I did for love! The bulls came at the students like Mack trucks, snorting and snarling, with blood flying everywhere.

Nonetheless, with the pot of gold that was Susana in the offing, I vowed to hold my ground. My vows came to naught when I was face-to-face with my first bull, a creature far scarier than Karloff's Frankenstein. All I had was this cape. It wasn't a fair match. When he first ran at me, I tried to dodge him, but he grazed my shoulder, knocking me fifteen feet across the ring. On his next furious pass, I gave up and ran out of the ring. I would have to get the girl some other, more orthodox way. Alas, I never got the chance. One day Oscar tapped me on the shoulder and told me, "George, it's time to go home. You're in big trouble." Oscar had just found out that my flame-to-be was the secret mistress of the Venezuelan president. "He would not be happy," Oscar said, explaining that the presidential wrath would put any bull to shame. I could see the interrogator in the torture room giving me shocks with a cattle prod trying to make me tell how far I had gone with El Presidente's señorita. End of romance. End of movie. Oh, Susana!

But there was good news along with the bad. As my mother always assured me, God looks out for us. Just as I was sweating being summoned before a firing squad, I got a telegram from my agent, Hy Sieger.

Crime had finally been released. It wasn't a *Kwai* home run, but it was a solid base hit. I got great reviews, even in the august *New York Times,* which lauded my "flashes of fire and torment that augur well for his future acting activities." MGM was so impressed that they were offering me a seven-year contract. Imagine. MGM, the gold standard of Hollywood, with "more stars than in heaven," the studio of Gable and Garbo and Tracy and Hepburn, the top dog, and they wanted *me.* California, here I come.

I decided to celebrate my good fortune by taking a roundabout island-hopping journey with Orty Woodward through the Caribbean. First stop was the Dominican Republic, where we deplaned at Ciudad Trujillo. Everything in the country was bugged; revolution was in the air, and the fear was palpable. We drank 1860 rum, locally known as "essence de Rubirosa" after the Dominican playboy whom Orty and I had met and idolized in Palm Beach. He, not Hugh Hefner, was the role model for all would-be bons vivants of the fifties. Next stop was Haiti, where we slept at the Grand Hotel Oloffson and had numerous adventures with the lovely mulattas, who helped me forget my Miss World in Caracas. Papa Doc Duvalier was in power and his machete-wielding, Nazi-dressed *tonton macoutes* scared the hell out of both of us.

Montego Bay, Jamaica, was a well-needed respite, a place to welcome in the new year of 1959. Orty got us put up at the luxurious Round Hill resort. He knew the owner, Englishman John Pringle, a great pal of James Bond's Ian Fleming, who lived in Jamaica. We had a wonderful lunch with Bill and Babe Paley and Moss Hart and Kitty Carlisle. Why these legends of the media would hang out with two nineteen-year-old brats seems odd, but, hey, I was a *movie star,* with an MGM contract. Who wouldn't want to hang with me? Such was the arrogance of ignorance. Moss and Kitty made a huge fuss over me and got the idea that I would make the perfect Moss in a film version of his best-selling autobiography, *Act One.* I first thought the idea of playing a Jewish playwright from the Bronx was even more absurd than my playing Simón Bolívar. But that was what acting was all about. The bigger the stretch, the greater the triumph. Moss had a huge ego, and I was flattered by his attention. Ironically, a few years later, after he died, this pipe dream became a reality.

We flew from Montego Bay to Havana, eager to hit the shows at the Nacional and the tables at the Montmartre, where Sean Flynn and I had partied and been served rum drinks underage as teenagers. Now that we were "grown up," we couldn't wait for the wild times ahead in this most decadent of playgrounds. But we never got to town. The party was over. José Martí airport was an armed camp. In January of '59 Castro had just taken over Havana. Batista had fallen. *Viva la revolución!* There were hundreds of soldiers with machine guns and beards. All flights had been canceled, and everyone was being arrested, including the two capitalist piglets, Orty and me.

Lucky for me that I had learned Spanish back in Acapulco and perfected it in the Caracas bullring. I struck up a conversation with our chief captor, one of Castro's top lieutenants. When I told him I was a Hollywood actor, he suddenly became my best friend. He had been a struggling actor himself in America and had done a season of summer stock at the Hyannis Playhouse before chucking it all for Fidel. When I mentioned the Bolívar project, he wanted to bring me to meet El Caudillo himself. I settled for a one-way passage to Miami. I had just seen firsthand how powerful a door opener Hollywood could be, the best visa in the world.

CHAPTER EIGHT
THE PLAYER

Somebody up there liked me, and that somebody, Vincente Minnelli, couldn't have been more up there than he was in 1959. His musical *Gigi* had just been nominated for nine Oscars and his drama *Some Came Running* for three. *Gigi* would soon sweep every category, including Best Picture and Best Director. Minnelli, already a film god for *An American in Paris,* was the lord of the movie realm, and he didn't need his ex-wife Judy Garland to enthrone him. He could write his own ticket, and, for some reason, he wanted me.

Vincente's next movie was *Home from the Hill,* which fit into the Southern dysfunctional family genre that had been so successful recently. *The Long Hot Summer, Cat on a Hot Tin Roof, The Sound and the Fury* had all tapped into a national nerve, a curiosity about the lives of the rich and incestuous below the Mason-Dixon Line. As Southern families went, my clan was less deranged than the typical Tennessee Williams creation, more like *Dobie Gillis* by comparison, but we did have our moments.

What Vincente later told me he saw in me was not my tortured soul but that I had the quality of a privileged but sensitive mama's boy. That was what he was seeking for *Home,* the incredibly convoluted and operatic tale of a debauched East Texas dynasty in which my character makes a mama out of his beneath-his-station girlfriend. He doesn't want to do the right thing by her, but his rugged illegitimate brother does. And that's only the subplot.

Vincente pitched me to his producers, Pandro Berman, Eddie Grainger, and Sol C. Siegel, a triumvirate of MGM's so-called College of Cardinals, the grand old men who made the movies. He screened *Crime and Punishment, USA* for them. Berman liked me, but Siegel thought I looked "too sophisticated," a curse that would come back to haunt me over and over again. Vincente had the bright idea of lightening my hair, which would somehow desophisticate me. The others told him to give the dye bottle a shot and then give me a screen test. This is what triggered my return from the tropics.

I met Minnelli on the MGM lot in Culver

City. In his midfifties, he was very elegant, wearing a yellow cashmere sweater, pleated mohair slacks, and black suede loafers. He drank wine and smoked cigarettes incessantly, holding them like Bette Davis and puckering his lips a lot. I came off the plane looking like a matador, slicked-down hair, tight pants — all I lacked was the cape. Vincente refrained from grimacing, but I could tell he was fairly horrified. He explained that I would be playing a "bumbling Southern boy," which was a long way from my Rudolph Valentino entrance.

Vincente sent me off to hair and makeup. I tested with the fine actress Shirley Knight, who didn't make the movie. Contract players did tests like that a lot. Vincente knew precisely what he wanted. He moved us around like props. "Four steps to the right, three back, lean left." He was very effete. "Pray continue," he'd say. And he stuttered. "C . . . c . . . c . . . cut!" If he laughed, it was very precise. Five *ha*'s. "Ha . . . ha . . . ha . . . ha . . . ha." But he always had the last laugh. He knew his stuff. Somehow the hair dye worked; I passed the test. I was ushered into the gorgeous art deco executive offices in the Thalberg Building and signed to that seven-year contract, which I could only assume would be a seven-year feast, not a seven-year itch.

The word on the street was that MGM, like all the Hollywood studios, was in terrible decline, a victim of television. Louis B. Mayer had left the company in 1951; Dore Schary, his replacement as studio chief, had been fired for giving the studio its first ever year in the red in 1956; the College of Cardinals, with their obsession with "classy" musicals and biopics and biblical epics, was getting old, as out of touch with the coming youthquake as their namesakes at the Vatican.

But when I got to MGM, you'd never know that the decline and fall of the celluloid empire was at hand. Its *Gigi* broke all records for a musical, its *Cat on a Hot Tin Roof* was the biggest moneymaker of 1958, its *Ben-Hur* came out the year I arrived, as did its Hitchcock masterpiece, *North by Northwest*. If this was failure, I wanted a big piece of it, with an Oscar on top.

Vincente's hair was receding and he was very shy and reserved, until he took charge. Then even De Mille would have run for cover. I never met anyone so sure of himself, and his certainty made you immediately doubt yourself. Hitchcock said actors were cattle. Vincente didn't say it, but he must have felt it. Having begun his career as a set decorator, Vincente often treated the talent as just another part of the scenery, scenery that only he was capable of putting together to make his impeccable films.

Vincente knew show business as well as anyone, since he was born into it. His father was the musical conductor of the Minnelli Brothers Dramatic Tent show, so Vincente spent his childhood on the road. He decided to become a costumer and Latinized his prosaic name of Lester Anthony to Vincente, sort of the way he played with his age. What did it matter? It was a world of make-believe, anyway.

Home promised to be a class act. The lead of the patriarch, originally intended for Clark Gable, who was indisposed, had gone to bad boy Robert Mitchum, whose drug bust was one of my earliest memories of the behind-the-scenes life of Hollywood. I was a huge fan. The mother of my mama's boy was going to be played by the elegant Eleanor Parker, now best remembered as the baroness in *The Sound of Music* but then on a roll with three Best Actress Oscar nominations in the past six years. The film was written by the famous screenwriting couple Irving Ravetch and Harriet Frank Jr. (a junior but a woman). They had penned *The Long Hot Summer* as well as *The Sound and the Fury,* which signified something: They had the best ear in the business for Southern dialogue, though that was one area where I didn't need any help.

Not so my fellow "discovery" in *Home,* though George Peppard would never admit he needed any help where acting was concerned. Vincente loved the idea of finding two newcomers as the two rival sons, but offscreen, he did nothing to foment a rivalry between us, which might have been natural. Vincente was anything but a "method" director. George, on the other hand, was a total method actor. He was an odd guy to be from New York's Actors Studio. A Detroit native, George had been a gunnery sergeant in the marines before studying civil engineering at Purdue, where he went from drill sergeant to party-hearty frat man. George could certainly drink, up there in the Mitchum league. In that sense he was ideally cast.

But George was the man who knew too much, certainly for control freak Vincente's taste. Even during rehearsals in Los Angeles, Vincente was having trouble getting what he wanted out of George. While I was grateful to do what I was told, to be directed by a master, George kept asking Vincente what his motivations were. This annoyed Vincente to no end. "Inside he may be a seething volcano," Vincente said to me, in near despair, "but there's nothing on his face." George and I would go on to do a number of films together, and the difference between us can be summed up by an incident that occurred in London, when we were making *The Victors*. A young boy came up to us, when we were in our soldiers' uniforms, and asked George if he was a movie star. "No," George snapped indignantly. "I'm an actor." Then the boy turned to me. Chastened by George's pique, he asked, with all British politesse, "Are you an actor?" "No," I said. "I'm a movie star."

The *real* movie star in this was the great Bob Mitchum. I never saw any star care less about being one. He was completely indifferent. Bob could talk your ear off, but the one thing he didn't want to talk about was his lines or the film. He liked to get drunk, and then sing songs, sea chanteys, Cockney ditties, Australian football songs, anything. He had a perfect mimic's ear and never stopped. What he would usually say to me was, "Gettin' any?" He certainly was. Bob would send me out to buy him liquor. On my first run back to his room in the hotel where billeted, I found him ramming away at a lovely townie whom he had splayed over a chair. He kept at it, motioning me to open the bottle and hand it to him. I was honored to be of service.

We shot on location in the elegant university town of Oxford, Mississippi, where Old Miss writer-in-residence William Faulkner would climb up in a tree and watch us film all day. When Bob Mitchum wasn't having sex with someone, he often just sat around in his boxer shorts and his priceless alligator cowboy boots in a rocking chair at our antebellum hotel, casting for imaginary trout with a fishing rod he used like Muslims use worry beads. He drank a lot and smoked a lot of dope. I don't know where he got it, but it was around. Star perks. He also took a lot of pills, which he kept in his own leather doctor's bag. One night I couldn't sleep and asked Bob if he had anything. Did he ever. He reached into his bag, opened a big bottle, and handed me a pill he called a "nighty night." I slept straight through my call the next morning and on into a second day.

While Bob may have been ahead of the Hollywood curve where illicit substances were concerned, in popping pills he was par for the show business course. Stars seemed to live on multiple prescription drugs, mother's little helpers, better living through chemistry. The Eisenhower era instilled an unlimited public faith in medicine, which had kept Ike alive through his White House heart attack. Bob once said to me, "They think I don't know my lines. It's not true. I'm just too drunk to say 'em." The studio sent production manager Eddie Wohler to keep Mitchum in line, but the minute Eddie walked into Bob's hotel room, Bob simply punched him out, knocking him through the door. The studio had no choice but to side with the star. Once Mitchum got comfortable with me, he would talk forever, about everything. He had a photographic memory. He was an expert on quarterhorses, of all things, and could go on about them, like a breeder or trainer, for hours. For years, Mitchum sent me Mother's Day cards. I was never sure why, but he gave me confidence that you could be a star in Hollywood on your own terms, not those of the studio or anyone else's.

Liza Minnelli was twelve when she came to visit the set. She had been named after the Gershwin song "Liza" popularized by Al Jolson in *Ziegfeld Follies* and directed by Vincente on Broadway, and she more than lived up to this awesome heritage, not to mention having Judy Garland for a mother. Liza had a bit of a crush on me. I had met her on the MGM lot and was deeply impressed with her exuberance and talent. Liza would go onto the sound stages and watch Fred Astaire and Cyd Charisse do their numbers and then replicate every step perfectly. She could do imitations of everyone, Marlene Dietrich, Ethel Merman, Mary Martin, everyone on Broadway. She got her hair cut in her trademark pixie style on the *Home* set because she had gotten some gum stuck in her hair and decided the best way to get it out was to cut it off.

The first time I ever saw her sing "professionally," was at the Cork & Bottle club in Dallas, when we were shooting the Texas part of *Home.* Bob Mitchum and I had taken her out, and there was a stage at the club. "Get up there and sing, Liza," I urged her. She did, and she brought the house down. But Judy was cold and discouraging to Liza. One night a couple of years later at L.A.'s Cocoanut Grove, they did a duet of "Itsy Bitsy Teeny Weeny Yellow Polka Dot Bikini." I told Judy how good I thought Liza was. "The kid doesn't have the timbre," Judy dismissed her. Mother doesn't always know best.

I had other adventures with Judy. One night we both found ourselves staying at the Plaza Hotel in New York. I had arrived there from London only to find that Judy had just flown in from London, too. I called her up and she said, "Let's go up to Westchester [to her country estate] and see the kids." It was near midnight and I was jet-lagged and tried to beg off. But you couldn't beg off with Judy Garland. "I just made the same trip," she teased me, "and I feel great. What's wrong with you?" So she herded me into her limousine and off we went, with a bottle of her favorite wine, the German Blue Nun, in an ice bucket in the backseat. When we arrived, the kids, Liza, Lorna, and Joey, were wide awake and raring to go, just like Mom, who made milk shakes for everyone. We sang songs and laughed like crazy. I think I went to bed in the pool guesthouse some time after three. I had never seen Judy happier.

The next morning, around eleven, I was awakened by the houseman, with a very somber expression. "Mr. Hamilton, I want you to come with me out the back way. I've got a car waiting for you." What's wrong, I asked him immediately. "Miss Garland tried to take her own life last night," he said. The press was all over the place, and the family didn't want me needlessly involved. I saw the three kids out by the pool, as if at a wake. I felt terrible, and I felt confused. I still have no idea why Judy would have tried to commit suicide that joyful night. I took the car and went back to the Plaza. I was vastly relieved when I found out that Judy survived.

Meanwhile, back on the set. My family was thrilled that they had sired a star. Moreover, I was the one true Southerner in the cast, the native son made good. Accordingly, Teeny and Bill arrived in Oxford to cheer me on. There they befriended a group of Mitchum's camp followers, the most bizarre entourage from nearby Memphis that Faulkner himself couldn't have cooked up. There was Brother Dave Garner, who was a poor man's Muddy Waters, replete with guitar and bottle of hooch. There was Allison Kimball, the alcoholic fallen beauty queen, who naturally had caught the Mitchum eye. There was Allison's best friend, an asexual chemist whose weird science appealed to Mitchum, and several other assorted misfit miscreants. If Hollywood wanted Southern dysfunction, here it was. I'm not sure what the staid Vincente made of it all, but he was used to the theater, and this was theater of the absurd.

I think the best acting I did on *Home* was concealing my mortification at the "Memphis Mafia." As far as my other acting went, Vincente destroyed my self-confidence. He was such an autocrat, a General Patton of a director, that by surrendering myself to him, I surrendered my own instincts and creativity. He would tell me to do stupid-seeming, overly mannered things that somehow would look wonderful on the screen. Who was I to doubt him? But I ended up doubting myself. I remember my first screen kiss with Luana Patten, who was perfect for the townie my snob was to fall for. If I knew anything at this point, it was how to kiss a woman, but Vincente made me as nervous as if it were my very first time, and I was paralyzed until he told me how to move my mouth.

The big set piece of *Home* was the wild boar hunt, through which my father was to turn my mother's boy character into a real, animal-killing he-male. The scene was a case study in the psychopathology of Vincente's perfectionism. We first started shooting in Mississippi with a boar imported from Russia. But when Vincente found out the boar wasn't indigenous to the American South, we ditched the "commie boar" and switched to a wild pig. We also moved to the sulfur flats of Paris, Texas, whose plumes of hellish brimstone brought out the old production designer in Vincente. I thought of Vincente's divinely glamorous *An American in Paris*. And here I was, with the master, an American in Paris, Texas. Where was Cyd Charisse? I despaired to myself. Texas didn't quite work either, so we finally moved the hunt to the back lot in Culver City. We got a new pig, which didn't seem fierce or scary enough. So Vincente hired the top orthodontist in Beverly Hills to rig up a pair of fake tusks for the beast. I joked to Vincente that we had to be careful that the pig didn't end up with better teeth than Mitchum. Vincente, always dead serious about his movies, didn't laugh.

Whatever the adventures on *Home,* the very fact that I had worked as a costar with Vincente Minnelli was to Hollywood what having a Harvard degree was to Wall Street. I was instantly acceptable. No more stealing turkeys. I was an MGM star. The grandest of the grandes dames I would soon get to know was Merle Oberon. I met Merle through Cobina Wright, the society columnist and a friend of Jesse Spalding. Cobina invited me to a party where I connected with Merle, who had just married an Italian-Mexican industrialist named Bruno Pagliai and lived mostly in Cuernavaca. But she still had her mansion on Ladera Drive in Holmby Hills and she invited me up. I had my mother's kick out of meeting legends. Merle was not even fifty when I met her, but she reminded me of Gloria Swanson playing Norma Desmond in *Sunset Boulevard.* It was midafternoon, and she was dressed in designer black and dripping in jewels, especially coral, which played well off her tan, and swept down her grand stairway the way Loretta Young did on her television show.

Merle hadn't been in a film for nearly a decade, but she still acted as if she ruled the business. She had joined European high society, was surrounded by aristocrats like the Cinis of Venice and the Mountbattens of England. Merle was invited all over the world, as well as to openings of new Hiltons (by Conrad himself) from Istanbul to Mexico City and other global galas to lend class and name value. Merle and Errol Flynn were the world's most famous Tasmanians, but Errol had teased her mercilessly saying she made it all up, and that she was really a low-caste, mixed-breed Indian. Oh! Calcutta!

Wherever Merle came from, she was now every inch the lady. We never discussed her roots, only her career as the star of *Wuthering Heights;* as Lady Korda, the former wife of director Sir Alexander; and as the wife of cinema's premier cinematographer, Lucien Ballard. Because Bruno was always away, I dressed up in black tie and went dancing with her at the Cocoanut Grove (thanks again, Mrs. deRham), or I dressed down in beach chic and went walking with her on the sands of Santa Monica.

Merle gave the best dinner parties in town. I was always the youngest guest, and she made a huge fuss over me, telling everyone I was the new hot star. The James Dean rebels of the era were not reliably good extra men the way I was. I met David Niven, who had almost married Merle himself, Gary Cooper, visiting Brits like Laurence Olivier, as well as Beverly Hills-based department store heirs like the Bloomingdales, the Orbachs, and the Mays, all of whom lived more lavishly than even the biggest stars. Also there were the moguls who owned the studios, Jules and Doris Stein, Bill and Edie Goetz, who was Louis B. Mayer's daughter and the prime social arbiter in the film colony.

The most unforgettable night of all was having dinner with the Duke and Duchess of Windsor, just the four of us, in black tie at Le Pavillon, the grandest French restaurant in New York. I was struck by how diminutive the impeccable duke was. With the duchess, he was almost like a little boy in tow with his mother. I got the impression that he would have preferred being home at the castle with his dogs. Merle seemed to like me because I was a throwback to a glorious era, her era, that wasn't here anymore. Imagine Dean or Brando dining with the

Windsors at Le Pavillon.

Merle was a stickler for perfect manners, and she kept me on my toes. But it wasn't all fancy dinners. She sent me to her masseuse, a woman with the great name of Thelma Thengwald, who'd rub me down with a mixture of egg yolks, kosher salt, olive oil, and lemon juice. I felt like a tossed salad afterward. Merle, like Gloria Swanson, was a health nut, and she got me interested in alternative medicine. Given my grandfather, I was already hooked on medicine, but it was Gloria who took me one step further, out into the twilight zone of longevity. Gloria, as well as Merle, had just started going to Switzerland to the wildly expensive Lausanne longevity clinic of Dr. Paul Niehans, who had achieved international celebrity by giving "sheep gland" shots to the ailing Pope Pius XII, as well as the Aga Khan and Christian Dior, for secular measure. The contents of the injections weren't really sheep glands, though that was the shorthand given by an incredulous press. But they did contain the cells of the embryos of lots of other animals. So when Gloria said she was strong as a bull, or hungry as a horse, there was a curious element of truth there. She swore by the Swiss clinic and claimed to feel twenty years younger, which put her within a decade of my tender age.

Merle, who drank only champagne, with ice to cut the acidity, frequently invited me down to her Mexico City architectural mansion and to her spectacular cliff-hugging Acapulco villa, Ghalal, a cross between the Alhambra and the Taj Mahal. England's Prince Philip would stay there, and President Johnson, and, later, Lynda Bird and I. Merle was definitely my first old-time superstar friend in the then fast-declining fairyland of Hollywood. She appreciated my ability to appreciate her.

Although *Home from the Hill* was a disappointment commercially, the high-prestige film got a lot of great reviews and put me on the map as a new movie star. MGM, which was not long on imagination in those days, elected to follow my typecasting and assign me to play another weak rich aristocrat in a dysfunctional family. Everyone thought this next film, which combined Southern Gothic with a biopic of jazzman Chet Baker, would be a winner. The movie had the awful title of *All the Fine Young Cannibals,* but it had nothing to do with Sam Spiegel's haut-cannibal opus *Suddenly, Last Summer.* If it had really followed the life of Chet Baker, the film would have been called *All the Fine Young Cannabis,* but these were square times, and

233

no one got high on this one.

The cast was intriguing. The main stars were the hottest, and prettiest, young couple in Hollywood, Robert Wagner and Natalie Wood, acting together for the first time. The costars were me and Susan Kohner, who was something of a dark Natalie-esque sultry beauty. Susan had garnered an Oscar nomination and a Golden Globe award for her role as a light-skinned black who passed for white in the hugely successful Ross Hunter near-camp classic *Imitation of Life.* We had the prestigious British director Michael Anderson, who had done *Around the World in 80 Days,* but he had no real feeling for the American South and its eccentricities.

Audiences, such as they were, roared with laughter at a scene in which Susan whips Bob Wagner with a riding crop, and they cheered at another wherein Bob drops down on his knees outside St. Patrick's Cathedral in New York and beseeches his maker, "Oh God! Don't let me have done this!" Still, there were lots of benefits to this "experimental" picture for me. I got to meet the great Pearl Bailey, who played a drunken blues singer, I became lifelong friends with Bob and Natalie, and I got to meet the woman I planned to marry. Susan was playing my sister in the film; we apparently matched up well.

For anyone who says that this gentleman prefers blondes, Susan Kohner, who was so good in *Imitation* that many people thought she was black in real life, was Exhibit A to the contrary. Susan was beautiful, brilliant, old world, aristocratic by any standards and not just her Hollywood pedigree. Her Central European father Paul was one of the premier agents in the business, representing the cream of Europe in Hollywood — Garbo, Dietrich, Chevalier, David Niven, Billy Wilder, and many more. Susan spoke five languages perfectly and she was a great and serious actress, having studied with Salka Viertel, who trained Garbo. What's more, she was sexy and sizzling enough that she was marked for stardom. And she loved me. Who could ask for anything more?

At this early stage of my career, I had learned, if nothing else, how to create the illusion of grandeur. It started with the clothes and continued with the cars. I asked myself, What would Gloria Swanson do? Gloria was a legend for having stood up to the studios and done it her way. So I decided that what Gloria would do was to buy the vintage Rolls-Royce that I had just seen and become obsessed with. It was a 1939 Sedanca de Ville, Phantom III, with a British Spitfire engine. It had been built specially for the king and queen of England, but the looming war made it seem too ostentatious even for them, so they sold it. It ended up out in Los Angeles and was owned by another Hamilton, a rich one, the heir to the Hamilton Beach blender fortune. The only problem with the car was that it had no back; it had lost its rear in a wreck. The owner wanted $5,000 for it. All I had was $1,500. At first the dealer balked, "This ain't for you, this is for kings." I closed the deal with a promise to make payments.

I found James Dean's former mechanic. Everyone in Hollywood has a pedigree, even grease monkeys. Baker to the stars. Butcher to the stars. Proctologist to the stars. I charmed Dean's man into letting me pay for the repairs on time as well. That took some real charm. Out of nowhere, I got a call from the studio, but it wasn't about a part. It was about the car. Someone had seen it and thought it would be perfect for a Rock Hudson movie. So I rented it to them for $100 a day, with the proviso that I get the car back at night. This paid off the dealer as well as the mechanic.

People were overwhelmed by that car. What great person owns it? was what everyone wanted to know. What a change from my early days at Hawthorne, hiding in the back of Tommy's jalopy. I got the next bright idea of renting a chauffeur's uniform as I drove the Rolls around, and whenever anyone asked who owned it, I'd say, "George Hamilton, of course." Eventually I dressed my gardener in my chauffeur's outfit and got him to drive me around. It worked. Hollywood began buzzing about George Hamilton.

If I was going to be a star and court a star, I wanted a star's salary, more than the $500 a week MGM was paying me. I wanted $1,000, which was serious money in 1960. I went to see Benny Thau, one of the bigwigs on the lot. I had my Rolls-Royce downstairs, and my guy in the chauffeur's uniform on the running board just below Thau's office in the Thalberg Building. I laid out my demands about salary and car. "We can get you a nice Chrysler," Thau said.

"I don't need a Chrysler. I already have a Rolls," I said. "And five hundred a week is nothing. My mother makes that." I took a very hard line. My entrance was worthy of Gloria Swanson.

"But you've got a Rolls-Royce, kid," Thau sputtered.

"I want a newer one."

They doubled my salary immediately. The only bad part about the Rolls was that it further locked me into this rich, preppy Eastern WASP image. Of course I was Southern, struggling, and hadn't gone beyond high school. But people believed what they wanted to believe. It wasn't as if I was the first preppy WASP to hit Hollywood. Humphrey Bogart was an Andover man. Jack Lemmon was a graduate of both Andover and Harvard. Jimmy Stewart was a preppy Princetonian. Rudy Vallee was a Yale man. Lex Barker, Tarzan himself, was Exeter and Princeton. This list could go on and on. But none of them, except maybe Rudy Vallee, played the part, and he had played it years before in the raccoon coat era when the preppy look was in vogue. Now nobody dared to play the prep, not in the James Dean-Marlon Brando era. Nobody but me.

Next up was *Where the Boys Are,* which put spring break on the map. The film was produced by schlockmeister Joe Pasternak, who was pretty much the hoodlum priest in MGM's College of Cardinals. While Pan Berman and Arthur Freed wore Savile Row suits, Joe was bargain basement, and proud of it. But he was a moneymaker, and MGM needed people like him, now more than ever. Joe had found this little script about kids going down to Florida over their spring break. What interested the studio was the racy subtext of a college girl getting knocked up. What also interested them was that they had all these young actors on contract whom they could plug into this quickie for a very low budget, people like Paula Prentiss, fresh out of Northwestern, Yvette Mimieux, Dolores Hart, Jim Hutton, and yours truly.

There was no real college scene in Fort Lauderdale when we made the film. It was simply a cheap location. It was also hot as hell and dead as a cemetery. *Boys* was shot in the brutal, torpid heat of summer. I couldn't go up to Palm Beach and lord my new stardom over my old pals, because no one was around in August. The best I could do was get a bit part for my friend Sean Flynn, so I would have some fun company to go drinking with in the few deserted bars that were open in summer. Imagine, me getting a job for the son of Errol Flynn. That sense of power was pure pleasure, maybe the only pleasing thing about this little nothing of a film.

Was I ever wrong. This time Joe Pasternak really brought home the bacon. *Boys* would become a cult and camp classic, thanks in large part to Connie Francis, who was also one of the stars. Connie's warbling of the title song went to number one on the *Billboard* charts, and the kids loved it. I starred as a Brown senior with a yacht, and I was enshrined nationally as the prototypical prep. My girlfriend in the film, for whom I drew the corny question mark in the sand to ask her if she loved me, was Dolores Hart. That question mark, which I improvised, also entered the zeitgeist. Funny what you get remembered for. Dolores would soon leave Hollywood to become a nun, though not on account of any hijinks on my part. In love with Susan Kohner, I behaved like the perfect gentleman I was playing. I had met and liked Dolores before the film. She was part of the pure and virginal Catholic set, a good friend of Gary Cooper's daughter Maria, who had gone to Marymount with other proper showbiz daughters like Mia Farrow and Candice Bergen. Dolores was so pure that she made two films with Elvis Presley and wouldn't let him kiss her good night. Today, the head of an abbey in Connecticut, she is said to chant in Latin eight times a day. I doubt the tune she sings is "Where the Boys Are," though it got so much airplay that most of America was brainwashed by it in 1960.

Even if I didn't return to Palm Beach in a blaze of glory, Palm Beach would soon come to me. The person who was most impressed by my breakthrough in Hollywood was brother Bill. He, however, didn't think I had a clue how to really milk it to the max. Sure, I got the Rolls, but there was so much more I could do. Accordingly, he came to Hollywood to become my personal mentor. He arrived with a rich socialite friend from Palm Beach named Liz Schafer. I had moved up from my initial rental on Wetherly to a much bigger house in Beverly Hills, but for Bill it wasn't anywhere big enough. Bill and Liz thus moved in and began the makeover.

In short order, Bill found a property worthy of what he wanted me to be. It was Grayhall, a 22,000-square-foot Tudor-style mansion built in 1912, the second house constructed in Beverly Hills. It was originally owned by Silsby Spalding, the first mayor of Beverly Hills. Bill loved the idea of provenance, that the house had been leased by Douglas Fairbanks while he and Mary Pickford were building Pickfair and had burrowed tunnels connecting the two estates. Now Bill had the idea that Teeny could move in and sneak through the underground passages for secret rendezvous with Buddy Rogers. There was a ballroom and twenty bathrooms, space aplenty to fill with the antiques Bill was planning to acquire with my newfound star money. With my family, it was one for all and all for one, and Grayhall was definitely for all.

Soon Teeny joined us. She had just gotten divorced and was at loose ends. I barely knew my most recent ex-stepfather, as Teeny had married him just as I was leaving high school. Like all the others, Jesse Spalding looked sublime on paper. He was the preppy heir I was playing, even if he no longer had the money to go with the lineage. After six months of bliss and three years of marriage, Teeny gave up on him. For her, my success was a saving grace, a new chapter in her wild and crazy life, her son, the movie star. My success gave Teeny and Bill an escape valve from Jesse Spalding. I wanted to do it for them; nothing could have made me happier than to be able to step up for my family. However, Teeny and Bill knew that Susan and the Kohners would give them the boot if we were married. They saw my impending marriage to Susan not as gaining a star but as losing one.

Teeny loved being back in Beverly Hills, living in my high style. No sooner had she arrived than she set up an evening at Pickfair, to see Buddy Rogers and to introduce me to Mary, "one star to another." Mary was around seventy, when seventy, at least in Beverly Hills, was a lot older than it is now. She wasn't the little girl with the curls anymore, but she was still blond. The first thing she said to me was, "Take your hands out of your pockets. A gentleman never puts his hands in his pockets." Another valuable lesson in etiquette.

Buddy took Teeny off somewhere in the vast estate, while Mary took care of me. We went into a room with several televisions that had giant magnifying screens so she could see. A butler brought her a big glass of milk. She gulped it down, then rang for another and downed it. "It's better with milk," she told me. What's better? I inquired. "The booze," she replied with a cackling laugh. Who would have guessed that Pollyanna was a lush? In fact, she was as naughty as the little girls she had been famous for playing. While I was with her, Mary had a brainstorm. "Let's give them a scare," she suggested. The idea was to pretend she was having a heart attack. She would fall to the floor and I would lie on top of her giving her mouth-to-mouth resuscitation. The actress in the Oscar winner had never died. And how could I refuse to take direction from the greatest woman in film? So I yelled for help as I breathed into her mouth and pounded on her chest. Somehow, Buddy and Teeny heard my cries. They came running in, piled on to help me. Mary came back to life with the biggest smile. "I'm glad to see that you care," she said.

Teeny set out to reconnect with all of her old Los Angeles friends, none of whom had the slightest desire to become old. No one treasured youth more than Gloria Swanson, whose Rolls-Royce was filled with health foods and vitamin supplements and blenders that she was constantly buying. We had dinner once with Gloria and a secret son of hers, whom Teeny told me was the issue of Gloria and Joe Kennedy. Gloria, like Merle Oberon, had her health and beauty routines that may have seemed obsessive-compulsive, but that drive was probably what made them stars to begin with. Why stop now?

Eventually, the moment of truth was at hand. My romance with Susan had developed to the point that it was time to meet the parents. Her father, Paul, seemed to like me, although he may have bought in too much to the publicity that portrayed me as an Eastern patrician. The Kohners were a very serious family. They refused to drive a Mercedes because of what the Germans had done, they wanted Susan to be a serious actress, and I think they wanted the same of me, more Minnelli, less Pasternak. But with three typecastings in a row, they were starting to have second thoughts about how serious I was about the craft and how crafty I seemed in avoiding seriousness. The two Rollses, Grayhall, the fancy threads — all this struck them as the height of frivolity. "How is my daughter going to *clean* this house?" Paul exclaimed as I showed him around my stately new home. Most of his famous clients didn't live in splendor like this. I was going to tell him that the maids would clean the house, not Susan, but Paul would have detested that decadent response.

The coup de grâce came when not only did Bill and Teeny arrive, but so did the bizarre Memphis Mafia from the *Home from the Hill* shoot. There was plenty of room at Grayhall, so why not? Bill went to every antique auction in California and filled the house with enough pieces to make Napoleon spin in his grave. Meanwhile, he and Teeny decided to staff the house to the hilt, hiring a retinue of maids, gardeners, butlers, and chauffeurs from an agency called HELP that specialized in rehabilitating ex-convicts through elegant service. I was able to pay for it all, not so much with my movie wages but on the easily available credit that allowed Californians to live the Good Life, far beyond their means.

The household was a comedy of errors — no, a farce. Our butler Sydney said he was a minister from Jamaica. He proved his point by converting our hellishly red velvet ballroom into a chapel for his sinners, more than a hundred of whom would pack the place every Sunday, then eat me out of house and home. When I confronted Sydney about not preparing a Sunday dinner for the Kohners, he told me, "The Lord has commanded me not to work on Sunday." I came back with, "Sydney, I just spoke to the Lord five minutes ago and he changed his mind. He wants you to work."

Bill, who was indifferent to food himself, gave one cocktail party after another, serving his many guests dog food on Ritz crackers as he'd done in New York. "These Hollywood people can't tell foie gras from Kal Kan," he said. And he was right. Everyone loved Bill's parties. Our chauffeur Harold, a six four giant with a rap sheet as long as he was tall, impressed Merle Oberon but horrified the Kohners, as did Teeny's Christian Science and her oft-articulated credo that "Divine love always has met, and always will meet, every human need." The Kohners began having second and third thoughts, and Susan, who was entirely dependent on her parents' approval, began having a crisis of faith. My love for her may have been divine, but I needed more than God to convince

Paul and Lupita to surrender their treasure to a madhouse like the Hamilton Grayhall.

Unable to summon the counsel of Gloria Swanson in matters of the heart, as opposed to matters of the studio, I turned to myself and decided to enlist the studio in my quest for the romantic holy grail. My equivalent of serenading the Kohners from under their balcony was to serenade them from the movie house itself. If I made better, more serious movies, maybe then the Kohners would take me, and my love, more seriously. Rule number one: no more preppies. I followed that rule to the extreme in my next outing, *Angel Baby,* a movie about a young evangelist like Marjoe Gortner before there ever was a Marjoe Gortner. Unfortunately, we may have beaten Marjoe to the punch, but we were a year behind *Elmer Gantry,* for which Burt Lancaster won the Oscar for his older version of my character. I loved getting up and preaching lines like, "You can't put off your appointment with Jesus!" But no one came to hear them.

It was hard enough to kiss a woman on-screen. It was even harder to hit one, which was what I was called on to do with my co-star in *Angel Baby,* the great Oscar-winning character actress Mercedes McCambridge. She was one tough broad and made fun of the Southern gent in me when I couldn't bring myself to give her the kind of violent whack the script called for. "Don't pull punches with me," she taunted. So I really let her have it. The next day she arrived in a neck brace, and I with my dislocated right arm in a sling. So much for this kind of method acting. We filmed in the Florida swamps (again, no bragging rights in Palm Beach), but I did get to work with the golden boy of my high school, Burt Reynolds, in his first role. Burt played second banana to me in this one. Years later, in *The Man Who Loved Cat Dancing,* I played second banana to him. Burt kept a picture of me hitting him in *Angel Baby,* where I seemed to be slugging everyone. "That's the last time that'll ever happen," Burt vowed, and he kept his promise.

My next move was of the if-you-can't-beat-'em-join-'em school. The Kohners couldn't get on my case if I was in the same film their daughter was in. That film was *By Love Possessed,* a big, sprawling melodrama of the kind you don't see anymore, and perhaps for good reason. *By Love* was an Ivy League *Peyton Place,* about the intersecting lives of three Yankee lawyers and their clients. Back to the Ivies again, I played a Harvard Law grad son forced to enter my father's (Efrem

248

Zimbalist Jr.) law firm. Susan played a virgin orphan heiress client (a mouthful; get the complexity?) of the firm whom I deflower and drive to suicide. She does herself in by drinking a can of cleaning fluid. I can't believe Paul Kohner let *either* of us do this one, but such legends as Lana Turner, Jason Robards Jr., Thomas Mitchell, and Barbara Bel Geddes made the same mistake.

The big thrill was Lana Turner. Lana was the actress with whom I would have the longest, and least felicitous, screen relationship. She was the most notorious woman in America right then, coming off the murder of gangster swain Johnny Stompanato. All the rumors were that Lana had stabbed him to death and gotten her teenage daughter to take the fall. But those rumors were never spoken anywhere near the Great One, just as India was never mentioned around Merle Oberon. Not that Lana and I hung out. Instead she hung *me* out, forcing me to do at least thirty takes of a scene in which all I had to do was help her on with her mink coat. The idea was to slide the mink to her neck, then let it drop away. Having learned from the master of the game, I thus became adept at putting endangered species on endangered species. I had a future in cloakrooms if all else failed.

And it did seem to be heading in that direction. Trying hard to avoid the Ivy curse, the best I could do was to play a West Point type dispatched to the West to kill Indians under the command of Richard Boone, who was everyone's favorite Western TV star as Paladin on *Have Gun — Will Travel.* But in those days it was hard to get people to pay in theaters for what they could get for free at home. Charles Bronson made an early appearance here, as a brutal ruffian, but he wasn't rough enough to create a buzz. The project had an impressive pedigree, with a script by James Warner Bellah, who wrote some of the best John Ford Westerns. My character, who lost the girl but gained his courage, was to embody the lesson of the piece, that "bachelors make the best soldiers. All they have to lose is their loneliness."

After *A Thunder of Drums,* I was faced with a mounting likelihood of bachelorhood myself. Susan had gotten a plum role opposite Montgomery Clift in the John Huston production of *Freud,* and she was heading off to her father's Vienna, and, in all likelihood, out of my life. I couldn't get on *Freud,* but I vowed to get myself to Europe. There was a movie starting in Rome at just the right time, *Light in the Piazza,* about a mentally handicapped American girl on holiday who falls for a young Italian boy. In crass Hollywood shorthand, it was *Summertime* with a mentally handicapped girl instead of a spinster. It was also what they called an "important" movie, remade decades later into a Tony Award-winning musical.

The film was being produced by Cardinals Arthur Freed and Pandro Berman, written by Julius Epstein, who cowrote *Casablanca*. *Summertime* heartthrob Rossano Brazzi was playing the boy's father; Olivia de Havilland, the girl's mother; Yvette Mimieux, the girl; and Tomas Milian, the Italian boy. The studio system was falling apart. Even though I was under contract, the prevailing attitude was, "We've got George Hamilton. Who else can we get?" Who they got was Tomas Milian, a young Cuban actor to play the Italian. Where did I fit in? I didn't. But I was resourceful enough to find a way.

I climbed into the MGM script cage at night to get the latest copy of the screenplay, hot off the mimeo machines. I learned every word by heart. I began working the lot at MGM, lobbying everyone from gate guards to casting directors to wardrobe mistresses to publicists to vice presidents to visiting theater owners to give me the part. Yvette was my pal from *Where the Boys Are,* so she got into my corner, knowing I would be good for at least a laugh or two in Rome. I argued that Milian was Cuban, not Italian, and that I could be a better Italian than he. His father was a general in Cuba, but he was a Batista general, hence in the age of Castro not available to cause me bodily harm.

I went to Gertrude Fogler, the chief voice coach, who trained me how to drop my voice and sound sexy, the same way she had taught Latin lover Fernando Lamas. I also sought out Rossano Brazzi and worked my charm on him, turning him into a one-man Berlitz blitz course in Italian. I then went to studio bigwig Benny Thau to get a screen test for *Light*. I arrived at lunchtime. "We got a guy," Benny said. "What are you bothering me for?"

"Mr. Thau, he's Cuban," I countered. "He's got an accent."

"Doesn't matter."

"Mr. Thau, there's a big difference between a Cuban accent and an Italian accent," I said.

"You don't speak either," Benny said.

"Mr. Thau, I have a perfect ear for this. I've studied. I can do the accent. I can play the character." I pleaded my case like Clarence Darrow.

"Do me a favor," Benny said. "Go down

there [on the MGM lot] and act. But not in this movie."

I wouldn't take no for an answer. Teeny knew a very rich man named Nathan Cummings, who was a major MGM shareholder. I even wrote him, saying how they were wasting the talent they were paying for. I went back again to Benny Thau. "I told you to find another picture, kid. You're becoming a pain in the ass."

In the course of my frantic lobbying for *Piazza,* I was chilled one day to see a once famous actor named Tom Drake (*Meet Me in St. Louis* and many more) I had watched on the big screen as a boy in Blytheville, now singing "Good Night, Irene" on a microphone at the meat counter of a grocery store in Beverly Hills. How fleeting these careers could be. I had to be even fleeter just to survive.

I went back to Thau's office another day around lunchtime to keep up my campaign. His secretary said he was busy. I cooled my heels for an hour. When the secretary took a break, I knocked on the door to the office myself. "Come in," a voice said. Thau was sitting there. He wasn't happy to see me.

"I want to talk to you."

"What about?"

"If you just give me a few minutes . . ."

253

"Just give *me* a few minutes," he said.

"Mr. Thau, I'd be delighted to give you a few minutes, but I've been waiting outside for over an hour."

"What's it about?"

"This movie. All I'm asking for is a test."

With this, I see a girl coming out from under his desk, having serviced him. She straightened her dress and walked into the other office. Benny didn't even bat an eye. Wow. This was Hollywood, I thought. Finally Benny spoke. "I'm considering you for the test," he said. "We'll keep this between us, won't we?"

"I didn't see anything, did you?" I replied with the straightest face I could muster. Now, that was real acting.

I finally got the test, and I was good. But the studio still had this commitment to Tomas Milian, and I couldn't get Benny to say yes. In fact, I couldn't get him at all. I found out from his secretary he was in Monaco on holiday. I wanted it so bad I flew over to meet him there. But I knew I needed another gimmick, as good as the Rolls. So I got into the Hôtel de Paris, tipped the waiter on Benny's floor $100, and we made a deal. "The first time he orders room service, you let me bring it in." I waited there for three hours. Finally he ordered and I brought it

into the suite overlooking the casino. Benny
was in his robe reading *Variety*. A girl was
lying in the bed, half naked.

"*Buon giorno,*" I said, in my best Italian.

"Yeah," Benny mumbled.

"Where you wanta me putta the food?
Over there?"

"Yeah."

"You wanta me pour you coffee?"

"Naw."

"You signora? She wanta me pour the coffee?"

"No." He was getting annoyed.

"You wanta signa the check?"

"Just put a tip on for yourself and go,"
Benny said.

"Why you tella me go? I come all the way
from the States."

He finally looked up at me. "Not you
again!" he groaned.

"Well," I said. "What do you say?"

"Get the hell outta here."

"Wait a minute," I said. "Mr. Thau, you
just thought I was a waiter, an Italian one.
If I could fool you, why couldn't I fool an
audience?"

He gave me the role.

CHAPTER NINE
MY DOLCE VITA

A funny thing happened on my way to the forum. Actually, lots and lots of funny things happened on my way to the forum, and I had a ringside seat, literally. My apartment, at 64 Via dei Foraggi, had one of the great views of the world, overlooking the eternal temples, arches, pillars, and columns, not to mention the beautiful tourists, junior year abroaders, and supermodels of the day on *Vogue* photo shoots. As far as I was concerned, every day was a Roman holiday — or the ides of March, depending on who was in town. To go with my killer view, I bought a killer car, a bright red Ferrari Daytona, for $18,000 (it costs well over a million now), and, for a lot less, I bought up the Via Condotti to dress like a modern Caesar, or at least an Agnelli. It wasn't bad for a twentysomething kid from Arkansas who got Cs in Latin and couldn't tell you the difference between Doric and Corinthian.

Arriving in 1962 to film *Light in the Piazza* and hanging around for *Two Weeks in Another Town,* I was part of the Hollywood invasion, which some stuffy Romans may have resented as much as they did the barbarians of yore, but most of them, including the noblest, embraced us as breathing life into a museum of a city devastated by World War II. Hollywood was there, rationally, because Rome was cheap. The lira was play money, and the Mussolini-built studios of Cinecittà ("Cinema City") gave you everything MGM or Fox did, at a fraction of the cost. But Hollywood was there because it was fun.

Eisenhower and television had ganged up to take the spirit and the glamour out of what was coming to be known as "old Hollywood." My contract at MGM had made me one of the last of a breed that was becoming extinct. But here in Rome, stars could act like stars. Stars were worshipped like popes and Caesars. Italians knew how to worship. The historic urban beauty, the restaurants, the clubs, and the total air of decadence (the city had been decaying elegantly for two thousand years; who could top that?) made for the sweet life that stars were meant to live. No wonder Elizabeth Taylor and company were here to shoot the most lavish film in history, *Cleopatra.* Shooting *Cleo* in Culver

City would have been a kind of sacrilege.

Adding to the fun was the presence of my old Hamptons flame, Betty Benson Spiegel, who always liked to be where the action was, although she was too modest to admit that the action was wherever she showed up. Her mogul husband, Sam, was taking full advantage of her endless tolerance, sailing around the Mediterranean on his new yacht, the *Malahne,* with his harem of socialites, aspiring actresses, and top-dollar *filles de jour,* Betty adored Rome. She had no aspirations to act, but she loved playing fairy godmother. Betty's best friend in New York was a girl named Denise Gigante, an elegant, understated, high-cheekboned Yugoslavian who had become, through Betty's *Hello, Dolly!* matchmaking, the girlfriend, and eventually wife, of my director and friend Vincente Minnelli.

I had fallen out with Betty when she had flown down to Caracas to have a fling with my pal Oscar Molinari Herrera. Even though Betty was married, I felt betrayed. But I got over it. If her own husband, the master of control, couldn't control Betty, who was I to try? She played by different rules, that is, whatever she felt like.

Vincente was coming to Rome to make *Two Weeks in Another Town,* an Irwin Shawwritten inside-Hollywood story starring Kirk Douglas and Edward G. Robinson as two has-beens who attempt a comeback in Rome. There was a part for a troubled, funky James Dean-type actor, for which I couldn't have been less appropriate. But Betty wanted to be in Rome, where the action was, and Betty told Denise I was good company and good value, so Denise leaned on Vincente, who was already predisposed to me, our flop notwithstanding. That wild pig with the Beverly Hills teeth had bonded us forever. I got the part.

Two Weeks was another A-list misfire. Maybe Vincente was so besotted with Denise that he had lost his vision. Hiring me to do a James Dean role may have been evidence of that. The Joe DiMaggio of MGM would swing for the fences with big budget movies like *The Sandpiper* (Liz and Dick) and *On a Clear Day You Can See Forever* (Streisand) for another decade, but he struck out every time. Maybe it was age, maybe it was the MGM curse. Movies were having an awful time of it then. *Two Weeks* was a sort of sequel to Vincente's earlier acclaimed inside look at Hollywood, *The Bad and the Beautiful.* This one was just *The Bad,* and most of the critics panned it as a rehash. My big nemesis at the outset of my career was

Bosley Crowther, chief film critic of the *New York Times*. Crowther had panned *Piazza,* noting that while Yvette Mimieux was supposed to seem retarded, she just seemed like a dumb Hollywood starlet, "no less bright in the upper story . . . than any doll played by Marilyn Monroe." The one who was "the real booby," Crowther hissed, was *me.* He called me "a bare cut above an idiot." On *Bad* Crowther let me off the hook and went after Kirk Douglas, noting that in this "drippy drama of degradation" he was "no more intelligible or convincing than Steve Reeves' Hercules." Such is the stuff of scrapbooks. At least I was in good company.

For me, even the worst movie was an education, a chance to work with legends. I was so in awe of Kirk Douglas and his terrifying intensity that two years later at a party at his house in Beverly Hills, I still felt the need to get inside my James Dean character for him. I got so inside that I passed out and ended up in Kirk's shower. Kirk made you "go for it," just as he did. Edward G. Robinson, in the land of the Caesars, was anything but Little Caesar in real life, as calm as Kirk was driven. Eddie was obsessed with art and had one of the great collections in America, and I learned more from him about Caravaggio than I did about Stanislavsky. Cyd Charisse was in the film, too, and her legs lived up to the legend. Because her husband, Tony Martin, was always right by her side, Cyd was one legend that remained intact.

Being in Rome put me in the heart of the world film colony at the time. The biggest news when I was making films there was the *Cleopatra* debacle, both on and off the set. It had a budget gone amok. Plus it had the biggest sex scandal in the history of film. I was at the Grand Hotel for Elizabeth Taylor's birthday party. She was thirtysomething, and she was the Cleopatra of the media world, the reigning queen of Hollywood. Richard Burton, her costar, sang a drunken, rambling paean to her, and everyone knew he was sleeping with her, everyone except poor Eddie Fisher, who was there as well. Eddie, who had done Debbie Reynolds wrong with Elizabeth, would soon be dying by the sword he lived by. Was it a cautionary tale to me? Not on your life. My own sword was badly in need of sharpening. Rome was the right place for it.

Aside from the film, my life in Rome was — like that of most men of most ages in most professions — about chasing women. For all my efforts, my relationship with Susan wasn't working out. The longer we waited to have our big Hollywood wedding, the less likely that big event was going to occur. While doing *Piazza* I had shuttled to Vienna, and she had shuttled to Rome, as she still did, from Hollywood or New York, but less frequently. Her own career was faring worse, far worse, than mine. *Freud* had been an unexpected bust, and Susan had begun doing episodic television, which was an ignominious admission of defeat back then. The unraveling of George and Susan came as a great relief to Teeny and Bill, who were living it up at Grayhall while this cat was away. I was very sad about my first experience with love at the top in Hollywood, and to salve my pain, I went out a lot.

I had become something of a hot property, thanks to being in the right place at the right time. That right place was the bar of the Hotel Cipriani at the Venice Film Festival. An angry woman began speaking to me, ranting about how awful Cyd Charisse was for avoiding her. I wasn't sure who the woman was — a spurned producer perhaps? maybe a publicist? I knew it wasn't a girlfriend, as Cyd and Tony were blissfully married. The woman finally exhausted her venom and changed the subject to one I preferred: me. "What do you do?" she asked.

"I'm an actor." It wasn't very original, but I was looking good in my new silk ascot.

"You look like a young Lord Byron," the woman said. What good taste she had. Then she got out a pad and began taking notes. "I was going to give the *Paris Match* cover to Cyd Charisse, but now it's going to be you," she said, announcing my good fortune. "I'll call you the next Lord Byron." The woman was as good as her word. The following week I was on the cover of *Match,* the *Life* of France. It made me the toast of Europe. The Cyd-spurned woman turned out to be Oriana Fallaci, who would become the very top female journalist of her generation. Normally she covered wars and revolutions. I was lucky she was going the glamour route for one of the rare times in her very serious career. Like Teeny, I could have the best timing when I least expected it.

In addition to my *Match* cover, I thought my Ferrari would be the ultimate aphrodisiac in Rome, but as far as Italian girls were concerned, I was dead wrong. In those days, Italian women were all show and no go, still under the virginal spell of the Catholic church. When they saw my Ferrari, they ran in the opposite direction; they assumed that any guy with a car like that was a pimp out to sell them into white slavery. That left me with the foreign girls, who leaped to no such dire conclusions, and, luckily, there were lots of foreign beauties on the make in Hollywood-on-the-Tiber. Their model was Anita Ekberg, of Fellini's *La Dolce Vita*, Swedish, voluptuous, bigger than life.

My first hot pursuit in this rich vein was one of Denise's fellow Yugoslavians, a ravishing basketball star named Ljuba Otanovic. Ljuba, who looked like Sophia Loren, only even more stunning, had been dating Cary Grant, who had vainly pursued Sophia in *The Pride and the Passion* (no pride on his part, no passion on hers), and was looking for a Sophia look-alike to salve his wounds. He was also showering her with jewels from Bulgari and Buccellati. I couldn't give her anything but love, but I was here in Rome, and Cary was not.

I took Ljuba to the disco of the moment, the Shaker (as in "movers and shakers") in Parioli on the Via Archimede, the ritziest residential area in Rome. King Farouk lived a block over, on Via Euclide. The Shaker was owned by two young Romans named Gigi Orlando and Stefano Orsini, who later brought their dolce vita style to Beverly Hills at their Caffé Roma, where Governor Schwarzenegger, among others, still smokes his Olympian stogies. One night, as Ljuba and I cruised up to the Shaker, my Ferrari was suddenly flanked by two matching Ferrari Californias, a more expensive model than mine, one black and one white. The Ferraris were his and hers, for the couple that obviously had everything. The drivers were the Baron Enrico "Ricky" di Portanova, the half-Italian heir to a great Texas oil fortune, which he would have to sue for before he came to own Houston and Acapulco, and his then girlfriend, a heroic Ekbergian Swede named Ingrid. Ricky was famous for his philosophy: The best things in life were "sun, sex, and spaghetti."

Inside the club, the dashing Ricky, whom I had never me before, made me quite a bold, bald proposition. He had fallen madly in love, as jet-set playboys tended to do, with Ljuba at first sight. He *had* to have her. Accordingly, he offered me Ingrid, of whom he had grown weary, as a swap. As part of the deal, he handed me the keys to Ingrid's heart: He told me she loved Ferraris and horses; he told me the name of her favorite restaurant on the Via Appia Antica and what to order for her. Ingrid, an amazing creature herself, was a slam dunk for me, and how could I compete with Cary Grant? By the same token, how could Ricky? Bottom line was that he could, and he did. He ended up marrying Ljuba. Despite all the inside info Ricky had provided,

265

I got nowhere with Ingrid.

One weekend, down on Capri, I spied another goddess sunning herself on the rocks of that storied isle. I was at the Canzone del Mare, a beach restaurant forerunner of Saint-Tropez's Club 55, where *tutto il mondo* hung out. The piano player was a handsome young American named Bob Crewe, who went on to write all the hits for the Four Seasons, songs like "Big Girls Don't Cry," and is celebrated in the hit musical *Jersey Girls*. Speaking of big girls, I was transfixed by this mermaid whose name was Jackie Lane. She was English; her sister was an aspiring actress in Rome. I don't remember what Jackie was aspiring to. All that mattered was that I aspired to her.

We made a date, but she wouldn't let me pick her up. Instead she insisted we meet at the Trevi Fountain, as in "three coins," the biggest tourist spot in Rome. I worried that she was blowing me off. But I went anyway, and lo and behold, there she was in all her splendor. I took her to dinner at Al Moro, which was Orson Welles's favorite trattoria, as well as a haunt of Fellini and Antonioni, famed for its spaghetti carbonara. Afterward, I took her to the hot disco Il Pipistrello (The Bat), and after that, well . . . and so to bed. Or so I thought.

But first we had to run the gauntlet of seventy paparazzi waiting outside the club on their Vespas and Lambrettas. Today's photo-stalkers of Lindsay, Britney, and Paris have nothing on these guys, who invented the profession. The Italian lensmen were ruthless and evil, to boot. I learned that the only way to deal with these vultures was to kill them with kindness, always stopping to pose and smile graciously. Resistance invited reprisal, and they always won.

But not tonight. I had my eye on the prize, and somehow I was able to sneak out the back door of Il Pipistrello and into the Excelsior Hotel on the Via Veneto, which was off-limits to the shooters. From there I tipped the concierge to get us a car in the service entrance, and from there it was straight to chez Jackie and, ostensibly, ecstasy. I remember taking my clothes off myself and folding them gingerly rather than the two of us rabidly undressing each other. I *loved* those clothes. Suit by Caraceni, shirt by Battistoni, shoes by Gatto. I had never dressed better in my life, all custom, all perfect. I didn't want any wrinkles. I was down to my Brooks Brothers briefs (some traditions die hard) and about to go to heaven when suddenly there was an ominous and insistent rapping at the door.

"It's him," Jackie gasped. "Oh, my God."

She showed me to the window. But it was a vertiginous third-floor apartment, and Roman ceilings were very high. The only way down was a drainpipe. Being no cat burglar, I instead found the maid's room, which, to my chagrin — and the maid's — was occupied. *"Mamma mia!"* she screamed, as I dived under her covers. To shut her up, I leaped out of bed and cowered in a dark corner. Through a cracked door I could see a violent man swinging Jackie around by her long, long hair like a rag doll.

I had to stand up for her honor, even if she couldn't, or hadn't. But how do you play Sir Galahad in your Brooks Brothers briefs? There was no elegant way out, but I did step forward. The guy stopped cold and stared deadly daggers at me. I recognized him as an American stuntman in the Steve Reeves Hercules pictures so ridiculed by Bosley Crowther, being shot at Cinecittà. Rome, movie Rome, was a small town. "It's my fault," I interceded. "All my fault." And, to my surprise — and relief — he released her.

"I'm gonna let you go," he said, "but I'm gonna get you, I promise." I took the threat — and the reprieve — as graciously as I could and beat a hasty exit down the stairs. I didn't dare take my clothes. A second's hesitation might have been fatal. I made it to the Excelsior in my briefs. Thank God even the paparazzi had gone to bed. I borrowed some money from the shocked concierge and bought the coat off the back of a cab-driver outside.

I never saw Jackie again, but a few years later, back in New York, I was eating a burger at the bar at P. J. Clarke's, the best burger in the world in those days, the burger that Jackie and Aristotle Onassis couldn't live without. As I reached for some ketchup, I was transfixed by the most beautiful outfit I'd ever seen. There was something familiar about it, though. And then it hit me: It was *my* suit, my shoes, the best that Rome had to offer. And the mad stuntman was wearing them. Right here in New York. I left that great burger on the bar and slipped out into the Manhattan night, awfully muggy, but the fresh air of freedom. Often clothes make the man, but there can be glaring exceptions.

Don't get the idea that because I stepped out of the way of that sartorial psychopath in Rome I wasn't capable of mixing it up, need be. Take, for instance, my smackdown with the premier lawyer to the stars, Greg Bautzer, immortalized as Joan Crawford's counsel in *Mommie Dearest*. Greg was not only Joan's lawyer; he represented everyone, including Howard Hughes. He was big and handsome, another Yugoslavian who had been a dockworker down at the port of L.A. in San Pedro before going to law school at night and beginning his amazing climb to the top. He was a great dancer and a nasty drunk. One night I was in New York at El Morocco with some friends, after I had broken up with Susan. Who should come in but Susan with Greg. He kept dancing her by my table, dipping her dangerously close to me, rubbing her in my face. I obviously was upset and called Greg aside. "You've got no manners," I told him. He jumped into action and put up his dukes. "You want it right here, kid? How do you want it? Fists, guns, karate? You name it. Let's do it." I backed off. I couldn't do a duel in front of Susan, not at El Morocco. Think of the publicity.

But I soon got a second chance, at a dinner at the home of Hedda Hopper. Greg was there, and he had it in for me. This time we went outside, and I knocked him out cold. Hedda, the ultimate gossip, didn't write it up. "Not at *my house!*" I ran into Greg a few days later in Beverly Hills, and instead of wanting to kill me, he was all hale fellow well met. He hugged me and called me "compadre." And from then on it was always "compadre." Sometimes the only way to join 'em is to beat 'em.

One legend I wanted to slug was John Huston. A dear friend of the Kohners, the he-man director felt that I wasn't worthy of this prize of prizes. I doubt that he thought any man was worthy of Susan. Whenever I was with him, he always tried to humiliate me. He was very sadistic. He'd offer me a cigar. I'd light up. He'd say, in that deep, baleful, mocking voice of his, "Do you know what kind of cigar you're smoking?" I'd have to say no. "You don't know anything, do you, boy?" I would go on to learn everything there was to know about cigars, thanks to him. If he saw me drinking champagne at a cocktail party, he'd ask me about the vintage and the brand. If I didn't know what the host had poured, and it would have been impolite to ask, he'd taunt me, "I wouldn't want to drink something I didn't know." I couldn't win with him. John was a brawler, itching for a fight. Scratch on, John, was my attitude.

Most of the lords of the Hollywood realm were, however, very nice to me, especially when I met them off their home turf, in places like the French Riviera. The idea was that if I were on the Riviera, I had to be all right. My first trip to the Côte d'Azur was with a character named Marvelous Marvin, who sounds like Gorgeous George but was not a wrestler. His full title, as he gave it, was "Dr. Marvin Finch, World Guest, Doctor Benson, Eminent Proctologist, and Bone Specialist to Friends." To me he was Marvin. Marvin was no more a doctor than "Prince" Mike Romanoff, who ran Beverly Hills's most star-studded restaurant, was Russian nobility. Both were audacious con men, but both were superb at faking it, putting on a great show, which is what show business is all about. They were the best "actors" in Hollywood. I very often found the gofers much more interesting than the powers they served. Guys like Marvin were genuine stars in their own right.

Marvin's great talent was assembling beautiful women, which endeared him to every studio mogul. He could pick up anybody, with Groucho Marxish machine-gun patter like, "Would you care for a drink or would you settle for the cash instead?" that left the recipients dazed and confused, at which point Marvin moved in for the kill. He was around sixty and looked very distinguished, like an American John Gielgud, with dapper clothes that had unusual touches like tartan linings under his jacket lapels. He could hustle girls, but he could also hustle cards, pool, horses, whatever. He had guts beyond belief.

"I'm a doer, goer, player, stayer, watcher, and a joiner," he'd riff. "Oh, hi!" was his classic greeting, drawn out for what seemed like a whole minute. His one drooping eye twinkled into a palsied wink. Marvin owned a nightclub in Hollywood called The Hague, and he was close to Huntington Hartford, whose billions and modeling agency provided the catnip that was Marvin's working capital.

I enjoyed brash extroverts like Marvin, because I was actually very shy around women. I had a hard time making that first move, going up to a stranger. It was much easier to let Marvin be my advance man, to blow my horn. My Southern gentility, which scorned being pushy, aggressive, "uppity," immobilized me from blowing my own horn. I could do it to get a job, but I couldn't do it to get a girl. I was a wallflower at the orgy compared to such contemporary lotharios as Bob Evans and Warren Beatty. There was no one with more chutzpah when it came to women than Evans. When I met him he was a struggling actor, still living large on his prodigious income as a Seventh Avenue *garmento*. Evans (né Shapera, his father a Harlem dentist) had played a toreador in *The Sun Also Rises,* but he was a far better salesman than a bullfighter. It would be a decade before he would sell his way into Paramount's executive suite and become the hottest producer in the business.

Judging from the spectacular female company he kept, Evans was already one of the hottest guys in town. The dress business and the film business have a lot in common, especially their obsession with gorgeous women. Bobby, as we called him, always had patronage to dispense, whether pants or parts. Warren Beatty, who came up in the "hot young actor" ranks almost simultaneously with me, was almost as aggressive as Evans. While Evans dealt in cool, seductive strategy, Warren was a raging bull who couldn't help himself. A beautiful woman incited a chemical reaction in him. His nostrils would flare, his ears would prick up, and he'd go into overdrive. You (if you were a guy) could be having the pleasantest conversation, and it would be over and you wouldn't exist anymore. His eyes would glaze over, he'd go a quart low, and, suddenly, you were gone.

That's why, for someone diffident, it was nice to be with Marvin. Once introduced, the ice broken, I could back into the deal and be a pretty good closer. But nobody opened like Marvin, who might steal your wallet to buy you dinner but whose company was worth the price. Somehow Marvin had showed up down in Florida when I was making *Where the Boys Are*. After shooting, he took me up to Gainesville, to the university, and used me as bait to replenish his phone book. About fifteen hundred kids showed up to meet me, Florida's newest gift to Hollywood. It was like a *Girls Gone Wild* audition. Marvin took the numbers of the fifty best looking and invited them to Hollywood for "screen tests." He also challenged one of the school's male tennis stars. Marvin, who was old and didn't even have tennis shoes, lured the golden boy out to the court for what seemed like the easiest of bets. With his leather street shoes on, Marvin blew the star away in straight sets. "All in a day's work," he'd say, then, "Oh, hi," to the next cheerleader crossing the quad.

So my first summer in Europe, he sent me a ticket to meet him at the Hôtel de Paris in Monte Carlo. As I entered the lobby, I saw Jack Warner, Fox head Darryl Zanuck, Columbia head Mike Frankovitch, Stavros Niarchos, Serge Semenenko, those kind of moguls. I didn't dare ask Marvin who was paying, but I was way out of my element. It was supposed to be the Summer of Sinatra, who was en route to perform at the Red Cross Gala, put on by Sinatra's dear friend Princess Grace. Sinatra was king of the world then, having been so instrumental in putting Jack Kennedy in the White House. Bob Neal, Texas-born heir to the Maxwell House fortune, who wore a T-shirt that had US DRINKING TEAM emblazoned on it, had chartered a 175-foot vintage steam yacht that had belonged to J. P. Morgan to cruise the Med with his pals, a floating Rat Pack that included Dean Martin, Sammy Davis, Peter Lawford, Jimmy Van Heusen, Mike Romanoff, Porfirio Rubirosa, the stud of studs, plus Marvelous Marvin and yours truly. Sinatra hated the boat, because it was old and ugly, so he threw one of his tantrums and left for Germany with Dean Martin. The rest of us stayed to watch Sammy's big show at the Sporting Club. Bob didn't care, as long as there were great women around.

Talk about feeling like the odd man out, with all these superstars around me. Marvin told me not to worry, that soon everyone on the Riviera would know who I was. To that end, he took me to the grand casino. Dressed in rare double-breasted custom-tailored dinner suits that Marvin had made for us, we made our grand entrance in a Lincoln Continental convertible that Marvin had had shipped over for Huntington Hartford to tool around in for the rest of the summer. Marvin gave me only one instruction: Shout "*banco*" as loud as I could once he got me to the chemin de fer table in the *salon privé*. I had no idea how to play the game, much less what *banco* meant. No matter, Marvin said.

We got into the salon in the over-the-top ornate gambling palace. Around the table were the same masters of the universe we saw at the Hôtel de Paris across the street, dressed to the nines, surrounded by a stable of tens, who, Marvin told me, were the top courtesans in Paris, all sent courtesy of Madame Claude, brothel keeper to the rich and famous. Actually the courtesy wasn't hers, but that of a gent at the table named Manfredo Horowitz, who was Harry Winston's main man in Europe. The courtesans, who were often titled aristocrats from Central European countries fallen on hard times, were loss leaders for the diamonds he planned to sell to the moguls for their wives, out of guilt for their current excesses. Fred Horowitz made a fortune in diamond commissions not only from Europe's crowned heads but even more from the Saudi royal family. An Arab king or prince couldn't just buy a million-dollar diamond for his wife; he had to buy one for *each* of his wives. There was a kind of democracy of consumption in the harem, and Fred milked it to become known as the Salesman of the Century.

Marvin punched me in the ribs to divert my attention from the Claude girls and onto the matter at hand. *"Banco!"* I shouted. The croupier looked up at me as if I were an alien. *"Vous n'avez pas crédit, monsieur,"* the croupier sneered. Marvin ribbed me again. *"Banco!"* I shouted to the frescoed ceiling. *"Banco!"* All the masters of the universe looked around. Who was this interloper? their daggered gazes asked. Jack Warner knew Marvin.

"Who the hell is he?" the tycoon asked.

"He's the new star at MGM," Marvin whispered to him, with all the confidence this con man could muster.

Jack Warner looked me up and down as if I were a piece of meat he was deciding whether to eat. I was trembling over the humiliation that could ensue.

"Let the kid have it," Warner snapped to the croupier.

The croupier turned the cards I had apparently bet on. It was a natural eight. I had just won $30,000. "See you at the bar," Marvelous Marvin said to me.

When I got there, six of Madame Claude's girls were in Marvin's tow. Like bank robber Willie Sutton, they went where the money was. Before I could begin squandering it,

Marvin came up and put the arm on me. "I want my half," he said. I asked him what would have happened if I had turned up a losing hand. "I wouldn't have known you," Marvin said.

That night in Monte Carlo was my coming-out party. It got me more buzz in Hollywood than any of my movies. Everybody wanted to know me, including Jack Warner himself, who, for all his imperial might, was considered the most uncouth man in an uncouth business. When Chiang Kai-shek was in Hollywood, he wanted to meet Warner, and to meet girls. The famed English publicist Richard Gully, whom I met through Merle Oberon, set up a doubles tennis match between the two emperors and two stars. Warner was so competitive that on the first volley he yelled to his partner, "Smash it to the Chink." No Warner Bros. films were shown in China until the generalissimo had to retreat to Taiwan. So much for diplomacy in Hollywood.

But Marvin's diplomacy worked for me, and I soon was signed for what promised to be one of the most prestigious projects in years, *The Victors,* shooting in London. This antiwar war movie about World War II was the directing debut of one of the greatest of all screenwriters, Carl Foreman, who wrote *High Noon.* He had been blacklisted as a

Communist sympathizer and moved to England, where he ghostwrote, for Sam Spiegel, *Bridge on the River Kwai*. Now the blacklist was over, and Carl had his own blockbuster as writer-producer of *Guns of Navarone*. I had never played a soldier, but I figured it would be an antidote to all those preppies. Besides, I would be in great feminine company, a brigade of goddesses including Melina Mercouri, Romy Schneider, Jeanne Moreau, and Elke Sommer, not to mention a film reunion with my *Home* boy, George Peppard.

Before I went to London, Marvin and I went to Paris, where I got to know better one of my great idols, Porfirio Rubirosa, whom I had met down in Monte Carlo. As a boy in Palm Beach, I used to watch Rubi, as he was known, play polo. He had actually lived there when he was married to Barbara Hutton. He was famous for having married both Barbara and Doris Duke, America's two greatest heiresses. Now Rubi was in his fifties, which was the twilight of his prime, but prime he was. I first met him at a dinner in Maxim's with Marvin and Bob Neal. A lot of the world-class playboys were there: Claude Terrail, who owned the rival Tour d'Argent; the Brazilian tycoon Baby Pignatari; another Brazilian, Jorge Guinle, who owned the Copacabana Palace Hotel in Rio; Gianni Agnelli; the wild fashion designer Jacques Fath; and Rubi and his new young pneumatic bride, Odile, his fifth, and this time for love, not money. Rubi ate a rice diet.

After dinner, Rubi took a bunch of us to his favorite boîte, Le Calvados, to listen to black American jazzmen. He himself serenaded the table on a guitar. Rubi invited me to the Bois de Boulogne the next morning, on zero sleep, to watch him play polo versus an Argentine team. Then we went riding, a skill that I had picked up at Gulfport and that alone made my military school ordeal worth it. He took me to his home, which had a boxing ring in the living room, and he took me on a white-knuckle ride in one of his Ferraris, the same one that he was killed in two years later while racing home from Calvados through the bois.

For a man who was supposedly bankrupt, it was whispered, his having gone through all the fortunes he had hunted, Rubi lived like a millionaire. For a womanizer, supposedly the greatest since Don Juan, Rubi had perfect manners. He set up a few dinners for us with a mix of royalty, top modeldom, and Madame Claude professionals, all world-class beauties, and he treated them all like ladies, not ladies of the evening. At the dinners, he seated all the women looking out into the restaurant, and all the men facing in, so that they couldn't be checking out other opportunities across the room. He knew how to focus, to pay total attention to the lady at hand. The key to women, he told me, was to *listen* to them and look deeply into their eyes, no matter what their age or beauty. That was the sure way to participate in their fantasies. It was a lesson I never forgot.

When I hit London, the Beatles were yet to arrive, but despite the black coal fog and the bad food and the postwar depression that still affected Albion, there were swinging times to be had. Marvin had turned me into a gambler, and there was great gaming to be done at Les Ambassadeurs, a private club in a height-of-empire mansion overlooking Hyde Park. There was great dancing to be done at Dolly's, a raffish disco owned by Johnny Gold, who would go on to create Tramp, which would become ground zero for British rock stars. For the royal set, Annabel's on Berkeley Square was just opening. As a movie star, I was welcome everywhere, the toast of the town.

I rented a town house in Chesham Mews in Knightsbridge with George Peppard. I spent many hours in the bathtub washing off the foxhole mud from our days playing soldiers in the British muck. We both wanted and needed *The Victors* to be a hit, and, to that end, followed the instructions of our studio publicist, Emily Torchia, to write letters to Hedda and Louella telling of our adventures and currying favor, being especially careful not to double-plant, as the two women were madly competitive and jealous of each other. I did as I was told, but on a visit to Hollywood on a break in shooting, I was cut dead by both of them. I soon found out why. George Peppard had bribed our joint secretary to switch letters, so Hedda got my mash note to Louella, and vice versa. I got so mad at George that I moved out and in with another costar, Jim Mitchum, who was laboring in the long shadow of his father, for whom he was a dead ringer.

True to my form, I insisted we live far beyond our means. We took an elegant house on Green Street in Mayfair, and I hired a Rolls-Royce with a chauffeur. Not bad for two doughboys. I started getting my hair cut at Vidal Sassoon, where I met the two "it" girls of early-sixties London, Christine Keeler and Mandy Rice-Davies, the two principals in the Profumo sex scandal that would break wide open while I was there.

These were two gorgeous Cockneys in Mayfair who fell under the spell of a society osteopath named Stephen Ward, who pimped these girls out to the Annabel's set of the high and mighty. Alas, he pimped Christine, a former stripper, too hard, getting her caught in a triangle with John Profumo, the British secretary of war, and Eugene Ivanov, the Russian naval attaché. I loved going dancing with these pop tarts, but things got too close for comfort when it turned out that my chauffeur was ferrying the girls to their assignations, on my shillings. I found this out only when a large sum of money, thousands of pounds I had won gambling, disappeared from our place and Scotland Yard showed up. My driver was, it appears, a master criminal using his chauffeur's cap as a disguise. Things got stickier as I fell hard for the luscious Mandy, not really aware until later of her expensive comings and goings. She even sent me some poetry, of the doggerel style.

Then the Profumo scandal broke open, and I got an SOS call from Mandy from Middlesex General Hospital, where she had gone after a suicide attempt. Get me out of here, she begged me. The Southern gentleman in me kicked in, and I had no choice but to respond to the call. Jim Mitchum's advice on the matter was to never write anything down, never tear anything up. I was headed off at the pass by Christine, who warned me, just in the nick of time, that the hospital was surrounded by journalists from all over the world. Mandy never mentioned my name to the press. It wasn't the first time that being a gentleman paid off for me. Mandy knew I had tried to rescue her, and she thus rescued me. Another friend of the girls, however, Douglas Fairbanks Jr., got caught in the glare of the tabloid spotlights. Doug had a good sense of humor, and we often joked about the adventure. Mandy went on to move to Israel and become the disco queen of Tel Aviv.

After my close brush with tabloid shame, I flew back to New York to make one last-ditch play for Susan Kohner. She sent me packing, and within a year would marry the German-born fashion designer John Weitz. Back in London, I vowed to avoid all "it" girls, no matter how beautiful they were. My romantic pendulum thus swung to Caterine Milinaire, an artsy *Vogue* editor and the daughter of the Duchess of Bedford. The Duke of Bedford, Caterine's stepfather, would become known in England as the Groovy Duke, because of his hippie haircut, psychedelic ties, and dancing naked in the

British production of *Hair.*

The duke was one of the first royals to open his stately home — Woburn Abbey, one of the stateliest — to the public. He added a zoo, a disco, and a peep show. He was fascinated by Hollywood and seemed to really like me. He wasn't one of those aristocrats who classed show people with the hired help. Caterine's mother, the new duchess, was a different matter. She had been married to a Hollywood producer and had been a Paris film producer herself, so she had a well-acquired distrust of Hollywood types. I was not the duchess's cup of Earl Grey tea. Some of Caterine's father's stuffier *Burke's Peerage* relatives also may have looked down on me, but Caterine was a free spirit.

Caterine drove a Mini and wore a mini, when it came on the radar. She was way ahead of the curve of trend. Alas, she also got ahead of the curve of the M1 motorway when she was speeding home from Woburn Abbey to a rendezvous we had planned on my return from America that night at the Dorchester. I assumed she had stood me up and had gone to bed. I was awakened at four A.M. by the duke. Caterine had been in a dreadful wreck, he told me. I sped to the hospital, where she was in shock. There was a long and painful recovery. She recuperated in the family home in Regent's Park. I went to see her and sat at her bed for days, where she lay unconscious. When she finally came to, she had no idea who I was. "Who are you? What do you do?" she asked. I was devastated. I remember watching the Kennedy assassination on television while sitting at her bedside. She still didn't know me. Sad days indeed. Caterine's mind did come back, but not much of her memory of the high times we had together. She would marry one of the Newport Cushings, who gave us Babe Paley and Betsey Whitney.

Part of *The Victors* was being shot in Salerno, south of Naples. Clotheshorse that I was, I decided to have my own sergeant's uniform made in London. Who said war had to be hell? It was the most beautiful outfit, made of sea island batiste, with epaulets. My orthopedic boots were the finest calfskin with metatarsal implants. I had an extralight balsa wood helmet. I was dressed for speed and style, not trench warfare. But wasn't this Hollywood?

My rented limo deposited me on the set in Salerno. It was as bloody and muddy as I was not. There were a thousand scruffy Yugoslavian extras who were working for a dollar a day and a Hershey bar, playing American soldiers in filthy uniforms. The place smelled awful. The explosives expert greeted me and pointed out the trip wires that would set off the explosions, warning me never to get behind one, as I could be blown to smithereens, even in this play-war we were doing.

George Peppard, my old nemesis, took one look at my uniform and called the director, Carl Foreman, over. "Did you see George Hamilton?" he asked.

Foreman came over to me like a drill sergeant, looking me up and down. "Who do you think you are?" he snarled at me. "General MacArthur?" He proceeded to dress me down for dressing up, in front of a thousand extras. I was glad they didn't comprehend a word of it. "What kind of uniform is this?" Foreman put it to me.

"It's a regular uniform," I said.

"There's nothing regular about it," Foreman snapped back.

"I had it made in London," I told him.

"You had it *made*?" The old left-winger was incredulous and furious. "Get out of it! Switch with him!" Foreman made me strip down on the spot and take the stinking outfit of one of the Yugoslavian extras. Now I weighed about a hundred pounds more. The pack weighed forty, the rifle twelve, the helmet was an iron pot on my head, the clunky shoes were from a torture chamber. I hadn't been so miserable since military school. The makeup people put dirt all over my face, and Foreman yelled, "Action!"

We were supposed to charge or retreat or whatever, but with the load I had on, I couldn't keep up with the army of extras. Then I saw one of those dreaded trip wires caught on the canteen of the guy running in front of me. Never get behind a trip wire, the explosives guy had warned me. Too late. I'm going to blow up, I thought to myself. *KABOOM!* I flew fifteen feet in the air. When I landed, in a foxhole, I was a cinema vérité bloody mess, with a broken hand and God knows what else. "Medic!" was the only cry I heard.

I was taken to an Italian hospital with several other of the injured players, one of whom was my costar, Vince Edwards, who was more terrified of hospitals than any person I've ever seen. "We can't take the tetanus shots," he warned me. "They can give us spinal meningitis." This was really something coming from the guy who played Ben Casey, one of the most famous television doctors in the world. "No shot, no movie," we were ordered. I ended up disguising myself and taking Vince's shot for him, so the show could go on.

In Europe in the jet-set early sixties, it was hard not to run into royalty, even without playing the Hollywood card. After my muddy wartime experiences in *The Victors,* I was in dire need of putting on a tux and going out on the town. An opportunity arose when I was invited to a black tie party at the castle of some count. I got all dressed up but was so exhausted from my fake war that I slept through my train stop and woke up a hundred miles farther down the boot. To give myself a consolation prize, I caught a ferry across the Bay of Naples to Capri, which was my idea of heaven.

I took a room at the Quisisana hotel and went for a walk around the island. All I had was my tux. People must have thought I was a waiter malingering from work. I went down to the Canzone del Mare, the clubby in-spot of the isle, to have a swim and eat lunch. While I had a drink, I asked a little boy to go and buy me a bathing suit. I gave him a wad of lira, and off he went. He came back with a swimsuit, but it was three times too big. I was too tired to care. I donned the suit, which made me look like a South Central rapper, and went into the pool. A stunning patrician woman began staring at me and burst out laughing. How can you wear such a big, baggy bathing suit? she asked.

Before I could answer, someone, at her command, was bringing me a new suit. I went in the cabana to put it on. In a flash, and I mean flash, I had gone from Snoop Dogg to American Gigolo. It was a Pucci men's bikini and it was skin tight, leaving less than' zero to the imagination. It would have been criminal exhibitionism to wear it; it would have been rude to my benefactress not to. I went with chivalry and squeezed into the slingshot.

The lady liked what she saw. And was she ever a lady. She introduced herself as a contessa, one of the rulers of the Capri social scene. When we finished our swim, she invited me to dine with her at nine. I put on my waiter's outfit, anything to get out of that slingshot, and went back to the Quisisana, stopping to buy a normal outfit for the upcoming enchanted evening with the countess. No sooner had I arrived at my room than there was a knock at the door. A bellman presented me a box from the contessa. I opened it and blushed. It was a phallic symbol with wings. A few hours later, a second gift arrived. This one was a sculpture of two donkeys, one on top of the other, and a note that read, "Until tonight. Love." I suddenly lost all interest in Italian nobility; they were more decadent here than the Emperor Nero. I couldn't handle it. I refused to answer my phone or any knock at the door. There were endless knocks and rings. But I stood up the barefoot contessa. At ten P.M., two hours later, the little boy from the club arrived at the hotel and presented me with an envelope. Inside was a bill for the Pucci bathing suit. With great relief, I paid it.

The Victors was not victorious, though socially it was magic. I went to the command performance royal premiere in London and met the Queen, Prince Philip, Prince Charles, Princess Margaret, and the Queen Mother. How I wished that Teeny and Bill, the true royalists, could have been there. The New York premiere was another matter. There, an old-time press agent got the bright idea that huge publicity for the film could be gained if a planted woman fainted in the audience during the scene where an American GI was executed for desertion. This was a fictionalized version of the shocking true-life execution of Private Slovik, a young American deserter who couldn't take the hell that war was, to Frank Sinatra singing "Have Yourself a Merry Little Christmas" on the sound track. This would get the whole world talking, it was successfully argued, and talking about me, since it was to be my task to pick up the fainting lady and gallantly carry her out of the theater.

The woman, who was planted beside me, was dressed in furs and looked to weigh even more than my uniform in Salerno. She moaned and groaned for an eternity before she finally crumpled to the floor. She fell under the seat, and I had to drag her out and then up the aisle for all the world to see. It was the heaviest load I ever bore, and I had to fake looking surprised, as a news photographer snapped away. I felt like Tony Perkins dragging Janet Leigh's body off to bury in *Psycho*, except Janet was a ton lighter. *Paris Match,* here I come again, I thought. *Life* too. Once the ordeal was accomplished and I was reflecting on what I would do for the sake of my art, the theater manager came up to me with a big smile. "It's all handled, Mr. Hamilton," he said proudly.

"What's handled?" I asked him.

"The pictures," he said. "I got that photographer, took his film, and tore it all up." He showed me the trophy of the shredded film. So much for publicity stunts.

Ultimately, no stunt would have done the job. *The Victors* was way too dark, foreshadowing the great paranoid movies of the later sixties, ahead of the bad times that seemed to begin with the Kennedy assassination. Imagine *Doctor Strangelove* without the humor. This, though, was the shell-shocked America I came back to after my first foray into jet-set living. The world, and my career, were about to get a lot more complicated, and the last place I would have imagined the jet stream was going to take me was the White House.

Photo 1: The entire family showed up for my premier engagement on August 12, 1939. I opened to rave reviews.

Photo 2: "Gee, what will I be when I grow up?" I was thinking to myself here, at age six. Policeman? Fireman? Soldier? Being an actor was the furthest thing from my mind.

Photo 3: Dad's pretty band singer, June Howard, together with Mom and Dad. Trouble was brewing, but there was still lots to smile about in these early days.

Photo 4: (Left to right) Dick Williams, Tommy Hunt, Carleton Hunt, Mom, David, Bill, and me in my military school -uniform—all assembled for Mom and Carleton's wedding in Boston.

Photo 5: Dad took a shot at the movie business when he appeared in films in 1937.

Photo 6: Bill in our Lincoln Continental (aka the Accident Waiting to Happen or Death Trap, for short) outside El Portal in Acapulco.

Photo 7: Beachside in Acapulco: David, Teeny, a local writer, and me. The sea was warm and the living was easy.

Photo 8: Glamour for Mom and Bill was an absolute necessity. Here they are at a Manhattan costume party with cohost David Shamay. Teeny dressed as a Ziegfeld girl, Bill as Rudolph Valentino.

Photo 9: On the set of Home from the Hill, *where we were awaiting the arrival of a live boar for the climactic hunting scene. (Left to right): Me, Eddy Grainger, Milton Krasner, Vincente Minnelli, and a very young Liza Minnelli.*

Photo 10: Hollywood socializing: Teeny, me, Susan Kohner, and Swifty Lazar.

Photo 11: Lunch at the LBJ ranch with Lynda Bird's father at the head of the table. Believe me, when the president talks, you listen.

Photo 12: Acapulco playtime with Lynda, joined by Merle Oberon and John Wayne.

Photo 13: On location filming Medusa in Rhodes for a working honeymoon with our dog, Georgie. Alana and I agreed that touristy Rhodes was a colossal dud.

Photo 14: Opening night in Las Vegas. Me, Lola Falana, and Johnny Harris.

Photo 15: Ashley shows up to steal the show from Alana, Mom, and me.

Photo 16: With beautiful girlfriend Liz Treadwell at Will Rogers State Historic Park. In truth, Liz was a better polo player than half the men on the field. She should have been riding the horse, and I should have been holding it.

Photos 17 and 18: The two most important guys in my life, my sons and pals, Ashley (above) and G.T. (below). Similar hair, don't you think?

CHAPTER TEN
THE EYES OF TEXAS

I had no idea that my decision to star in a B picture about Hank Williams would win the hearts and minds of the family of Lyndon Johnson, but it did. The whole first family loved *Your Cheatin' Heart.* If only a few more families had seen it. The Johnsons thought that I did Southern right. It wasn't hard. I was just going back to my roots, or at least the other side of the tracks of my roots. *Cheatin'* was maybe the first MTV movie long before there was MTV, a country music biopic, a hayseed *Glenn Miller Story* or *Night and Day,* but the hayseed was prime stock. Hank Williams was the first entertainer to put country music on the pop charts, the first crossover. And what music it was, every bit as much the sound track of my youth as the big band classics Dad played.

MGM's music division somehow owned the rights to the Hank Williams songbook. One of the cardinals thought it was a perfect vehicle for Elvis Presley, but Elvis's Svengali manager, Colonel Tom Parker, said no. I had met the colonel on the lot, and he had taken a shine to me. Not enough of a shine to manage me, as I begged him to do. The colonel's heart belonged to Elvis and Elvis alone. The Dutchman had begun his career as a barker in carnival sideshows and made it as the manager of country singer Eddy Arnold, assuming the Kentucky colonel mystique. He told me I could always come to him for free advice, which was all I could afford anyhow. I would have loved him to manage me formally, but as he said, anything he *could* do for me, he *should* be doing for Elvis.

The colonel was the one who put me onto Hank and to his widow, Audrey, who was the executor of his estate. I had grown up on Hank Williams. His songs were among the greatest American music: "Jambalaya," "Hey, Good Lookin'," "I'm So Lonesome I Could Cry," and the title song of the film, to name just a few. These were the songs I cried my own blues to while marooned at Gulf Coast Military Academy. Plus Hank's story had both noble and tragic proportions. Hank literally came from Alabama with a banjo on his knee, and nothing else. By his twenties he was a superstar with eleven number-one country hits. Tony Bennett covered "Cold

Cold Heart" and made it *Billboard*'s number one, and "I Saw the Light" became a standard in churches around the world. He met Audrey Sheppard in a redneck bar, and she became his manager and wife. But because of a childhood spinal deformity, Hank had become addicted to morphine and alcohol. He died at age twenty-nine. I was twenty-four when I discovered his story. Forget the tuxedos and the debutantes and the polo ponies. This was the story I *had* to do, and the colonel showed me how.

The top brass at MGM laughed in my face. With Elvis out of the picture, and Nick Adams having turned it down as well, they had revised their concept of the film as quickie drive-in fare that might sell some records in the South, and maybe to some crossover *Beverly Hillbillies* fans. To that end, they assigned it to their producer Sam Katzman, known in Hollywood as the King of Schlock. Whatever they saw, they didn't see their stock company preppy playboy playing a drug addict honky-tonk crooner. Colonel Parker urged me to press on and to go to Nashville to plead my case to Audrey Williams herself. So I took his advice and went home to Tennessee.

Audrey was a domineering, slightly depressive, brassy blonde with a definite country glamour. She was the Jackie Kennedy of the Grand Ole Opry. She knew everyone in the South and took an instant shine to me as a fellow traveler. I knew I was in when she invited me to drive down to Montgomery with her to meet her friend Governor George Wallace. We never made it because we hit a cow in the middle of the road and totaled the Caddy. Audrey noted that Hank would have had a Cadillac for every direction on the compass. I met Hank's father, Lonnie, a retired train conductor, who took me to visit one of the schools Hank had dropped out of. During the visit, I got a nasty splinter in my finger from Hank's schoolboy desk. I regarded it as a good omen, and, while it hurt like the devil, I didn't get it removed until we finished shooting the movie. I figured I needed all the pain I could get to play this part right.

Audrey wanted the movie to happen, especially to make her son Hank Williams Jr. a singing star the same way she had pushed Big Hank to stardom. The idea was that Hank Jr., who was all of fifteen at the time (he had begun singing in shows with Jerry Lee Lewis at eight), would dub my singing in the movie and release the sound track album under his name. Having immersed myself in Hank Williamsiana, I felt that I could sing the songs myself. I wanted so much to sing them. That was the key to the character. But the only way I would get the part was to eat humble pie and play the studio game. I consoled myself that Ava Gardner had been similarly disappointed in *Showboat,* Audrey Hepburn in *My Fair Lady,* and Natalie Wood in *West Side Story.* Audrey Williams was a powerful woman, a born manager who had overcome horrible obstacles to make Hank a legend. Who was I to stand in her way? After all, this was her story. Colonel Parker advised me to get on her train and ride it to the bank. MGM was listening to Audrey, not to me. "You get what you want only when they start screaming," the colonel told me. Audrey made them scream. Hank Jr. got the sound track. I got the part. The colonel was as pleased as I was that I had won the chance to change my image. My MGM contract having lapsed, the studio had to buy me back.

I was very excited by the project though apprehensive about the producer, who didn't fit the College of Cardinals at all. But the college was flunking out at the box office. Sam Katzman, in addition to having created the Dead End Kids in the thirties, the Johnny Weissmuller Jungle Jim series in the forties (hence Katzman's nickname, "Jungle

Sam"), and the Superman and Batman serials in the fifties, was the master of the rock movie, having invented the seminal *Rock Around the Clock*.

Jungle Sam had done a number of Elvis movies and thereby had the imprimatur of the colonel. He was famous for his quick shoots and low budgets, for simply and coldly ripping out scenes when a film was over budget. He warned me coming in that he would pull the plug on the film on the thirteenth day at six P.M., whether we were finished or not. He had a trademark collection of walking sticks, which he pounded the floor with insistently whenever we were behind schedule. Jungle Sam cracked the whip, whacked the cane, and the whole film was in the can right on time. But he gave me free rein creatively, and our director, an ex-dancer named Gene Nelson, brought in something memorable, and even Sam knew it. At five forty-five on the thirteenth day, just as I finished Hank's death scene, Sam arrived with a beautiful Martin D-28 guitar as a gift for me. It remains one of my proudest possessions.

At the end of it all, I got some wonderful country outfits, I learned to play the guitar, and I got the best reviews of my career. Even the *New York Times* loved the film and singled me out. "This young actor, heretofore a rather vapid, sleek movie commodity, is perfectly cast as the homespun hero," they wrote. The movie made me a hero in the South. But because it was a small film, it didn't get the exposure it deserved in the rest of the country. But Colonel Parker loved it. And so did Lynda Bird. And so did Alana Kaye Collins. And that was enough to change my life.

But it took a while. After *Heart,* I became as depressed about Hollywood as I had been after shooting *Crime and Punishment, USA* and having to do *Rin Tin Tin* episodes. This was on top of the failure of *Act One.* Yes, just as the Harts had predicted down at Round Hill, I'd been cast as Moss Hart, but this acting George had gathered no Moss. I could blame my director, MGM head Dore Schary, fulfilling a fantasy to be behind the camera. Oddly enough, MGM didn't even do this film; Warners did. Schary de-ethnicized the entire production and took out the brilliance for good measure.

It was at this point in my career that I took my first shot at Broadway. Or maybe Broadway took its first shot at me, depending on how you look at it. Having just finished playing a past king of Broadway, Moss Hart, I got a call from the office of a current king, Alan Jay Lerner, offering me a shot at the lead of his new musical, *On a Clear Day You Can See Forever*. Lerner was world famous, with his partner Fritz Loewe, for creating *My Fair Lady,* not to mention *Brigadoon, Camelot,* and *Gigi*. This was the big time. I flew to New York for the audition that could make me a Broadway star and checked in at my old home, the Alrae. At two A.M. my first night, I was awakened by Lerner's secretary saying that Mr. Lerner was waiting for me. At two A.M.? Well, you don't keep Alan Jay Lerner waiting, at any hour, so I pulled myself together.

A car and a chauffeur had been sent for me to take me to Lerner's office at the Waldorf Towers, where I used to hang out with Arthur MacArthur. Lerner's suite was as busy, in the dead of night, as if it were high noon. There was a pool of secretaries typing away. I was shown into Lerner's palatial office overlooking the dark spires of midtown. In his forties, young for such a legend, Lerner was sitting at a piano, wearing white gloves. "I want to know what you think of this song I'm writing." He began playing and singing, "On a clear day . . ." He stopped and we began talking about the show, which involved clairvoyance and past lives, but soon

Lerner dozed off in midsentence. I sat there awhile. He woke up, started talking again, then nodded out. This happened a few more times until he was down for the count. I gave up and went back to the hotel around four A.M.

A few hours later, at seven thirty, I was awakened by another call. "Mr. Lerner will see you now." I dutifully went back to the Waldorf. He still had those white gloves on, but he was away from the piano, on the floor with his young son building a plastic fort from one of those Plasticville kits. It took a while to get his attention. At some point the gloves came off and I could see that his fingers were all bloody and scabbed up. I noticed he bit his nails, and his fingers, too, like some sort of caged tiger. With the music that came from those fingers, I supposed this was the price of genius. He gave me a song he wanted me to learn and told me to come to the Mark Hellinger Theatre that night to sing it for him.

I arrived around midnight. The place was empty, with a pianist onstage waiting for me, and Lerner in the front row fast asleep. He never woke up. After waiting for an hour, the secretary came up to me and said, "Mr. Lerner needs to nap right now. We'll call you." Back to the Alrae I went, only to be roused around five A.M. with a call from Lerner himself. This time he asked me to audition by doing the score of *My Fair Lady*. He didn't say which song or songs, so I got the songbook and spent the next three days learning every one of them, from "With a Little Bit of Luck" to "Get Me to the Church on Time." I went back to the theater. He had me sing every single song, in four or five different ways. The problem was, he kept falling asleep, so I'd have to leave and start the whole process again whenever he woke up, which could be any time. "I could have danced all night" were the truest lyrics ever written, for I did dance all night — and all day, too.

This torture went on for a month. I lost seventeen pounds. I figured it would be worth it to get the part of a lifetime. But I didn't get it. The role went to John Cullum, who won a Tony for it. What I did find out was the cause of Lerner's narcolepsy? He was going to Dr. Max Jacobson, the famous Dr. Feelgood, whose huge roster of celebrity patients included Lerner's Choate and Harvard classmate John F. Kennedy and his wife, Jackie. Jacobson's "vitamin shots" were actually huge doses of amphetamines, which gave his patients the grand illusion of superhuman creative energy but ended up turning them into zombies like the half-conscious schizoid speedy-sleepy Lerner. Jacobson was eventually disgraced and de-licensed. A few months later I saw the normally sedate Eddie Fisher onstage in Vegas, rocking it up like Chuck Berry. Then I saw a strange man in the wings, who turned out to be an emissary of Dr. Feelgood, and I understood everything.

By the time I had tried a Broadway Jew and a Grand Ole Opry redneck, I had run the casting gamut from A to Z. I decided to go to Acapulco and do something meaningful with my life: work on my tan. "You're not a quitter," Teeny challenged me. "You must fight." Bill teased me that I would soon be back onscreen in Mexican films, south-of-the-border sex farces in which I'd be wearing boxer shorts, garters, and a pencil-thin mustache. I had no comeback at the time, not even realizing that I had just begun to fight.

Acapulco had evolved from a sleepy fishing village into the last resort of the jet set in the decade since we had made our ill-fated family road trip there. I checked into the new Las Brisas hotel, a spectacular Maya pyramid built into a cliffside. I hadn't been in the bay waterskiing for fifteen minutes when a motor launch bearing a familiar face pulled up to me. It was Marina Cicogna, a Venetian countess from a dogelike family. She was a charter member of the jet set whom I had met in Rome, and she knew my family socially. Like so many jet-setters with excess time on their hands, Marina had begun producing movies. She was in Mexico visiting her good friend, French director Louis Malle, who, she said, was making a movie in Cuernavaca that he wanted me to be in. This wasn't a Mexican movie. It was *French* movie, and, in the sixties, nothing was hipper and smarter than a French movie. And not only was it a French movie, but a French movie starring the two goddesses of the world, Brigitte Bardot and Jeanne Moreau. And further sweetening the prize was Louis Malle, the scion of the French sugar dynasty and a Nouvelle Vague disciple whose brilliant first films showed that you could be rich and talented at the same time. But why me, of all people? To replace Alain Delon, who had just dropped out for some reason. I couldn't have been more flattered. It was a miracle on Acapulco Bay — pennies, or pesos, from heaven. Just as Teeny said, divine love will meet every human need.

Not that it really mattered, but I asked Marina what the film, by the way, was all about. She gave me the briefest plot synopsis. Two

306

dance hall girls, both named Maria, are working the bars in a banana republic when a revolution breaks out, and they get into a ménage à trois with Pancho Villa, who leads the charge. Villa would be me. How French, how fun! Marina took me in a Cadillac convertible on the four-hour mountain drive to Cuernavaca to meet *les girls*. Douglas Fairbanks Jr. happened to be in Acapulco and rode with us, along with a guitar player he brought to serenade us an route. We talked about Mary Pickford and Grayhall and, yes, Mandy Rice-Davies and Christine Keeler. Cuernavaca was where all the rich people of Mexico City went for country weekends. I had been here briefly before when we drove to Acapulco, but now I was coming with a whole new grown-up perspective. Cuernavaca was high in the mountains, with supposedly the most perfect climate on earth and lavish vegetation to go with the lavish villas. Peacocks strutted through the gardens. It felt like paradise.

Louis Malle was very charming. I told him I didn't speak French. "You will learn," he said, with the caveat that the final say on my casting wasn't his but that of his two femme stars. Suddenly, Brigitte Bardot swept through the villa, tailed by an army of paparazzi. An hour later, a door to the terrace where we were drinking tequila opened and BB poked her head out for a second and stared at me. A few minutes later, Marina emerged. "She likes you," she said. So far so good. The next day I met La Moreau, upon whom I, and every other man I knew, had had a huge crush since seeing her in *Jules et Jim*. She liked me, too. Wow! "The best way to learn French," she told me, "is in bed." Double wow.

My first scene, however, was less than auspicious. I had written out a phonetic pronunciation of my lines and had practiced all night. I was on a horse and I said to Jeanne, in French, "I saw you exiting the ball." *"Dégueulasse!"* she interrupted me before I could even get into the flirt. *Dégueulasse* means disgusting. She stormed off the set, leaving me alone on my horse.

Louis Malle came up to me with a grim face. "Your accent is horrible," he said.

Nothing offends the French more than a bad accent, not even a bad croissant. I told him that I had worked all night, with the aid of one of the French crew members, trying to be perfect. Louis wasn't amused. The crew just shot the movie. I was playing a Mexican and was supposed to speak French with a perfect *Mexican* accent. Aha! So I found a Mexican student, explained the situation in my pretty good Spanish, and made him my dialogue coach. *"C'est formidable,"* Louis said to me on my next take.

I could say the same about Jeanne. While I never got at all close to Brigitte Bardot, Jeanne helped tutor me in "Frexican" and in other arts as well. We would lie in bed together pronouncing the Aztec names of volcanoes, which turned out to be very sexy. Anything Jeanne Moreau said was sexy, but this especially. Po-po-ca-te-pet-el. Tak-ka-wan-na-me-na-ku. Iz-ta-chi-chi-wa-tel. You get the idea. It was Aztec baby talk, and I would talk the talk, as long as it allowed me to walk the walk. Eventually I walked the plank. After the film's premiere in Paris, I went to visit Jeanne in the country for a little stroll down memory lane. But when I arrived, she was doing another picture, and another actor. It's okay to lose your mind on a film set, but don't lose your heart.

My French film credit suddenly gave me a certain cachet abroad. Now I was an "international film star," which meant I couldn't get any decent parts in Hollywood but could find work abroad. In the midsixties, when America was destroying itself with assassinations and racial hatred and Vietnam, Europe was a wonderful place to sit out the turmoil, not to mention being one of the biggest bargains in history.

I was doing a film in Spain called *The Man from Marrakech,* a knockoff of Philippe de Broca's wonderful *That Man from Rio,* with spies and intrigue and whatever. The James Bond series had started a few years before, and everyone wanted a piece of the espionage pie. This one was about a gold heist in the Moroccan desert; it was never released anywhere I know of, not even Morocco. You've never heard of anyone in it, and neither had I. But it was a payday and a free season in sunny Spain. We were in Almería, where they had shot parts of *Lawrence of Arabia.* All that was left was a forlorn girl with a gold tooth and a more forlorn camel. Almería was described as "3,360 dangerous curves from Marbella." My friend Sean Flynn came down to visit. He, too, had tried to be an actor, with far greater expectations than I had and far worse results. He was making pictures with the identical twins Pili and Mili, whoever they were. "What the hell happened to our careers?" he despaired.

Not that there weren't great times to be had. I have cinematic amnesia about what transpired on the *Marrakech* shoot, but after hours, the adventures were unforgettable. One occurred in Madrid, where I had gone for the weekend after a long week's shoot

These were Franco times, and the city was very buttoned up and shut down. I asked my hotel where I could get a drink, and they sent me off to a brothel. Apparently, in Franco Spain, where everything else was forbidden, brothels were the only place where anything went, and everyone went to do it. There were no discos, only whorehouses. The first woman I ran into at the bar of this very louche establishment was a hooker with her dress on backward, the shoulder pads inside out. And then I heard a very familiar voice, so familiar it was surreal. I looked around the bar, and who was there but my mother, with none other than Ava Gardner.

"What in the world are you doing here?" I asked my mother.

"I should ask the same of you," Teeny shot back.

Ava, who had moved to Madrid to date bullfighters and escape Frank Sinatra, was the biggest Hollywood star in this increasingly Hollywood town. Because Ava was the second most prodigious drinker in show business, her nights hosting Teeny turned into days. Teeny had come over to see me, but knowing Ava was icing on an already sweet cake. The biggest female partyer was Tyrone Power's fiery ex, Linda Christian, who had been discovered in Mexico by none other than Errol Flynn. I dated her myself, but she drank me way under the table. Also partying with us that night were two other very different ladies, the French Bond Girl Claudine Auger and Jo-Carroll Dennison, the wife of Phil Silvers. Sergeant Bilko was on duty back in TV land, so Jo-Carroll was up for an evening out, and Ava gave it to her.

There was a big movie contingent in Madrid, which had replaced Rome's Cinecittà as home base for spaghetti Westerns. Clint Eastwood was here, and Ty Hardin, and Guy Madison. The *vita* there was less *dolce* than in Rome, but it could get pretty wild on its own. Ava set up another wild night (Teeny sat this one out), where our caravan of limos followed a troupe of gypsy entertainers from a Madrid club home to a far rougher native club in the hills outside the city to see a flamenco show, eat dozens of roast chickens, and drink a few barrels of Marquis de Riscal wine. Ava went back early, which for her was before dawn, around five. When the sun rose and it was time to settle — that is, for gallant me to settle — the check came to $3,000. That was like thirty grand today and a fortune in midsixties Spain, where a lot of people still rode around in oxcarts. When I questioned the bill, the gypsy owner pulled out a huge hunting knife. Jo-Carroll began to scream in terror, so I sent the ladies to the cars. I would take care of matters. I knew I'd have to think fast, which was hard to do in my sleep-deprived and drunken state.

I began by asking the owner for a break-down of the bill. "How much wine did we drink?"

"Twenty bottles," he said.

"And how many chickens did we eat?"

"Four dozen."

"And how many dances did your people do?"

"Thirty."

"All for three thousand dollars. That's pretty cheap," I said.

"Cheap?" The owner had never heard that word before in this clip joint.

I told the owner that I sang as well, having been a frequent guest on the *Ed Sullivan Show* after my "musical" debut in *Your Cheatin' Heart*. I mentioned, with all due modesty, that they paid me $20,000 to sing one song. Then I asked the owner for the guitar. I started playing a song until he begged me to stop, in the name of harmony. "You're terrible," he told me, in no uncertain terms, and that I should fork over the three grand and leave him in peace.

"I may be terrible," I said, "but you owe

me seventeen thousand dollars."

He hated my math, but he couldn't argue with my quote. He put away the knife. "How much have you got on you?" he asked. I looked in my wallet. I had about $60 in Spanish money. "I'll take it," he said. I gave him the cash, and out I ran, only to find our cars all gone. So run, run, run I did down the gypsy hill, until I found the car parked below. It was one more great lesson, that wit and humor can get you out of the most serious predicaments. I also learned restraint. When Ava called to set up one more night of oblivion, I was smart enough to just say no.

All the action in Madrid seemed to take place in bordellos. At another house of mirth I got into a scrape on behalf of the actor John Ireland, a dear friend of Errol Flynn whom I met through Sean. John was famous for his tough-guy roles, Oscar-nominated for *All the King's Men.* In insider circles he was famous for his endowment and his obsession with young starlets. When he was in his forties, he dated Natalie Wood, *Lolita*'s Sue Lyon, and Tuesday Weld, all in their teens. Times had gotten tough in Hollywood for John, so he too was in Europe trading on his noir reputation. John took me to a brothel, just as Ava had taken Teeny. Because of my Spanish skills, John asked me to translate to his obscure object of desire what his specific desire was. I blush to tell you, so I won't, but it had something to do with a rare set of pearls John had bought for his wife, Daphne, in Majorca.

The next morning, John called me in a panic. He had left the pearls at the brothel, Daphne was flying in imminently from London, so could I go and retrieve them for him? Let me tell you that there is no place sadder than a Spanish brothel in the dead of morning. Bodies were everywhere; it looked more like Gettysburg than an orgy. There was no trace of Daphne's pearls. Surely the girl had absconded with them. But as I played my Inspector Clouseau act, I discovered that the girl in question was the consort of the owner. The owner called her to task. She was still drunk, but then she woke up. Of course the pearls weren't in plain sight. They were still in the unmentionable orifice where John kinkily had placed them. I got them back and left a huge tip. I arrived back at the hotel with the pearls just as Daphne was arriving. Daphne was never the wiser, but for John and me, "Daphne's pearls" became a running joke that had us laughing for years.

One of the biggest problems about doing *Marrakech* had been getting paid. I was always chasing down my fee. One reason I was in Madrid was to corner the producer. Typically, he wasn't there. He was in Murcia, with his wife and dog, but he promised he was driving up to Madrid the next day, with my cash in a bag. It was a Spanish version of "your check is in the mail" — "Your cash is on the *autopista*." He never showed. But he did call, in the frailest voice, saying he had gotten into a terrible wreck on the *autopista* and was in the hospital.

I decided to call his bluff and drove to Murcia myself. And lo and behold, there he was in the hospital, in traction, bandaged head to toe like Boris Karloff in *The Mummy*. He begged me to keep working for two more weeks to finish the picture, without pay, of course. How could I say no to this poor accident victim? So I worked and worked. And never got paid. The producer fled to the Caribbean or Tibet or the sands of Africa. Who knows? What a miraculous recovery, I marveled. When I told Sean Flynn, he couldn't stop laughing. This same producer had pulled the same stunt on Errol Flynn decades before. He pretended to be in a wreck, made a deal with the hospital to fake his mummification, and stiffed Errol for his fee. Hollywood could be hazardous to your health, but these offshore films were invariably fatal.

I should have learned a lesson from Judy Garland, whom I went to see in a show she was doing in Boston. Judy's husband, Sid Luft, had invited me to see her at the Shubert Theatre. But the afternoon before the show Sid invited me over to their suite at the Copley Plaza. I thought it was a little early and tried to beg off, but Sid insisted. "Judy's dying to see you," he pleaded. When I arrived at the suite, the normally ebullient Sid looked glum. I didn't see Judy. "Where is she?" I asked.

"In there," he said, motioning to a closed door. I knocked. Nothing. Then I turned the doorknob. It was locked. I knocked again.

"Who is it?" Judy asked.

"George, George Hamilton."

She still wouldn't open the door. "Ah, George. Be so sweet and get me a bottle of Blue Nun," her favorite wine.

"Why won't you open the door?" I asked.

"Because Sid is stealing all my money. And because the bastard theater owner won't pay me, and I'm on strike till they pay me. Get me the Blue Nun. And get me the producer." Sid could be charming, but he could also be a cad.

While I was standing there the producer arrived in a major sweat. Judy wouldn't open

317

the door. "I want my money," she insisted. "In cash."

"I've got a whole row of war veterans in wheelchairs," the producer begged. "They're waiting for you."

"You wheeled them in, you can wheel them out." Judy held the line.

"I'll have the cash for you at the theater," the producer conceded.

There was no time for me to get the wine. We hightailed it to the Shubert. Liza, Lorna, and Joey were there. A martini was waiting in the wings for Judy, who gunned it down and then came onstage. Without any fanfare, she took her case to a jury of thousands of her loving fans. "Ladies and gentlemen, I'm so sorry I'm late," she began, "but, you know, in show business, if you don't get paid, you don't play. No pay, no play. The manager told me that if I came here, all that money that you paid tonight, I would get some. Don't you think I should have it onstage right now?" Of course the audience went wild, cheering her on.

The mortified producer emerged from the wings with a big bag of cash. Judy took it, smiled, and proceeded to do a rendition of "Over the Rainbow" that had the veterans rising from their wheelchairs in a standing ovation. She continued to sing her heart out for the next two and a half hours. Like I said, I should have taken that lesson on the road with me.

It wasn't all brothels and gypsies and scoundrel producers. One day the former American ambassador to Spain, formerly JFK's and LBJ's White House chief of protocol, Angier Biddle Duke, called me to the embassy in Madrid. What the hell had I done now? First Ambassador Duke, the tobacco heir, joked with me about how little he had to do other than tell people that the president sends his best and deliver boxes of then unknown California wine. Worrying this was all a prelude to a deportation, I was vastly relieved when the ambassador calmed my nerves by extending me an invitation to the White House to a dinner for Princess Margaret and Lord Snowdon. To what did I owe this honor? I queried him. To Lynda Bird Johnson, who had never gotten over seeing me in *Your Cheatin' Heart,* he said. I only hoped that she wouldn't somehow get a print of *The Man from Marrakech* and ruin the grand illusion.

I had actually met Lynda Bird the summer before at a dinner party in New York given by Charlotte Ford (daughter of Henry II), whom I was dating. Given how rough-and-tumble LBJ seemed, when I met Lynda I was struck by how delicate and sensitive she was. She was a bit sad, too, because she had just broken off her engagement to a young officer named Bernard Rosenbach and was dating a young man named David Le-Fevre. She was a college girl then, having just transferred to George Washington from the University of Texas, and she was brainy and bookish. She was also extremely tall, five ten or more, and I sensed that somewhere inside that bookworm was a babe trying to get out. Once we reconnected at that White House dinner, I would get my chance to play Pygmalion with her.

I stopped in Washington on my way back to L.A. from Spain and stayed at the Mayflower Hotel. In addition to the British royal guests of honor, I met Jay Rockefeller and his wife, Sharon Percy, daughter of the handsome new JFK-like senator from Illinois. Sharon's sister had been murdered in a terrible unsolved mystery during her father's campaign. She was a Christian Scientist, so we had a lot to talk about. I also met the all-powerful Lady Bird Johnson press secretary Liz Carpenter, who would guide Lynda and me through lots of shark-infested waters in the years ahead.

At the dinner I reconnected with Lynda. Like everyone else in the world, she was fascinated by the movies, by my so-called glamorous life. Hollywood seemed to intrigue her far more than Washington, but the Astroturf is always greener on the other side of the red carpet. Lynda asked me where I was going next. I told her Acapulco, to go waterskiing, to recuperate from my low-budget moviemaking in Spain. I didn't tell her the awful truth, not wanting to burst her bubble. I asked her offhandedly if she had ever been there and would she like to come down. Don't mind if I do, she said.

I thought Lynda's interest in having fun in Acapulco was just idle White House chatter. I was out on the bay, when, just as Marina Cicogna had come up to me in a speedboat bearing the gift of Jeanne Moreau, two Secret Servicemen roared up on a motor launch bearing news that Lynda would be arriving that evening. She would be flying down on a private Twin Air and was being "chaperoned" by San Antonio LBJ family friends. The family went by the ominous name of Mr. and Mrs. Earl Deathe. They had hosted the Kennedy family a few years before. This was one case where being at Deathes' door wasn't as bad as it sounded.

We had a wonderful weekend. It was just after Thanksgiving, and Lynda was pale as a ghost. I tried to get her into the tanning mode; this ghost blew me away by lasting longer in the sun than I could. Her secret weapon, she told me, was that a Texas pharmacy had given her their latest lotion, with the highest SPF ever created. Whatever time we didn't spend on the water, we were dancing at Tequila a Go-Go. Lynda seemed dead set on showing the world that she could swing with the swinging times we were in. She was very much aware that her little sister, Luci Baines, was viewed by the press as "the sexy one." The girls' Secret Service names told the story. Lynda was "Velvet," Luci "Venus." Luci seemed to be less dutiful to LBJ's rules. She also looked like she was going to beat Lynda to the altar. Luci, eighteen, was close to being engaged to a young Marquette grad named Pat Nugent, and there was talk of one of the biggest White House weddings in memory. Pat wasn't at all flashy or pedigreed; he wasn't a Niarchos, or even a Deathe. This was pure love. Lynda was surely now feeling her own pressures to have a White House wedding. A true Johnson at heart, she didn't cotton to the idea of being overshadowed.

Lynda got her wish. We next went to the Sugar Bowl in New Orleans, and then we went back for Mardi Gras, where we danced at the Rex Ball and stayed with kingpin Senator Hale Boggs and his wife, Lindy. Lynda Bird and I became front-page news all over the world, especially when I invited her to be my date at the 1966 Oscars that coming April. She had reciprocated in advance by inviting me for Easter at the LBJ ranch. It was a family affair, with LBJ and Lady Bird, whom I was crazy about, Pat and Luci and Lynda and me, as well as Mathilde and Arthur Krim, a genuine movie mogul and head of United Artists who also happened to be a leading Democratic moneyman. The Johnsons had their own growing Texas empire of radio and television stations, so the weekend conversation was fairly divided between resurrection and acquisition.

It was a beautiful Easter, with bluebonnets and buttercups in full bloom. The president avoided most of the showbiz small talk by driving around in his Lincoln convertible, surveying his herds of cattle and pigs. Easter dinner was Texas steak, Texas corn, Texas strawberries, and Sara Lee angel food cake. The press quoted several teenage female parishioners at St. Barnabas Episcopal Church in Fredericksburg, where we attended services, who said how excited they were to see me there. Shades of the Beatlemania that had recently swept the country.

The next week at the Oscars, I gave Lynda

a small dinner for twelve at Grayhall to meet Teeny and Bill, plus such thespian friends as Samantha Eggar (an ex from my London days), Tony Curtis, and Eddie Fisher. I'm not sure how those two womanizers made the list, but if the idea was to get Lynda as far away from the White House as I could, those Hollywood playboys were perfect. Even better for Lynda was my introduction of her to George Masters, probably the preeminent hairdresser to the stars, or at least in the running with Jay Sebring and Gene Shacove. I had been calling around asking who might do her hair, and Masters just showed up at Grayhall in his truck wearing cut-off shorts and boots, with a big hair dryer in the back. Before I knew it, he had Lynda in a chair, whipped out a razor, and began shaving her forehead to create a higher hairline. "If you make a mistake here, buddy," I cautioned him, "you're a dead man." And me, too, I thought. Masters was great. He exchanged the Dallas bouffant style for something fresh and natural, tweezed Lynda's eyebrows, and toned down the oil baroness makeup.

By Oscar night, Masters had transformed Lynda into a sleek lioness. *Women's Wear Daily* had previously put all three Johnson women on their Worst Dressed list. Now they would eat their words. When we arrived for the ceremony at the Santa Monica Civic Auditorium, me in white tie and tails, Lynda in a clingy peach-colored Luis Estevez silk evening dress, the world press was blown away, not to mention a lot of jealous movie stars who found themselves upstaged by what *Variety* would have called a "nonpro." Even Julie Christie, who won the Oscar for *Darling,* was lost in the shuffle when she came into Lynda's orbit at the Governors Ball.

Bob Hope, the emcee, made one political joke after another, teasing attendees Senator George Murphy and then gubernatorial hopeful Ronald Reagan for their political ambitions, and noting that it was a nice switch, someone from Washington coming to Hollywood, as opposed to vice versa, for a change. Hope made a joke that if I played my cards right, I might be the second Hamilton in the White house, erroneously assuming that Alexander Hamilton had been president.

With so much publicity, the inevitable sniping soon began. I was derided as a failed actor/fortune hunter using the hapless presidential progeny as a jump start to a dead career. It was circulated that LBJ knew just what a scoundrel I was and nicknamed me Charlie, which was what GIs called the enemy Vietcong in Vietnam. He actually called me Georgie.

Things got much nastier when I appeared at Luci Baines's extravagant White House wedding in August 1966, as Lynda's date, and presumably the first movie star to take up residence in the White House, or so I thought until I saw the showerhead in the Lincoln Bedroom with the inscription "To Jack and Jackie, Love, Peter Lawford." I had indeed spent many a night there, having gone swimming with LBJ in the White House Roosevelt pool and eaten tapioca pudding with him from the White House fridge. Lynda and I spent a lot of "quality time" together. Although protocol demanded that we sleep in separate bedrooms, the Secret Service gave us plenty of time to ourselves. But on the wedding day, all the eyes of Texas, and the nation, were on us as I did the twist with the bride to Peter Duchin's society orchestra, and Lynda caught her sister's bouquet. Later that day on the radio I heard the Kinks singing "Who'll Be the Next in Line?" Were they playing our song?

As the putative LBJ son-in-law, I was subject to incredible scrutiny. The press dug up that I had a Selective Service classification of 3A, which gave me a draft deferment on the grounds of "extreme hardship," because

I was the sole support of my family. That was true. Bill, dabbling at interior decoration, mostly of Grayhall, certainly wasn't in the profit mode, and David was way out of the limelight, having made his escape from Teeny and Bill to the University of Florida. I was the family breadwinner, and happy to be so. Naturally, the press had a field day with the deferment, especially given that my possible future brother-in-law Pat Nugent had joined the Air Force to fight in what the world saw and despised as "LBJ's war." And what was I, the Hollywood playboy, doing for the cause? Draft dodging, was what the president's many critics screamed.

I am sure I was the first actor ever to be denounced on the floor of Congress. Wisconsin representative Alvin O'Konski, the senior Republican on the House Armed Services Committee, attacked the draft system as "undemocratic and un-American." Not one of the hundred men drafted in his congressional district in the past six months had a family income of more than $5,000. O'Konski contrasted that with "a young Hollywood actor with a $200,000 home, a $30,000 Rolls-Royce, and a $100,000 income" deferred for supporting his four-times-married mother. "It nauseates me," the lawmaker said. He refused to speak my name, but the whole world knew whom he was talking about.

In fact, at twenty-six I was above the age where men were being called to war. But this time age didn't matter. This was all about publicity, and I was on the wrong end of it. To counter the attacks I did an interview with Vincent Canby of the *New York Times,* the successor to my nemesis Bosley Crowther. Canby noted that my salary was higher than Lyndon Johnson's, and that I made it from such nonheroic endeavors as those bad offshore films, hosting the pop music show *Hullabaloo,* guesting on the *Milton Berle Show,* and doing a road show of *Gigi.* I tried to defend myself and my lifestyle, lightly, very lightly, by saying that "I invest in myself, instead of oil wells and bowling alleys. An actor expresses his attitude in the way he lives." Admitting that I did enjoy living well, I added, "I happen to be in a business that supports my habits."

The president was not amused. It was suggested that I come down to Texas to the ranch to have a heart-to-heart about "this little problem." I flew down to Texas on a commercial flight and was met in San Antonio by LBJ's King Air. Waiting for me on the landing strip of the ranch, LBJ was driving the open Continental, with "Tennessee Waltz" blasting from an eight-track car stereo. He didn't mention the deferment. "We're goin' huntin'," he told me, and motioned me to get in the backseat. Then he handed me a Winchester 30-30 rifle. There I was, sitting behind the president of the United States with a loaded rifle. With visions of John Wilkes Booth running through my mind, I feared that the Secret Service, following in the distance, might kill me.

LBJ tore off into the fields in a presidential cloud of dust. He proudly pointed out his prime Santa Gertrudis cattle, his endless grasslands. Then he screeched to a halt, backed up, and went forward a few times, nearly jarring my teeth out. Was he going to execute me himself, out on the range? No. He had just run over a big snake and wanted to make sure he got him.

Then he spied a deer in the distance. "Get 'im," my commander in chief commanded. I got out of the Lincoln with the rifle, fell to the ground in sharpshooter position, and nailed the deer on the first shot. Thank God for those shooting lessons Teeny's friend had given me when we were husband hunting in St. Louis. The Secret Service retrieved the deer and proceeded to skin it. LBJ, swigging one Texas-bottled Dr Pepper after another, stopped again. We got out of the car. He walked over to me and handed me his empty Dr Pepper bottle. "Thanks," LBJ said, unzipping the presidential fly. He began to pee, home on the range indeed. Without ever looking down, I held the bottle. "You're a regular Daniel Boone," he said, paying me the ultimate compliment on my shot.

Meanwhile, back at the ranch, he presented me with some homemade venison sausage to take back to Hollywood. He asked his cook, Zephyr, what she was making us to eat. When she replied chicken, he screamed. "I lived through the Depression. I don't want any more goddamn chicken."

LBJ got to the matter at hand only the next day when we were on Air Force One flying back to Washington. "Georgie," the president said. "It's not enough to do good. You got to look good. And we don't look good right now." While he didn't suggest that I enlist in the army, for the good of the nation, and for the good of the Johnsons, the implication was that if I would waive my "extreme hardship" maternal care deferment, I'd be handing out volleyballs at Fort Ord; he'd make sure I wasn't sent to Vietnam to be cannon fodder, but rather be given a safe desk job.

When I got back to Hollywood, I sought the advice of Colonel Parker. "Sign up," was all he said. For some reason, I decided that would be the coward's way out. I thus defied both the colonel and the president. I was heading off to Germany to make another offshore film, *Jack of Diamonds,* about a natty cat burglar, à la Cary Grant in *To Catch a Thief.* I thought I'd make the film, then enlist in Germany on my own volition. I was planning to report to the nearest base, where I would be given a physical and be reclassified. Elvis served in Germany; so could I, even though agewise I was over the hill. But I didn't want to be branded as a draft dodger all my life, not a good ol' Southern boy like myself who had gone to military school, for Stonewall Jackson's sake.

Before leaving for Germany, Lynda and I had some wonderful weekends in New York. The press followed us everywhere and made up wildly romantic stories, such as my serenading Lynda with songs like "Love Is a Many-Splendored Thing" at smoky boîtes. Bands did play the old standard "Linda" everywhere we went. It was like our theme. We went to *Man of La Mancha* and ate Nathan's hot dogs and held hands a lot and stayed up late. I couldn't wait to see her again.

But then scandal intervened. Teeny had a dubious society friend from El Morocco, Butler, a dapper man-about-town about whom everything, including his claimed blue bloodlines, was fake. Butler was the kind of man who dressed his elderly father in livery and passed him off as his manservant. A consummate gossip, his sources of income were questionable, and his luck was running out. The IRS was onto him, and he needed to save himself. To do so, he began dangling damaging inside information he claimed to have about my brother Bill's *"liaisons dangereuses."* Butler was gay and indiscreet. Bill was gay and discreet. But "gay" was the dirtiest word anyone could have used in and around the Johnson White House, which had been extremely lucky not to have faced a scandal of Profumo proportions in the case of LBJ's long-term right-hand man Walter Jenkins.

In 1964, just before the presidential election, as it was explained to me, Jenkins was arrested in a YMCA bathroom performing "unnatural acts" with a Hungarian. The problem was, it wasn't the first time. Jenkins had been arrested in the same toilet six years before. In those days homosexuality was the sin of sins, particularly in politics, let alone with a Communist. LBJ supposedly dispatched his chief lawyer, Abe Fortas, whom he later appointed to the Supreme Court, to hush the matter up. Even Fortas failed; the press would not be suppressed on this one. JFK's infidelities, maybe, but not a gay man in LBJ's macho Dixie corps. That was too hot not to handle. Fortunately for all concerned, geopolitics kept Walter Jenkins in the back pages. At the same time of his disgrace, China exploded its first nuclear test, and, even bigger, Nikita Khrushchev was deposed in Russia.

LBJ slipped off the hook, but damned if George Hamilton was going to hang him there again. A draft problem was nothing compared to a gay problem. Talk about bad appearances. Although I was hardly my brother's keeper. I *was* his keeper financially. As far as homosexual scandals were concerned, the legal doctrine of "fruit of the poisoned tree" often applied, fair or not. If Bill were outed, I would be inevitably tarred with that sweet brush, my whole life of Don Juanism notwithstanding. In short, I didn't want my family dragged into the mud. Butler would have said anything — about Bill, Teeny, me — just to get his slippery neck out of the ringer. Beware friendships forged at El Morocco.

My last tango with Lynda Bird took place not in Paris but in Marbella. We were having a wonderful rendezvous, putting all the awful gossip an ocean away, where it belonged. Then enter another El Morocco friend of Teeny's, Johnny Meyer, formerly the Mr. Fixit of Howard Hughes, now having assumed the same capacity for Aristotle Onassis, whose great yacht, *Cristina,* was anchored there. Johnny wined and dined us for two days and then made his inevitable pitch. Onassis wanted us on the *Cristina* as his very honored guests. It sounded like the *Love Boat* of a lifetime but would have actually been *Voyage of the Damned.* Onassis, it transpired, had huge American tax problems. LBJ, it so happened, saw Onassis as persona non grata because of tax reasons. If Lynda Bird set foot on that boat, she would be walking the plank of fatal compromise. Johnny Meyer had found out that we were heading to Marbella and sailed the *Cristina* there to tempt us with its poisoned fruit. He had also tried and failed to tempt Teeny with promises of huge sums of offshore money if she could get me to take the Greek bait.

There was just too much sleaze out there. I had thought Hollywood was bad, but it was nothing like politics.

Lynda Bird, the child of the most political animal on the planet, ended up following her genetic destiny. Within a few months she got engaged to Charles Robb. They wed in 1967, and he went on to become governor of Virginia. I received an invitation to that inaugural, and I couldn't help thinking it might have been me. Lynda and I never stopped being friends and the Johnsons insisted I come to the second White House wedding. Maybe they needed a good dancer. I did have a conflict, though. I was doing *Barefoot in the Park* in Chicago, and the show had to go on, White House or not. But Liz Carpenter said that she would not take no for an RSVP.

A helicopter was dispatched to pick me up on the roof of the theater following the matinee, zip me to the airport, where I was jetted to Washington and then helicoptered to the ceremony, where I had arranged to meet Merle Oberon and Henry and Christina Ford. I was going to sit with them, until Henry, remembering my recent denunciation in Congress, suggested after one Bloody Mary that it might be better if I made a separate entrance all by myself.

The ceremony lasted all of seventeen minutes. I was then whisked back to Chicago just in time for the evening curtain. Whether or not I would make it had more suspense than any Hitchcock movie. I ran onto stage breathless with no makeup and ad-libbed to the full house, most of whom were fully aware of my continuing soap opera with the first family, "Ladies and gentleman, I just had a helluva day in Washington . . ." I didn't get the girl, but I did get a standing ovation.

CHAPTER ELEVEN
MODEL BEHAVIOR

Is there life after the White House? There had to be. A lot of people were worried that my star would be tarnished by me, Hollywood's ostensible grandmaster of the dating game, losing the president's daughter to a mere mortal military man. I just took it in stride. It was all part of that dating game, the game of love, and, romantic recidivist that I was, I simply went back to the craps tables of courtship. I was hooked and I couldn't help myself.

I doubt that anyone in Hollywood has had more "dates" than I have. Cinema seems to be the universal aphrodisiac, sort of the way charcoal is the universal antidote. I had been extremely fortunate, having gone out with the first daughter and the Crown Princess of the Motor City (Charlotte Ford), all while I was in my tender twenties. I had even had a fling with the Countess of Couture, Jacqueline de Ribes, who was as influential a chic role model in France as her look-alike Jackie Kennedy was in America. I suppose she found me worthy of her company because I was the youngest man to make fashion czarina Eleanor Lambert's Lifetime Best-Dressed List, up there in a pantheon with Prince Phillip, the Duke of Windsor, Lord Lichfield, Hubert de Givenchy, and downhill racer Jean-Claude Killy. Fast company indeed.

Jacqueline was old enough to be my . . . well, big sister, fabulous enough for me to be smitten by, and sophisticated enough for her marriage not to be an issue. She was five ten, way beyond rich and thin, and probably the most glamorous woman I ever met. Then again, that's what she was famous for. She was one person who lived up to the hype. When I escorted her for a week in the Med on Gianni Agnelli's yacht *Agneta,* Jacqueline traveled with forty pieces of matched Vuitton luggage, when Vuitton was still chic and exclusive. I had felt like a prima donna with my own twelve, so being a clotheshorse is a relative affair.

Jacqueline was a balletomane who was responsible for Rudolf Nureyev defecting to the West. I would have defected for her myself, trunks and all. Her favorite restaurant was Le Coq Hardi in Bougival, outside

Paris, which was one of the most romantic of all restaurants, a living version of Renoir's *Luncheon of the Boating Party*. Sipping champagne and talking Baudelaire amid the hydrangeas with the most stylish woman in the most stylish country was about as good as it gets. It seemed unreal, and in fact it wasn't real. Jacqueline, the vicomtesse, had a husband who had a very grand title and a very grand banker. This was one *bateau* you couldn't exactly rock.

When I had first arrived at MGM, the studio enjoyed the publicity value of stars dating stars, and the publicists played matchmakers. My first star date was the bombshell Mamie Van Doren, who had been married to the bandleader Ray Anthony. So we actually had something to talk about. I even had a date with Marilyn Monroe, to escort her to an A-list dinner party at the home of Jennifer Jones and David O. Selznick. I was terribly intimidated. She had just broken up with Arthur Miller, but she was still in a highly intellectual mode, going on about philosophy and anthropology and other brainy subjects where I was clueless. I had absolutely no idea what she was saying. All I could say to her was that I had been an errand boy for her New York lawyer, Frank Delaney, which was not exactly the kind of gambit that led to fireworks with Hollywood's leading icon. Dumb blonde? Forget it. How I wish I had caught her coming off Joe DiMaggio.

Most of the stars and starlets I was fixed up with in my early days were wearing so much makeup and so many foundation garments that the prospect of ever seeing them in the flesh was as daunting as Houdini trying to get out of one of his chained straitjackets. There was nothing natural about early sixties Hollywood, not until the miniskirts came on and the cantilevered bras came off, but by then the pendulum had swung so far in the other direction that the mystery and the romance completely disappeared. Thank God for the Jacqueline de Ribeses of the world.

There were so many opportunities knocking at the door of Grayhall and I was simply too young and full of wild oats to look the other way. I often tried to push my luck, just to see how wild my oats could be. There was a weekend in Palm Springs where I set out to juggle four gorgeous starlets, one of whom was the lovely Tuesday Weld, who had come from a blue-blooded but downwardly mobile Eastern WASP family. I had a whole French farce set up — breakfast with Tuesday, tennis at the Racquet Club with another, a horseback ride in the canyons with a third, dinner with a fourth, and back to Tuesday for a nightcap, with the excuse that I was out playing polo or croquet with the guys. But the ladies were onto me and were conspiring to have me make love to all of them, all the time, until I was a dead man. Wear me out they did, and I ended up falling asleep alone in my car.

In the aftermath of the Lynda Bird affair, I needed to salve my romantic wounds and begin dating my blues away. I suppose I was embracing my inner cad, having as much fun as a movie star could have, which was endless, without putting my fragile heart on the line. In those days, when the going got tough, George Hamilton got going to Acapulco, which was a magic venue then, as well as a lucky charm. I had embraced two of my fellow cads to go down to Mexico for a little tequila a-go-go. One of my companions for this spring break, Hollywood style, was Tony Curtis. Tony was an inspiration to me. For all his great films — *Sweet Smell of Success, The Defiant Ones, Some Like It Hot* — Tony was far more impassioned about his lifestyle than his career, the latter existing only to support the former. Tony somehow was able to fuse Cary Grant with Bernie Schwartz. He was one of the best-dressed men in the business, a veritable Beau Brummel. His father had been a tailor, and clothes were in his blood, although not as much as women. He had had the prototypical Hollywood fifties dream marriage with Janet Leigh. I figured if that didn't work, what could? Tony had just split from his second wife, the elegant German actress Christine Kaufmann, who was all of seventeen when Tony left Janet for her. Fame and fidelity were a tough fit.

Our other fellow traveler was Gene Shacove, the motorcycle-riding stud hairdresser to the stars who inspired the Warren Beatty character in *Shampoo*. Gene was so heterosexual that he single-handedly balanced the scales between all the gay hairdressers in the business. He cut my hair, as well as that of every hot actress in town, from Jill St. John to Marlene Dietrich. To further our own romantic pursuits, Tony, Gene, and I had become investors in the Candy Store, which was the disco of the minute in Beverly Hills.

The Three Musketeers, as we saw ourselves, were psyched for this "hunting trip" to paradise. Tony had bought us all Mickey Mouse watches to wear on the flight down, and we rented a whole floor of Teddy Stauffer's Villa Vera to accommodate our conquests. We planned a big party for ourselves and stocked our suite with the best wines and hors d'oeuvres, a host of servants, and a mariachi band. However, not one girl showed up. Each of us thought one of the others was in charge of feminine companionship, although Tony and Gene ganged up and blamed me for turning the debauch into a stag night. We ended up dancing by ourselves and pretending to sweet-talk all the imaginary girls, competing to come up with the most outrageous pickup lines. We got incredibly drunk on the unused spirits. The servants thought we were completely loco, and we were. Such were the dubious pleasures of bachelorhood.

The next day, or whenever we came to, we went out on the bay, and that's where I met Alana. She was so tall and blond and natural and American dream stunning that she could have only been a Ford model, which she was, but it took me a month to find out. At the moment, she was very much possessed, in the company of a Mexican actor named Hugo Stieglitz. Even though Hugo was short and not an obviously worthy match for this goddess, Alana didn't seem particularly interested in me. Nevertheless, her hypnotic blue eyes and her equally hypnotic derriere, rare for a model, stayed in my tequila-marinated mind.

A month later in New York, this vision

emerged again at Le Club, which was the Annabel's of the Manhattan moment. Le Club, a members-only disco off Sutton Place, was a former carriage house converted by jet-set columnist Igor Cassini into what looked like the living room of a European castle. Pre-electricity. The room was so dark you could barely see anyone, which made groping permissible; that may have been the whole point. Even in this festive but very dark boîte, Alana's catlike eyes glowed in the dark, though not at me. She was with the tycoon and trophy-girlfriend collector David Gilmore, who later would create Fiji Water, and with whom I was familiar from the Annabel-Regine-Castel-Cabala Euro nightclub circuit, but not familiar enough to crash his turf. I had my own date, whom I quickly forgot, but the vision remained of the impossible dream.

But amazingly, the vision soon showed up on my home turf at the Candy Store. This time she was alone, with a girlfriend, shaking that heroic booty on the dance floor. In these halcyon days before sexual harassment, when knighthood was in flower, I made the chivalrous gesture of pinching Alana on her prime asset. And because of the times, and the manners, she not only didn't slap me, she began flirting, enough that I could get her L.A. number and invite her to visit my own prime asset, Grayhall. She took a long time to call me.

After drinks at the mansion and dancing at the Candy Store, I had learned a lot about Alana Collins, and I was smitten. She was all of twenty but seemed much more mature than I, which wasn't saying that much. She had grown up in the cow town of Nacogdoches, in East Texas, which wasn't far from Arkansas. We had small-town Southern geography in common, as well as a desire for escape.

Alana had done it the hard way, working as an air hostess for the puddle-jumping Trans-Texas Airways. Alana was panicked to fly. "We're all going to die," she often screamed on takeoff, and the passengers would have to come to her aid. Somehow she survived to earn enough money for a one-way ticket to New York so she could introduce herself to superagent Eileen Ford, who was as smitten as I was. She had been dispatched by Ford to Paris and Milan to make her name as a model, which she had done, as well as meeting the battery of playboys like David Gilmore. She had been to Acapulco on photo shoots, where she had met the Mexican actor I saw her with on the boat. Letting down her guard, she admitted that, on a previous trip, she had seen me with Lynda Bird at a party at Merle Oberon's. She also admitted that she was a big fan of *Your Cheatin' Heart,* just as Lynda Bird had been. How I owed Hank. I began believing that I had some special connection with Texas girls.

Before we left Grayhall, my mother swept in, in her Auntie Mame fashion, and took a long, hard look a Alana. "Is that Miss Sally?" she asked, nearly queering the deal by referring to another of my hot pursuits. But before the boom could fall, she paid Alana, who was resplendent in a Pucci mini-dress, the ultimate compliment. "How chic you look!" Teeny exclaimed, and went about her merry way.

In addition to her looks, I was captivated by Alana's spunk and drive, not to mention her precocious wit and sense of humor. She had been raised by her grandmother, having been virtually abandoned by her four-times-married mother, a beautiful dead ringer for Gene Tierney, with similar psychiatric problems. Alana had had to grow up fast, and the travails of Texas poverty had only sharpened her wit and spirit. I was so enraptured that I invited Alana to come to Europe with me the following week, where I was to begin production on *The Survivors,* a glamorous new prime-time soap opera about a rich and depraved banking family, created by the bard of jet-set excess, Harold Robbins. Alana begged off. How could she not? She didn't know me well enough yet. She didn't know me at all. Still, I pressed my case. One night while she was still in L.A. for her photo shoot, I rented a shit-kicking Texas-style white Cadillac convertible from Rent-A-Wreck, donned one of my Hank Williams purple and white checked Western shirts, and took the super-health-conscious Alana to that pioneering temple of organic gastronomy, the Aware Inn.

On another night, I had Lilla, our cook at Grayhall, who happened to be from Huntsville, Texas, make Alana a country feast of biscuits and gravy and fried chicken. The idea was to convince Alana that I was a simpatico Dixie homeboy, not the highfalutin lockjawed Ivy twit I played on-screen. I even flew the red eye back to New York with Alana, dropping her off en route to Europe. She was, however, a little nonplussed when I changed into an entirely new outfit prior to landing. MGM having taught me the importance of entrances and exits, I always wanted to look my best, but I'm not sure my fastidious chic would have played in Nacogdoches.

No sooner had I gotten to Europe and

begun learning my lines for the series, where I would star as a souped-up, or rather soaped-up, Harold Robbins version of a Rothschild scion, than I got a call from Alana. Eileen Ford had just offered her a last-minute assignment in London. We could meet there, then go down to Saint-Tropez, where *Survivors* was being shot. Yes, there is a God, I said to myself.

While Alana went to work on her shoot, I flew down to the Hotel du Cap to pick up a red Ferrari I had bought at a fire sale price from Bob Neal. I was trying awfully hard, but I was falling for Alana and wanted her to see the Riviera in style. I soon saw why the Ferrari was so cheap. Neal the Heel hadn't disclosed to me that it had British right-hand drive. It was hard enough to drive a normal car on the hairpin turns and vertiginous cliffs of the Côte d'Azur. Not being able to see was the stuff of daredevils. I prayed Alana would be impressed. I prayed that we would live out the weeks ahead.

Things started out great. Alana arrived in high spirits and we took a suite at Le Byblos in Saint-Tropez, which is where Mick Jagger would marry Bianca and was ground zero for Riviera cool. Alana shared my love of the sun and was attached to her reflecting screen the way most Saint-Tropeziens were tied to their gold chains. She was a quarter Cherokee and bronzed like a champion. She should have been the Bain de Soleil girl. She was also a great waterskier. On the other hand, she was the pickiest eater of all time. She had gotten hepatitis from Mexican clams on one of her Acapulco shoots and had become a health nut and a walking food allergy. All the wonderful French champagne and foie gras and bouillabaisse was wasted on her. I loved ordering for my women, but she wouldn't hear of it. Instead, she insisted on interrogating the waiters herself. When the meal invariably failed to measure up, Alana would send the food back to the kitchen and the waiter back to his native land.

Aside from our restaurant stalemates, we had our first (of thousands) big fight at a Saint-Tropez party where, lubricated with Domaine Ott *vin rosé,* I got up with the band and began doing my best Chuck Berry on "Memphis." I liked the band so much that I jammed them all into the Ferrari when the party ended and turned it into a movable debauch at an all-night club. Alana was not amused. She thought I could have killed us all driving blind in a Ferrari-turned-sardine-can. She also thought I was showing off and accused me of gross narcissism, plus paying more attention to the band then to her.

She told me it was over, before it had even begun, left me, and walked back to the Byblos. When I finally returned, she was asleep. I decided that enough was enough. I would pack my bags and leave and she would wake up all alone. However, I had so many bags that after a few hours of trying to pack, I gave up. It was easier just to stay and fight it out. By the morning's sun, we were thrilled to see each other. If it hadn't been for that excess baggage of mine, we might never have gotten married.

We took the wrong-way Ferrari on to Monte Carlo, Alana being my Seeing Eye dog, stopping en route at the Hotel du Cap to fetch a few more trunks of my clothes that I had stored there, about which Alana teased me mercilessly. Next stop was Portofino, where Alana and I had a big fight when I ordered her *pesca* instead of *pesce*. She wanted a big fish; she got a little peach, by which time the kitchen had shut down and was unable to remedy my linguistic gaffe. It was bad enough to show off. It was something else to starve a hungry girl. In Florence, we had another set-to when a famous restaurant by the Duomo put alcohol in Alana's fruit salad. She swore that by three A.M. she would be sick as a dog. I set my alarm for three to wake her and remind her it was time to be ill. Our trip was a version of *Two for the Road* crossed with the *Guide Michelin*. The *Michelin* part came into play when the Ferrari blew up on the autostrada.

Somehow we made it to Rome, where our Roman holiday was interrupted by emergency phone calls from the Candy Store saying that brother Bill had run up shockingly huge tabs purchasing most of the vintage champagne in France and charging it to my account. This was the first of endless family financial crises that Alana became a party to. I called Bill in L.A. He laughed the whole thing off. This wasn't an *extravagance,* he explained in his always cool Southern drawl, it was an *investment,* just like the hundreds of thousands in Jérôme Bonaparte antiques that he had charged to me as well. Bill's position, he told me, was like that of a stockbroker or, today, an investment adviser. He wasn't bathing in the champagne, he was collecting it for me, and he made me feel like a philistine ingrate for questioning his impeccable taste and judgment. If I couldn't trust my own family, then who? Certainly not this barely postadolescent but precocious model I was dragging around Europe with me and whom I had jokingly rechristened the Duchess of Nacogdoches.

Alana was very direct. She had never had

money to throw around and now that she was making money as a model, she wouldn't let her wild and crazy mother squander it. Of course I was totally defensive about my family. For all my success, I still felt privileged to serve them in any way I could. I was their vassal; they were my lieges. Grayhall was the family castle; that I paid for it was incidental, just our family's particular division of labor. It was just the beginning, but Alana was dead set on teaching me a word that was not in my vocabulary. That word was "no."

I wasn't really price sensitive at this point because I was making a lot of money, thanks to my quasi godfather Colonel Parker. *Survivors,* based on a nine-page synopsis Harold Robbins had conjured up for a cool million, was the most expensive television show thus far created, a joint venture of ABC and Universal Pictures. I was to play the half brother of my former leading lady Lana Turner, whose mink I could never put on to her exigent taste. Lana was being paid the huge sum of $12,500 a week to lure the superstar to perform on the small screen. I had been offered $8,000. A huge order of fifty-two episodes had been scheduled, so those paychecks would add up fast. I told the colonel my good news, and he told me to turn it down. I thought he was crazy, crazy like a fox.

So I ordered my near-apoplectic agents at William Morris, Abe Lastfogel and Stan Kamen, to whom, incidentally, the colonel had introduced me, to say no. They kept saying no until the poker-faced mogul of Universal, Lew Wasserman, who looked and acted like a Vegas pit boss, began calling the agents and, uncharacteristically sweet and sugary, asking them to take the deal, offering to throw in Ferraris and Savile Row wardrobes to sweeten the package. I did exactly as the colonel said, which was to say no, no, no, until we finally arrived $17,500 per episode, a record of media avarice in those days. The colonel said he wouldn't take it, that he would hold out for more. But I wasn't greedy. I took it and got two pay-or-play deals to make films at $150,000 each as part of the package. For me, it was Christmas in July. Now Lana hit the roof, but she didn't have the colonel in her corner. At one point she threatened to commit suicide over being outpaid by me, but she was talked into having a new face-lift instead. Lana remained at $12,500. I would have gladly ceded her top billing as a consolation prize, but Universal wouldn't let me. The actor who gets paid the most gets the top credit. It was another valuable Hollywood lesson I learned: If you get the money, the rest follows. Anyway, you can't eat billing.

I met Robbins himself, who looked more like a bookie than an author. He wore a flowered hat, big collars, more chains than a sommelier. When he told me I was just what he was looking for, I wasn't sure whether to be flattered or insulted. He had a big yacht in Cannes and a big house in Beverly Hills, all white marble. It looked like a disco in Tehran. But you couldn't argue with Harold's success. Sex sold, and his formula of melding sex, glamour, and caricatures of the rich and famous became the template for best sellers by Judith Krantz, Sidney Sheldon, Jackie Collins, and others. His *Carpetbaggers* was, at the time, the fourth biggest-selling book in history.

Unfortunately, Harold played far less well on the small screen than on the paperback page, possibly because he had absolutely nothing to do with the series other than take the "created by" money and run. The shoot was a major disaster, and if I missed not having Alana around to spar with (she had to go back to New York to model), Lana more than made up for it by trying to batter my self-esteem every single day. This once most super of superstars was traumatized at having to step down to television and still enraged at my outearning her. She picked on me mercilessly, typically accusing me of upstaging her by wearing a bright coral-colored tie that in fact had been given to me by costumer Luis Estevez. She required a real chinchilla coat, but even this wasteful production drew the line when Lana said she could not work in fake jewels and demanded the real deal from Van Cleef. Luxury, genuine luxury, was the "method" for this actress, but the TV people told Lana that only a big-screen production could accommodate her wants and needs. In my case, they provided me everything I wanted — cars, clothes, food, assistants — everything except a good script.

Despite the Riviera settings and the prestige cast, which included Ralph Bellamy and Kevin McCarthy, *The Survivors* did not survive past the first season. Lana got a midnight call from Stan Kamen, who was her agent, too, advising her that she had been let go. They couldn't afford to fire me. I had a pay-or-play deal and I was being paid too much to be thrown away. The entire production, or what was left of it, was downsized and brought back to Universal City. What a comedown from St.-Jean-Cap-Ferrat. The emasculated series, renamed *Paris 7000,* was now set in the American embassy in

Paris and the Rothschild heir I was playing was transformed into an embassy clerk who helped wayward Americans find their lost passports or locate a dentist if they broke a tooth on a partridge bone at Maxim's. We had weekly guest stars, aging legends in need of a paycheck like E. G. Marshall and Anne Baxter, but the series went nowhere.

The saving grace was my huge two-picture pay-or-play deal. Unfortunately, Universal wanted to back out of the deal, and pressure was put on my agents for the studio to be let out of its contract. "But I'm pay or play," I told them, which meant that they either had to make the movie and play me, or pay me to go away.

"Won't happen," the agents said. Universal wanted *me* to go away. "It's Lew Wasserman," said the agents, who always sided with the power, regardless of whom they were supposedly representing, invoking the most feared name in Hollywood, the man who ran Universal, the smartest, coldest wheeler-dealer in town who knew every single card in the deck, a deck stacked in his favor. Don't mess with Lew, or Mr. Wasserman, as he insisted on being called.

Somehow I held my ground. For the first of my "play" movies, Universal offered me the worst script in the history of film. The idea was that it was so bad I would say no and they wouldn't have to pay me. The thing could drag on forever with me never seeing a cent. So I said yes and learned every horrible line and showed up on the lot for the start of shooting. But when I arrived, there was no crew and no picture. Universal had no intention of making that turkey. They were just playing a card game with me. I played right back. I grabbed a broom and began sweeping the soundstage. Somehow, the Universal executives got the point. "You're owed money," they conceded.

"Yes," I said, "and when the second picture is due, I'll be down here sweeping again." Universal knew from then on that they had a rough customer. Soon my lawyers called me. They had gotten as call from Lew Wasserman saying, "We *have* to make a deal." The whole town was shaking. Soon I personally got a call from the boss of bosses. I had met him and his wife, Edie, one of the queens of the entertainment world, about five times socially, but I had never really connected with this cold-as-ice businessman.

"George, how are you doing?" he opened the conversation.

"Mr. Wasserman . . ." I began, but he cut me off.

"Call me Lew."

Wow. Nobody calls him Lew, except maybe Jules Stein, who founded the place. "I'm sorry about this situation," I said.

"Edie and I always enjoy seeing you. You must come up to the house sometime."

"Mr. Wasserman . . ."

"Lew."

"I'd love to come for dinner . . ."

He turned to business. "We have big plans for you here at the studio. We want to fit you in."

"I'd love to fit in."

"What if I just send you a check for the movie and call it quits?" Lew got straight to the point.

"But," I said, "there are two pictures we're talking about, not just one."

"I know," Lew said. "But you're getting a lot of money and you don't have to do anything. It's a great deal for both of us."

I realized then and there it was one of those offers that could not be refused. "If you insist," I said.

"My man will be there in a half hour with the check," Lew said, closing the deal.

"Well, Lew, it's been great. I would love to see you and Edie soon . . ." I tried to make the most of being steamrollered.

"You can call me Mr. Wasserman now," he said, and hung up.

I had been nowhere in television before, on a 1964 series called *The Rogues* about a family of con men. David Niven, Charles Boyer, and Gig Young played crooked cousins, English, French, and Yank. I played Charles Boyer's son. I had fun watching these great stars ham it up, each trying to upstage the others with a cocked brow, an attention-getting cough, a derisive sneer, but never a loud tie, as Lana accused me. The worst thing an actor could do to another — same sex, at least — was to touch him. That meant that the touchee was less important than the toucher, and the *Rogues* set was often a game of tag.

The best part of these small-screen exercises, aside from the paychecks, was the opportunity to eat at the Universal commissary with the likes of Alfred Hitchcock and Ronald Reagan. But I had to start thinking about getting back onto the big screen, and pronto, if I was going to be able to keep my family in the style to which I had gotten them accustomed, not to mention pushing my Duchess of Nacogdoches, who was being hit on constantly by every playboy of the Western world. Alana had a way of drifting into my life, then drifting out, her independence inspiring fits of jealousy and insecurity that no other woman had ever inflicted on me. To make myself feel secure, I vowed to succeed.

My brainstorm that would, I was certain, lead to this holy grail of success, or at least box office, occurred at the Universal commissary. I had been talking to a producer named John Strong about locating a stunt man for one of the episodes of *Paris 7000*. He mentioned Evel Knievel to me. We traded calls about coming out to see me about the job. One day John and I were lunching at the commissary when the maître d' called me to the phone. There's a man at the gate, a Mr. Knievel, wanting to get on the lot, he said. Send him in, I said. "There's a problem," the maître d' said. "He can't walk."

I arranged to get some help. A broken-up-looking man was carried to our booth by two assistants. He looked like he could barely make it, but he was dressed like Elvis in his latter days, or Liberace, with big blond hair, a huge belt, a cape, and other accoutrements befitting a magician. The whole commissary was watching, people like Hitchcock, all the bigwigs. This guy, whoever he was, had star quality. This guy was Evel Knievel. "I wanted you for this stunt," I said, "but you're obviously indisposed."

"I'll heal," Evel said. "I want the job." That's why he was here. He explained that he was going in for an operation to put eleven pounds of metal in his leg. "I'll be ready in a week."

It seemed like the most deluded wishful thinking I'd ever heard. On the day before he was supposed to show up to do the stunt, Evel called me, wanting to get all the parameters of the stunt that was to be done. "I like to be precise," he said. We talked awhile. Then the phone went dead. After a minute, a woman picked up. It was a nurse in the intensive care unit of the hospital where Evel had been operated on. The man, the wild man, had just passed out cold on the hospital floor. I scrubbed the stunt but realized I had something more. A week later Evel called, ready to go. "Forget the stunt," I told him. "You're the most outrageous character I've ever met. I want to do your life story." Here was an American original, all right, a modern gladiator who adhered to the honor code of the Wild West. This was way more than a stunt. Here was my next movie.

John Strong flashed on the idea. He sent me to see Evel at St. Joseph's Hospital in the San Fernando Valley to tie up his life rights, while there was still a life to tie up. This guy was heroic like no one else. He was also a showman like no one else, a daredevil Hank Williams. Evel was a mountain man, from

Butte, Montana. He had worked the copper mines as a young man, doing wheelies with the earth movers. He had worked as a rodeo rider and a ski jumper, as well as a semipro hockey player.

Evel was a one-man death wish minstrel show, traveling the country and doing longer and longer jumps until he got his fifteen minutes of fame on the *Joey Bishop Show*. His proximity to the Rat Pack led him to Vegas and Caesars Palace, where John Derek and his then wife Linda Evans filmed his near-death crash. America loved near death, and now Evel was ready for his close-up. Alana would love it, I was sure. So would Lynda Bird. So would everyone in America. Here was the last American hero. I was sure this one would lead me back to the White House for a command performance. This time I vowed I would do my subject commercial justice and not let a moribund studio like MGM relegate the film to Southern drive-ins. I had the colonel, I had William Morris, and I had Evel Knievel. What else was there?

Well, there was the matter of a script, which often gets overlooked when "hot properties" are acquired. At this point I was being represented by superagent Mike Medavoy, who would go on to be a major studio head. He loved the Evel project and saw it as a way to "package" a number of his clients. Consequently, Mike began sending me one A-list writer after another: Willard Huyck of *American Graffiti,* Paul Schrader, even George Lucas himself. I settled on John Milius, who had just done an uncredited rewrite on *Dirty Harry* (he came up with the classic line, "Go ahead, make my day") and would go on to fame in writing *Apocalypse Now.* I chose John because of his right-wing macho persona, which I thought would enable him to "get" Evel. A member of the National Rifle Association, he had tried to join the marines after film school at USC but was rejected because of asthma, so he tried his best to compensate with a *semper fi* spirit on the page.

Another of John's attractions was that I could hire him cheaply, always a virtue in overpriced Hollywood. What John said he was interested in was "girls, gold, and guns." He had tried to get me to pay him in arms, but I hadn't met Adnan Khashoggi yet. The gold was one carrot here, Evel would later supply Purdy shotguns, and, for the girls, I installed John in a house in Palm Springs and hired a succession of hookers to sunbathe naked by the pool but with specific orders not to let John lay a finger on them until he completed the script. I proved to be a better motivator than Dale Carnegie. John soon delivered to me, via telegrams to the Plaza Hotel in New York, where I was staying, a 130-page masterpiece, an anachronistic, over-the-top character study of the craziest of all American heroes.

I tracked down Evel at the divey Hollywoodland Motel to share our good fortune. I brought the script over personally for him to read. Evel was lying in the seedy room with a Kotex pad wrapped around a wound on his leg, drinking a case of Wild Turkey. Problem was that Evel didn't read, an aversion he shared with a good many movie stars, who rarely read an entire script, only their own lines. Evel went the big stars one better. He ordered me to read the script aloud to him.

I declined. "I don't read scripts. I act them."

"Read," Evel demanded and literally put a gun to my head. And cocked it. Read, he said. And so I read. For more than two hours. I gave the performance of a lifetime, as if it might be my last, which was clearly the case. Evel liked what he heard. He liked it so much that he began adopting John's fictionalized dialogue and style as his own, life imitating art this time. Thank my lucky stars. Problem was that Evel got so into it that he became as grandiose as a Roman emperor.

Although I had hired a stuntman for the lesser jumps, I was planning to film the maestro himself doing one of the biggest jumps of his career, a world record of nineteen cars at the Ontario Motor Speedway east of Los Angeles. This was going to be my "money shot," and Evel, knowing this, decided to hold me up for more money. No pay, no jump. He had me over a barrel or, more precisely, he had me over nineteen barrels.

"I want more money," Evel insisted.

"But we have a deal." I tried to talk reason.

"You had a deal with a man under narcotic sedation. That ain't a deal. I'll take you to court over it."

"You're always under sedation," I countered, turning to Evel's doctor, standing nearby.

The doctor complained that Evel was always messing up the great surgery he did. "I have this beautiful metal in him, and he's always twisting it up."

I paid. That blood money still did not ensure Evel's good behavior. He smashed two cameras with his wood-covered lead cane, a deceptive weapon out of James Bond, plus he showed up at Universal with a baseball bat to beat the life out of Shelley Saltzman, a writer-producer who was trying to write a book that Evel feared would expose his infidelities. Before our big shoot in the Astrodome in Houston, Evel beat up a waiter in a restaurant, and I had to bail him out of jail to save the picture. My all-American hero had turned out to be a raving psychopath, with a far worse temper than Frank Sinatra, heretofore the angriest man in show business.

During the preparation of the film, I met Evel's grandmother, who told me Evel had been a nice boy until he hit his head on an ice rink. From then on he was crazy. He was part Colonel Parker showman, part Charles Manson ax murderer. Once, in Butte, Montana, he was taken to court for assaulting a woman. He showed up on crutches and pleaded with the judge that he was a cripple, an invalid who couldn't harm a fly. The judge dismissed the case, whereupon Evel cornered the woman in the courthouse elevator and beat the hell out of her once again, smashing up both his crutches in the process. Evel tried to pick up Alana, who had a bit part, when we were shooting in Montana. They rode horses together. I can't believe she said no and lived to tell the tale.

For all his rage, Evel retained a low hustler's business savvy. The day of the Ontario shoot, I found him drinking Wild Turkey from the bottle as he plotted the trajectory of his leap, talking angles and ballistics like an MIT scientist. "That crowd wants to see me splatter," he observed matter-of-factly. The scene outside evoked the Roman Colosseum. I've never heard so much noise, tens of thousands screaming for blood. "We want Evel," they shouted. "Dead" was understood. I watched Evel drink, and he must have seen the disapproval or disbelief in my face. "Wouldn't you?" he asked, motioning to the endless row of cars that faced him.

Suddenly Evel balled up all the architectural plans, drained the Wild Turkey bottle, and limped with his cane to his bike and taped his broken wrist to one of the handlebars. He revved up, blasted off, and flew through the air in the longest few seconds I ever experienced. But then he crashed. I raced to the side of the man I was supposed to be playing but could never capture. When I reached Evel's bloody, mangled body, there was a smile on his face. He gave me a big wink. I wasn't sure whether it was expression of joy at having survived, or one of having pulled off a great con. It was probably both. Anything short of death Evel regarded as a fast one.

Evel hated me for trying to play him, but he loved the movie. It was a pure ego trip for this pure egomaniac. I was as disappointed in the finished film as I was in Evel himself. What John Milius had written was a sophisticated parody of fame. But the director, an Emmy-winning television veteran named Marvin Chomsky, who would years later direct me as a slave owner in *Roots,* took Evel dead seriously. I was so down over the results that I decided I didn't belong in show business at all. Adding insult to injury was Alana's frustration at my failure to say "no" to my family and say "I do" to her. It had become put up or shut up for her. I decided to exit, and in came Lord Lichfield, the great English photographer and first cousin of the queen. The Duchess of Nacogdoches was now going to become Lady Lichfield with her own stately home, Shugborough Hall in Staffordshire. The joke was on me.

I decided to change my life around completely. Christian Science notwithstanding, I would follow my grandfather Docky's tradition and become a doctor, which was the only career I had ever had any passion about, from the moment as a Blytheville kid when I had begun to "examine" my beautiful little neighbor. Why not get a license and do some good for the world? There was, of course, the small matter of degrees. I had not even finished high school, never gone to college. Playing Harvard men didn't count. But I figured out that if I moved to England, I could go right to medical school without having to get an undergraduate degree. I had just turned thirty. I had plenty of time. Life would begin at thirty, instead of ending, as it seemed to be doing. To England I would go. To medicine. To the Hippocratic oath.

I took off for Europe for one last fling before hitting the books. I was always having one last fling. This time I was going to be flinging with my dear friend Leslie Bricusse, the brilliant Cambridge-educated songwriter who had collaborated with Anthony Newley on the hit plays *Stop the World — I Want to Get Off* and *The Roar of the Greasepaint — The Smell of the Crowd*. Leslie had written the smash "Goldfinger," and had won the Oscar for "Talk to the Animals" in *Doctor Doolittle*. The wages of his brilliance were high indeed; Leslie lived better than anyone else in Hollywood, with fabulous homes in Beverly Hills, Acapulco, and Saint Paul de Vence. He lived the way I always assumed Hollywood successes lived, but few ever did. Most stars have huge houses, but all they usually do in them is watch television and eat takeout from McDonald's. When they travel, they eat room service in their expensive suites at the Ritz and watch more television.

Not Leslie. He was a true man of the world whose parties, wherever he was, were the fulcrum of the sophisticated British film colony. His best friends were David Niven, Michael Caine, Roger Moore, Dudley Moore, Albert Finney, and the man beyond borders, Sammy Davis Jr., who had such a hit with Leslie's "What Kind of Fool Am I?" These were all global bons vivants of the highest order. I had met Leslie in the south of France while filming *The Survivors*. He and Harold Robbins were friends because they both had multiple homes in the same prime locales. Leslie was deeply amused, as was I, at Harold's self-perception as the reincarnation of Charles Dickens, and by Harold's thumbing his nose at the critics. "Who's on the yacht in Cannes?" was Harold's attitude.

That summer, though, we were both down and out. Leslie had separated from his wife, Evie, a ravishing Maltese actress whose thespian claim to fame was having costarred, as Yvonne Romain, with Elvis Presley in *Double Trouble* after being a pin-up girl in Britain for her many horror movies like *Devil Doll*. Now the Devil Doll had taken the Duchess of Nacogdoches down to the Bricusses' Acapulco villa, so the only appropriate tit for tat was for Brickman, as he was known, to take Hamilton down to the Côte d'Azur.

We drove from Paris and stopped at the picturesque town of Avallon, staying at the Hôtel de la Poste, which was filled with Napoleonic antiques that made me think of Bill and all the money of mine he was spending. How could I keep my family on a med student's nonwages? I didn't have long to contemplate finance, however, before a vision of blondness in a white Mercedes convertible pulled up next to us near the hotel. It was Britt Ekland, the Swedish bombshell who had been married to Leslie's dear friend Peter Sellers. She was the prototype of the big-eyed Swedish goddess, except that, contrary to the drool-inducing stereotype, Britt was petite, proof that the best things do come in small blond packages. I still don't know whether Britt's arrival was a simple twist of fate or arranged by Leslie, who was a master of the surprise party. If it was the latter, you can see why I have treasured his friendship for decades.

Britt and I connected immediately. We had a lot in common. She was just coming off a relationship with Warren Beatty. In her autobiography, *True Britt,* she wrote that she found me as handsome as Warren and vastly funnier. She said it, not I, but I'll take the compliment. There was also the coincidence that, pre-Beatty, Britt had had a torrid affair with my current nemesis, Lord Lichfield. He had proposed to her, and she turned him down, queen and all. Britt was also close to the other royal lensman, Lord Snowdon, Princess Margaret's husband, whom she deemed the better photographer, though it wasn't Lichfield's camerawork that led to her refusal. Even though the lord's blood was blue, his accounts were red. He was an artist, and artists, even royal ones, struggled, especially in down-at-the-heels, tax-the-rich pre-Thatcher England. Shugborough Hall was open to the public through the National Trust; the lord and Britt had only a small wing and had to use the servants' entrance. That was no way to treat a would-be lady. I shuddered to think how Britt would feel about my plans to sell Grayhall and become a poor medical student. At least the lord still had a wing.

Britt was an unforgettable two weeks of heaven, but when it was over, I was still in pain. I headed for Palm Springs, where I had been renting a house, for the sun, the horses, the escape from the Beverly Hills party circuit to a much shorter circuit out here. The other thing that never looked so good was Alana, who was here collecting her things in preparation for her move to England and ladyship. Lord Lichfield had gone to Fiji for his last bachelor flying and would be picking up Alana on his way back in a few days. We had something of a farewell dinner with Colonel Parker, who lived not far from us. Seeing how sad I was, the colonel took me aside and gave me some fatherly and managerial advice. I had to handle Alana like a negotiation, he said. She may be bluffing, but you care too much to risk losing her. "You better stay in the game," he concluded. "She's a lot smarter than you, boy. You better marry her." To seal the deal, the colonel offered me Elvis's plane to fly to Vegas and tie the knot. There was one caveat. If I was going to do it, I had to do it now. Right now. "There's a ten o'clock movie I want to watch on TV tonight," the colonel said. "We've got to be back for that."

As always I took the colonel's advice, though I thought in this case it would be impossible to compete with a thousand years of British pomp and circumstance. But, oddly enough, Alana, like Britt, was somehow put off by the long lines of tourists at Shugborough Hall paying to see how the other half lived. I knew that Alana had been obsessed with show business all her life, far more so than English castles. I also knew that, because of this obsession, Alana wanted an actor, not a doctor. So as much as I wanted to chuck it all and become a doctor, I wanted Alana more. An actor I would remain.

I got down on my knees, and Alana said yes, and off we went in Elvisair, with the colonel and Alana's cockapoo, Georgie. The colonel had reserved the top suite of the International, the hotel that Elvis had built, for the ceremony, and he rounded up a drunk preacher to whom I paid $30 for the vows. The colonel was my best man, Georgie the dog was the maid of honor, and aside from a dazed waiter we enlisted as a witness, the only other people present were the International's head man, Sam Belkin, and the pit boss Artie Newman, who had been Meyer Lansky's man in Havana. We had some drinks, then called our respective mothers (Teeny was disappointed, to say the least). The colonel and I went and played some roulette and won $15,000. Then we got back on the flying Elvis and spent our wedding night at home in Palm Springs, while the colonel watched his movie. It was a far cry from what may have awaited Alana at Westminster Abbey. It was a far cry from any wedding I might have imagined for myself, though conjuring up ceremonies wasn't exactly how I spent my leisure time. But now I was married, somewhat in shock, and it was time to figure out at last what I was going to do now that I had officially grown up.

CHAPTER TWELVE
WORLDLY POSSESSIONS

My brilliant medical career was short-lived. No sooner had I tied the knot with Alana than the gods of Hollywood took mercy on me, and for all its shortcomings, *Evel Knievel* opened to big numbers. Americans wanted to see Evel, even if they were only seeing me as a stand-in. Furthermore, having now made it legal with Alana, I had to be responsible and support her. There was a catch here, though. An addendum to my vows with Alana was that in choosing her, I was unchoosing my mother and brother — not the love but the financial support.

Never has a family expressed such betrayal and outrage as when I told Teeny and Bill I was going to sell Grayhall. To them it was like asking Scarlett O'Hara to part with Tara. I gave them an option: They could have either the house or the furniture. To them neither choice was acceptable. Bill thought I was the biggest fool on earth. You *never* sell this house, and you *never* sell these antiques. They may have cost a fortune, but they would appreciate every year and be worth a bigger fortune than I could ever make in the movies.

As it turns out, Bill was absolutely right. Grayhall sold most recently for $28 million. But I wasn't thinking of the future, only of changing the present, and a promise was a promise, especially to Alana. It got so heated that Bill and I had a vicious Cain and Abel shoving match atop Grayhall's grand staircase that could have easily resulted in two brothers tumbling to their deaths. In the end, Teeny and Bill chose the furniture and sold it for a princely sum that enabled them to move back to Palm Beach in high style and buy two mansions. Those antiques would have been worth $100 million today, but it's the carrying costs that get you and force you to sell. As my pal Gould Morrison always said, hard times make the organ-grinder's monkey eat red peppers.

I sold Grayhall to the rogue financier Bernie Cornfeld for about $1 million. Bill was aghast at the idea of selling to Bernie for any amount. That was Bill, as impractical as he was artistic. "You can't sell to *him!*" Bill said with all the contempt on earth. But I did. Teeny and Bill then sued me for support, which was as low as a family could get. Bill's rationale was that this supporting role had saved my life by keeping me out of the army and out of the Vietnam line of fire. But being dragged into court by my own flesh and blood, being shaken down for a payoff, made me feel that I would have rather taken my chances with the Vietcong. I didn't speak to my family again for several years.

I needed to escape Bill and Teeny, I needed a new movie, and I needed to take my bride on a honeymoon. I was able to kill three birds with one stone thanks to a production of *Medusa,* a wrong-man Hitchcockian thriller shooting in the Greek isles. I was to play a George Hamiltonian drunken playboy accused of the brutal killing of a stewardess. Because of the shocking 1968 wedding of American idol Jackie Kennedy to the very un-American Greek tycoon Aristotle Onassis, among other reasons, the Greek isles were the most wanted honeymoon spot on earth in 1972.

Aside from the location shoot on Rhodes, there was one major touch of class to this foreign film. The producer was Lady Sarah Consuelo Spencer-Churchill, niece of Winston, whose grandmother was the heiress Consuelo Vanderbilt and who had grown up in Blenheim Palace, without ever having to admit paying tourists. With Sarah behind the production, this was one offshore film where I didn't have to worry about getting stiffed, financially, if not critically. Sarah was doing the film to humor her twenty-years-younger Greek husband, a wannabe actor-producer Adonis named Theo Roubanis. I never cease to be amazed at how film captivates the entire world, high and low, but here we were, with one of the world's great aristocrats backing a B, if not C, picture.

The longer the lineage, the shorter the patience with pomposity. Sarah was as unpretentious as anyone I've ever met. Tall and slender, she wore mostly blazers, slacks, and pearls, with no makeup except a dab of lipstick. She had a whole kennel of Jack Russells and did a lot of needlepoint, always keeping her glasses on.

Sarah would do anything for Theo, her third husband, the proof of which was *Medusa*. We had an English television director at the helm, and the only name in the cast other than mine was the great character actor Cameron Mitchell, who did heavies better than anyone else except maybe Broderick Crawford. Cameron played a gangster here, what else? There were a lot of Greeks playing Greeks, and we did have our own Bond girl, Luciana Paluzzi, the villainess in *Thunderball*. There was another beautiful girl in the cast, a Swedish extra who put some major strains of temptation on my new marital vows. She kept telling me about her nice older boyfriend in Israel, and I thought she would be a pushover, if I chose to push. Then one day she showed me his picture. It was Meyer Lansky. My ardor was permanently chilled. No woman was worth competing with Murder, Incorporated.

Before Alana and I left for the honeymoon/shoot, we went to New York for an appearance on the *Ed Sullivan Show*. Ed had loved *Your Cheatin' Heart,* and every year since he would have me on to sing country songs. I won his heart by buying him one of the first pairs of Gucci loafers ever seen in America. You never thought of Ed as being chic, but he loved the idea. This time I sang Buck Owens's "Act Naturally" in a gold lamé outfit made by the famed Western cowboy tailor Nudie. I gave the outfit as a gift to Jerri Hall years later. My second number was the Beatles' "And I Love Her," dedicated to my new bride.

In Athens we stayed in the Churchill villa and went out every night, smashing plates in tavernas in the Plaka. Alana loved it, but things took a downturn when the flight to Rhodes wouldn't let her take her beloved

Georgie on the plane. So we had to take a slow and rocky boat to Rhodes that reminded me of the one in *Zorba the Greek* in which everyone threw up during the rough passage. Rhodes, for all its history and medieval charms, evoked nothing but nausea from Alana. The place was full of low-rent package tourists and lots of drunk Germans in lederhosen, the hotel where we were billeted was a divey tourist trap, and after a few meals Alana got sick of the unvarying diet of moussaka, feta, and bad retsina that she couldn't even drink to kill the taste of the food. The only thing that kept her from a total meltdown was her bit part in the film, which she, determined thinker that she was, talked herself into believing would be the first step on the road to an Oscar. Sadly, the movie was never released in America. I'm not sure where it played, maybe in drive-ins in Thessaloníki.

What saved the honeymoon was the arrival of my new pal and house customer Bernie Cornfeld, who picked us up in Greece in one of his last company planes, an old DC-3, and took us to Israel. Bernie had been born in Istanbul and knew the region well. His father had been an actor and theatrical producer in Romania before immigrating to America, and Bernie had a lifelong fascination with show business. He seemed to think I walked on water because I was a movie star, however fast that star might be fading, thanks to duds like *Medusa.*

Bernie had brought mopeds for all of us to ride, so we each exited the plane on two wheels and scootered around Jerusalem like Gregory Peck and Audrey Hepburn in *Roman Holiday.* He got us the Menachem Begin suite at the King David, the Ritz of Jerusalem, which Begin had blown up when it was British headquarters on the eve of Israel's statehood. Bernie put a yarmulke on my head and took us to pray at the Wailing Wall. But Alana was a tough convert, because the way to her soul was through her delicate stomach, and the only good food in Israel was what the Arabs cooked in the Old City and on the West Bank. But she kept the faith and was very moved by all the Christian sites, such as the Church of the Holy Sepulchre and the stations of the cross, which brought her back to her grandmother's old-time religion Southern Baptist Sundays in Nacogdoches. Her only disappointment was the tour guides elbowing aside nuns to show their flocks the plastic Jesus in the manger in Bethlehem. Soon enough, it was back to America and back to work, whatever that might mean.

When it comes to big business in America, no one I know is a greater tycoon than my best friend from Hackley, Herbert "Spike" Allen, the high financier whose Sun Valley conference is the ultimate summer camp for the rich and famous. Spike was a highly original prankster at Hackley, and some of us felt he kept out of trouble only because his family were generous benefactors of the school. In 1973, Spike got into show business when his family firm, Allen & Company, took over Columbia Pictures. Oh lucky day, I thought to myself. With my best boyhood chum a movie mogul, I had it made. I was certain he would make me head of Columbia, or at least give me a massive production deal on the lot, just when I really needed it. I called Spike immediately to congratulate him and told him I wanted to see him. Come on, he insisted.

I met him at the Carlyle Hotel in New York City, where he deflated me somewhat by telling me that his old family friend Ray Stark would be running the studio for him. Ray, the husband of Fanny Brice's daughter and the producer of the Streisand smash *Funny Girl*, was already one of the most powerful men in entertainment. But he wasn't George Hamilton. "Spike," I said, "Ray's great, but who can you trust more than me?"

"Herbert," Spike corrected me. "It's Herbert now."

"Can't I call you Spike, Herbert?" I teased him.

"George, I love you, you're the best," he said, "but I need someone deeply in the business to advise me."

"Who's been in it longer than me?" I pressed him. "We'll do great things together."

"It's great to have old friends like you, George. Let me think about it." Spike played for time. He took me out into the lobby, where I was going to get a car to take me to the airport and back to L.A. "Listen, George," Spike said. "I need a favor from you."

"Anything," I said.

He pointed out a very old and frail woman stretched out on a lobby sofa, her walker in front of her. "That's my grandmother. Can you take her back to California with you? I don't want her to travel alone."

I took a look at the woman, surrounded by eight pieces of plastic luggage. There's one in every family, I thought to myself. "Of course I will, pal. I'll take great care of her."

"Thanks, George. You're the best," Spike said.

I called a car and helped the lady in, with

all her bags. On the way out to JFK I tried to make small talk with her. "He's a wonderful guy, Spike, Herbert to you, Spike to me . . ."

The old woman gave me a very blank stare.

We rode on. I tried again. "It's terrific how much Herbert's accomplished . . ." Another blank stare. "Herbert, your grandson, the man who put you in the car with me . . ."

Then, in a deep Yiddish accent, the woman said to me, "I never saw that man before in my whole life. He found me in the lobby. He said you were going to the airport and could give me a ride."

This wasn't Spike's grandmother at all but another of his Oscar-worthy practical jokes. He loved playing those jokes, even more than he loved owning a studio. He never called me about the deal at Columbia, but we're still great pals. Just remember that having friends in high places doesn't always pay off like you think it will.

Despite the revenues from *Evel, Medusa* made it hard to get any more big-screen starring roles, even as my stereotypical East Coast preppy playboy. These were the anti-war, Watergate seventies, when East Coast playboys were considered retro Republicans and despised like Richard Nixon. After *Easy*

Rider, the movies had gotten "real" — and dark and paranoid — and I was perceived as a time capsule item, not a bankable presence. I supported myself with the odd television series guest-starring role, which was the kiss of death back then, before the era when small-screen shows like *Dallas* and *Dynasty* could raise the big-screen dead.

Meanwhile Alana and I moved permanently to Palm Springs to a house we bought from Gloria Swanson. To try to maintain a desert version of the old Grayhall grandeur I hired as my valet George Jacobs, the legendary man Friday of Swifty Lazar and Frank Sinatra. Frank had just fired George after fifteen years of service when gossip queen Rona Barrett shocked the world by reporting that the Chairman's handsome black right hand had been seen doing the Watusi at my Candy Store with Frank's soon to be ex, Mia Farrow.

Even though I would later make a bad movie in Yugoslavia with Peter Lawford and become a good friend of Sammy Davis Jr., I was never in Frank's orbit or part of the Rat Pack or, for that matter, any other Hollywood clique. I was a loner, and I liked it that way. I would meet all the Kennedys, but aside from my naked encounter with JFK in Palm Beach, I wasn't close with any of them.

My impression of the clan was that JFK was the life of the party, RFK the ultimate party pooper, and Teddy the party animal.

Alana would become best friends with Tina Sinatra and take me to Sinatra parties in Palm Springs, but I was always worried that Old Blue Eyes, for all his politeness (he called me "pally"), was giving me the evil eye because we had inadvertently crossed swords over Queen Soraya of Persia early on in my career. Soraya was certainly the most beautiful, glamorous, and mysterious monarch in the world in early 1960 when I met her. She had been on the cover of *Life.* She had ridden to her wedding in a solid gold Rolls-Royce. Joseph Stalin had sent her a $150,000 Russian mink coat as a wedding gift. Christian Dior designed her silver lamé wedding gown and studded it with six thousand diamonds. This was straight out of the Arabian Nights.

When we met, Soraya had just been divorced from the shah for being unable to bear him a son. She was in her late twenties, footloose, with a king's ransom at her disposal and more gorgeous than ever, the catch of all catches. She was visiting Hollywood under the wing of my MGM publicist Lee Anderson. Lee would go on to become Hollywood royalty herself by marrying Vincente Minnelli. Soraya had expressed a desire to become an actress, sort of a reverse Grace Kelly, from throne queen to screen queen. I was highly flattered to be one of only two actors Lee had invited to an exclusive dinner party for the queen at her apartment in Westwood. The other actor at the dinner was George Nader, who was born in Amman, Jordan, and was one of the rare Arabs in the film business. All he and I had in common was that we were both dark. I guess Omar Sharif wasn't available.

Soraya looked ravishingly sophisticated that night in Chanel. I was instantly smitten by her beauty, particularly those emerald green, almond-shaped eyes, her lustrous raven hair, and her smoldering German-accented voice. Soraya's mother, a Russian-born beauty, had married a Persian noble who had become Iran's ambassador to Germany. Soraya had grown up in Europe and exuded an intimidating worldliness, if not indifference.

Everyone else at the dinner was married, a table of tycoons and their trophy wives, not even in "the biz." I can't remember what we all talked about, the Cuban missile crisis, desegregation at Old Miss, Linus Pauling's Nobel Prize, but whatever it was seemed to bore the queen to death. She became animated only when the conversation shifted to show business, where she seemed fascinated by even the silliest television shows, like *Gunsmoke* and *Dobie Gillis,* not to mention the big stuff Hollywood was doing, like *Spartacus* and *The Alamo.* She asked me about my upcoming acting projects. To me they were just jobs; to Soraya, "art." Of course I humored her to the hilt. At some point in the evening she told me she was interested in going out to Palm Springs. She also mentioned that she had an invitation from Old Blue Eyes.

"Old Blue Eyes?" I asked.

"Yes, Frankie Boy. Frank Sinatra," she said in that heavy German accent.

Getting invited by Frank Sinatra to Palm Springs was like getting invited by the pope to the Vatican. "But I said no. He is too old," she said, almost with a yawn. Rejecting the Chairman of the Board, I supposed, was the prerogative of queens. But she still wanted to see Palm Springs, and by the end of the evening I volunteered to drive her down in my Bentley, and the queen accepted.

Lee Anderson was, if possible, even more thrilled than I was. She arranged for us to be "invited" to Palm Springs for the weekend by a local socialite named Ruth Cutten, who had one of those great sprawling desert modern fifties estates. En route, I got a sense of what royalty really was when Soraya said she felt like some mint tea. We stopped at a coffee shop that happened to be owned by Iranians, a burgeoning ethnic group in the area. Someone recognized Soraya, and it was as if they'd all seen Allah. The entire restaurant, staff, kitchen, and customers all got out of their booths and came from behind the counter to bow down before her. When we left, the queen was far less impressed by the display of power than I was. "I'm not amused," she said. "It's so boring." She said that a lot.

When we reached the desert, we decided to get a bite for dinner before settling in at our hostess's hacienda. We stopped at a joint called Ruby's Dunes, a great favorite of the Hollywood set. By now Palm Springs was becoming the world's resort. President Eisenhower, obsessive golfer that he was, had retired here. And President Kennedy had spent so much time here with his brother-in-law Peter Lawford and the Rat Pack that Frank Sinatra's huge compound was for a time the de facto Western White House. Democrats and Republicans, stars and gangsters alike, all mixed it up at Ruby's Dunes. I thought Soraya would find it entertaining.

She was not entertained, however, when I

tried to order a bottle of champagne and the tuxedoed old-school Italian waiter looked at me and asked, "How old are you?"

"What are you talking about?" I asked. I was only twenty at the time and under the drinking age in California.

"I have to see some identification," he replied.

I stood up and tried to pull him aside. "I'm with the queen," I whispered. "Soraya. Please. Just bring us a bottle of champagne."

He was hard as nails. "I need some ID."

I was in a panic. I sat back down and turned to Soraya. "They don't have the year I want," I improvised. "Let's go."

Discretion being the better part of valor, I led the queen to the door. Suddenly, "You Make Me Feel So Young" came up on the jukebox, belted out by Frank Sinatra. I looked up and saw an amber spotlight shining down on none other than the Chairman himself in a corner of the restaurant with his crew of guys and dolls boisterously yukking it up. Frank was Hollywood's undisputed king of mean practical jokes, and he had just pulled a huge one on me. Still smarting from having recently been snubbed by the queen, Frank was in his nastiest mode.

I'm sure Soraya, who hadn't noticed Sinatra, would have been thrilled to death to hobnob with the legend, even if she didn't want to date him. But I didn't want to push my luck. Frank might have bought us a jeroboam of champagne; then again, he might have poured it on us. You just never knew. We made our way to our digs at the lovely Cutten estate, hard up against the towering mountains of this American Marrakech. We were billeted in separate rooms, with all due propriety. It was all terribly chaste, much more fifties than swinging sixties. We remained strangers in the Palm Springs night.

The next day began formally. Horses had been arranged at Smoketree Stables, and we went for a long ride into the desert canyons. I knew this lady was not for me. She was dressed in jodhpurs and boots. I was in blue jeans. The wide-open desert stretched before us. But then we saw someone else, a silver-haired, darkly tanned man riding all by himself on a white Arabian horse. As we got closer to this lone rider, he greeted me with, "Hello, George," in the most unmistakable accent in show business. It was Cary Grant, now a silver fox, but Cary Grant nonetheless, riding an Arabian beauty of a steed.

We had met when I first arrived on the MGM lot. I was tanning myself with a sun reflector between takes on the sunny side of a sound studio, and Cary was in front of another parallel stage doing the exact same thing. Cary, as big a sun worshipper as I, was delighted to find a man after his own heart. So we became friendly, and he gave me a lot of encouragement in my new career. I obviously idolized him, as did everyone else on earth, and so did Soraya, who was breathless when I introduced her on horseback.

For a queen who had met the most important leaders of the world, Soraya was speechless in Cary's presence, as if he were Muhammad himself. Cary began talking bizarrely, about how everyone would soon be going to the moon. Instead of "Shine On, Harvest Moon," Cary observed, we would be singing, "Shine On, Harvest Earth." Then he rode off. Soraya was deeply impressed. She said he was so brilliant. I found out later that Cary was just entering his LSD phase, and was taking an acid trip on horseback. Cary became the Timothy Leary of Hollywood, long before Leary himself came to town.

Despite his recent megabit *North by Northwest,* Cary was starting to scale back on his film career. Been there, done that, was his attitude. He told me he didn't want to grow old on film. He preferred to be remembered young. With his name permanently up in

lights, he was now looking for enlighten-
ment. Movies to him, he often told me when
he was lucid, were simply a job. "Nobody
impersonates Cary Grant better than me,"
he would say.

That evening our hostess Ruth Cutten
gave a dinner party for us, and Cary Grant
dropped by, not in black tie, as the other
guests, but in dungarees, as if he had ridden
his horse over. Palm Springs was still a small
town, and everyone knew everyone else. The
rest of the guests, as at Lee's party, consisted
of the resident tycoonery, with no memorable showbiz types in attendance. But with
Cary Grant there, you didn't need anyone
else. Cary was not appreciably less spaced-
out than he had been earlier in the day. But
he was holding his hands up oddly in front
of him, as if he were a doctor just scrubbed
for an operation, waiting for a nurse to put
on his gloves. He also told some Henny
Youngman "take my wife"-style corny jokes.
He didn't like conversation; he preferred
jokes, for he felt, as I often do, that humor
kept things going. "He's so brilliant," was all
the queen could say.

Soraya wanted to ask him about what mattered to her, that is, what it was like playing
opposite that *other* princess, Grace Kelly,
in *To Catch a Thief,* and Sophia Loren in

Houseboat. Soraya knew more about the film business than any agent I had met. Poor Cary, in search of higher meaning, didn't know what to do with her. He kept spouting old chestnuts: "Two Irishman walk out of a bar . . . Could happen." Here was a queen of the Middle East who wanted to be on planet Hollywood, and here was a king of Hollywood who wanted to be in another galaxy.

By evening's end I was totally emboldened, by the champagne, by the full moon over the desert, by the twinkling stars in the sky. Somehow, once everyone else was gone, I was able to steer us back to my room. About to make my big move and kiss her, I told Soraya how amazing her eyes were.

"My eyes," she said in that accent. "Are they too close together?"

"No," I said. "Your eyes are beautiful." I tried again to kiss her.

"My hairline. They want to move back my hairline. And do you think I should change my eyebrows?"

When I raved about her silken hair, all she wanted to know was, in my professional opinion, should she color it? Her beautiful mouth? Should I get my teeth straightened? Her creamy shoulders? Am I too fat? Her sleek legs? Am I too short? Do I need different makeup? This queen was a royal nutcase. She was treating me not as a suitor, not as a star, but as a stylist, a hairdresser, her own personal Wally Westmore. I was an insider, and the queen wanted an inside opinion, because the queen, more than anything on earth, wanted to be a movie star. Cut and print! If Frank only knew what he had been missing, he probably would have thanked me for sparing him the experience.

That had been well over a decade earlier, but Sinatra had never shown any sign of forgetting or forgiving. And so I had no compunctions about hiring George Jacobs. The one with compunctions was Alana. Tina Sinatra was Alana's best friend and would become godmother to our Ashley and later to Alana's son Sean by Rod Stewart. Alana wasn't cool on Gorgeous George because he was trying to hit on her. It was because he wouldn't do any work. He loved dressing stylishly as much as I did, and wouldn't be caught dead in any sort of livery or even a white jacket. His style was hippie jeans, gold chains, cashmere sweaters. As George said, "You want linguine at two A.M. for twelve, I'm your man. But don't ask me to wear butler shit." George wouldn't clean, and although a great Italian cook, he would barely do that either, save on special occasions.

He was happiest having drinks with us by the pool. Frank had basically made George the fifth Beatle; he had paid him lavishly to hang out with him. Other servants did the dirty work. In the end, I couldn't afford the luxury of a trophy employee like George.

My best friend in Palm Springs was Colonel Parker, who lived four blocks away, but if you think we were having wild times with Elvis and the Memphis Mafia, forget it. Elvis and the colonel were all about TCB, "taking care of business" being Elvis's motto. But once the business was done, Elvis partied only with "the guys," not us. Instead, Alana and I would have five o'clock early bird dinners at a place called the Little Lamb House with the colonel and his wife, Marie, whom he had met in the circus when she was running the cookhouse. He called her Miss Rie and was absolutely devoted to her. The colonel had every opportunity to be a swinger, for Elvis had countless girls around him, and Elvis's girls were passionate groupies. They would have done anything for the Man Who Made the King.

But the colonel wasn't the slightest bit interested. He didn't cheat, and he didn't drink, not anything stronger that Mountain Valley Water from Arkansas, which he always had restaurants serve in a champagne bucket.

The colonel's weakness was gambling, which is why he loved Vegas, and why Vegas loved him, for he usually lost most of the fortune Vegas paid him for Elvis at the tables. He might have done his gambling at tonier spots like Monte Carlo and Deauville, but I had heard that the colonel was an illegal alien who didn't dare venture outside America for fear of never being let back in. That's why he never let Elvis perform abroad. He also paid his taxes, to the penny, long in advance. The colonel had done enough tricky business earlier in life that his golden years were all on the very straight and narrow. The old carny wanted nothing more than to be legit.

Palm Springs was where the colonel cared for Miss Rie, who was beginning to get dementia. He had four round-the-clock nurses for her. It became the joint task of Alana and Jane Morgan, the singer wife of the colonel's aide and mogul-to-be Jerry Weintraub, to serve as Miss Rie's best friends, playing games like mah-jongg and Yahtzee. An old-fashioned European, the colonel was as male chauvinist as it got and saw nothing wrong with making our wives be best friends.

This didn't exactly play well with my jet-set model wife, who would have preferred greeting the tourists as Shugborough Hall to playing caregiver for Miss Rie. Alana was having enough problems with her own aging mother, who was drinking and pilling herself into oblivion; she had no need to take on another mom. Plus she hated the idea of eating those poor little lambs at the Little Lamb House that the colonel preferred to Romanoff's. Even though Palm Springs was losing its old cachet as a spa for polo players like Hawks and Zanuck, there were still plenty of glamorous, if aging, stars around: Cary Grant, Sinatra, Elvis himself. But we didn't see them. That wasn't our circle. Our circle was the colonel and Miss Rie, the golden-age producer Hal Wallis, who had done all the Elvis films, and the golden-age manager Bullets Durgom. Alana began champing at the bit, feeling she had given up Grayhall for a retirement home. For all the Hollywood action she wasn't getting, she might as well have stayed in Nacogdoches.

I wouldn't let Alana bite the hand that might be feeding us. At a low fiscal ebb, the colonel, who never charged me a cent, came up with a plan to replenish my coffers. He found out that the International in Vegas had an open week in the dog days of August between Perry Como and Aretha Franklin, and he could get me the gig. I would earn a cool hundred grand, which was big money, Elvis money, in those days. George Hamilton playing Vegas? Don't mind if I do. On second thought, I froze. Aside from the *Ed Sullivan Show,* I had never sung for a crowd. The Big Room of the International was Vegas's largest and hardest room to fill. What would I sing? Who would come? In a panic I turned to my friend Leslie Bricusse, the avatar of all things musical.

Leslie called Sammy Davis Jr., the master showman, for advice. Come on over, Sammy said. Sammy lived close by in Palm Springs, but he wasn't there. He was in Chicago, doing a show. Come on over, to a guy like Sammy, meant a hop, skip, and a jet. Fortunately, Leslie, master logistician, knew where to get the jet. He called Hugh Hefner, who just happened to be flying to Chicago that night on the Playboy DC-9, known as the Black Bunny. Not only would Hef give us an airlift, he would put us up in the Playboy Mansion in Chicago, when that address was the center of the sexual universe. We were surrounded by wall-to-wall pneumatic Playmates, basically dressed in nothing, but I don't think I even noticed. Paralyzed with stage fright, I was amused by one bunny who didn't like the taste of the rare Château Lafite she was being served and began putting sugar in it to make it taste like a soft drink. I took the bottle off her hands and calmed my nerves in high style.

In those days it was said in Hollywood that true insecurity is thinking that Sammy Davis doesn't love you. There has never been a more generous star. The moment he heard my plight over dinner at the Playboy Mansion, Sammy leaped into the breach. Acknowledging how tough the Big Room was, Sammy offered to produce the whole thing, free of charge. The date was only three weeks away, but Sammy dropped everything and came to Vegas to put this extravaganza together. Colonel Parker had envisioned something very modest, like one guitar player, but Sammy would settle for nothing less than a twenty-piece orchestra with a full rhythm section. He got me Lola Falana to open; Elvis's musical director, Joe Guercio; Tom Jones's composer, Johnny Harris; his own costumer, Bernhard; an army of backup singers and dancers; and Sammy's conductor George Rhodes to rehearse me. We did the rehearsals at the Cocoanut Grove in Los Angeles, before going to Vegas. Sammy showed up every day, all day, to try to imbue this white man with rhythm. He was in great spirits. My spirits were brandy Alexanders. I think I had maybe fifteen of them before I hit the stage opening night.

The house was packed, all eighteen hundred seats, probably more than the grand total who saw *Your Cheatin' Heart*. I couldn't believe so many people would come out to hear me sing. I began singing offstage, the Beatles' "What would you do if I sang out of tune, would you stand up and walk out on me?" Although the staging was all Sammy's idea, no words could ever have been more sincerely sung. Then I came onstage, in a tuxedo, to amazingly huge applause, and I read a bunch of congratulatory telegrams, all made up, that allowed me to do impersonations of Cary Grant, Gregory Peck, Jimmy Stewart, and others. The audience seemed to be buying it. I launched into "Wichita Lineman," "The End of a Love Affair," "MacArthur Park," and "This Time We Almost Made it." At this point my microphone went dead. What a disaster! But Sammy stepped out of the shadows to save the show and promptly stole it, but it was all his to steal.

One major glitch was that the great Bernhard's costumes never arrived. Per Sammy's directions, I went offstage and ditched the tux and changed into jeans, and Lola, Sammy, and I got down and got funky, dancing and singing to "Proud Mary" and "Light My Fire." I can't remember the rest, it was such a blur. There were endless standing ovations.

I had pulled off a miracle, with a lot of help from my friends. Backstage Sammy gave me a huge gold necklace, which would be de rigueur if I were to remain a player in Vegas. I was congratulated by Alex "the Cleaver" Shoofey, who ran the International for its shadowy owner Kirk Kerkorian. Shoofey's scary presence made me wonder if I were really cut out to be the next Tom Jones, but I basked in the moment. Alana took pictures of me in front of the Hilton marquee at five A.M. It looked as if I had truly "arrived."

The next day, I slept until five P.M. then got up and did it all over again. This time, however, only a thousand of the seats were filled. The next night it was down to six hundred, and by the weekend, at most two hundred poor souls paid to see me. They kept moving the amps in and closing the curtains to make the room seem more intimate, like the incredible shrinking show. At the end, there were more people onstage than in the audience. I heard a couple ask, "Is he still on?" The second coming of Tom Jones was not to be me. I may have bombed, but at least I was earning a hundred thousand, I consoled myself. Wrong again. The Cleaver burst my bubble when I went to collect. The money was all gone. Sammy had spent thousands upon thousands on orchestra, rehearsals, all the frills. I would get nothing. I had bombed, big time, and you didn't argue with the Cleaver. All I could do was call the colonel. "Come see me," he said.

The colonel convened a five P.M. Sunday dinner in Palm Springs with me, Alana, and Alex Shoofey. And then who should walk in but the King himself. Alana's knees began to shake, just as Teeny's had when she got around one of the men of her dreams. Elvis was dressed in some sort of white cape and a ton of gold chains, sort of a daytime Dracula. He made a lot of small talk, mostly about germs. He showed off the Federal Drug Administration badge President Nixon had given him, his most prized possession: Elvis the narc. Colonel Parker rolled his eyes. It was surreal. We ate our fried chicken, then we got down to business. "How did George do?" the colonel asked Shoofey.

"We lost money," the Cleaver replied, deadpan.

"Did George make money?"

Dead silence.

The colonel went on. "Does that mean if Elvis played and lost money, you wouldn't pay him his guarantee?"

"Elvis doesn't lose," the Cleaver replied, annoyed at the absurdity of the proposition.

"But what if he did?" the colonel pressed.

The Cleaver shot a glance at the King, who was distractedly fondling his badge. "We'd pay Elvis," he grunted. Then Shoofey turned to me, with a look that could kill. "Come see me Monday."

I did, and I collected my hundred grand.

The colonel remained my best friend and father confessor and unofficial manager. He occasionally played games to test my loyalty to him, as he did with anyone he wanted to allow into his orbit. He would call me for a ride back from Palm Springs while I was in L.A., which would have necessitated my driving the long road out there and back. The moment I was in the car about to get going, he'd let me off the hook. Or he would ask for $15,000 in cash, on very short notice, just to see if I could raise it. Nor could I miss those early bird weekend dinners with Miss Rie and her son Bitsy. I always rose to the colonel's occasions and passed all his tests. He was worth it.

I got my best chance to return his many favors several years later. On August 16, 1977, I received a phone call from Colonel Parker advising me of Elvis Presley's funeral arrangements. He simply said that Elvis's private plane, the *Lisa Marie*, was being dispatched from Las Vegas and would pick me up in Los Angeles and fly me to Memphis.

Typical of the colonel, it was short notice. But I wanted to be there. I genuinely admired Elvis. More than that, I was indebted to both him and the colonel for helping me collect my money after my ill-fated Vegas debut.

I didn't recognize most of the people boarding the plane, except for Elvis's backup singers, the Sweet Inspirations. On the flight, the hostess told me about a couple of strange things had happened aboard the plane on the way to L.A. For no reason, the heating blanket on the King's bed had burned up. Then the container that Elvis used to drink his favorite peanut butter milk shakes had broken. Spooky, I thought.

When we arrived at Graceland, the colonel was standing on the porch, silver-headed cane in hand, talking to the Sun Records people. He greeted me, and then barked orders to Joe Esposito to secure Elvis's memorabilia, including what was in Madison, Tennessee, because the public would soon be on a rampage for Elvis souvenirs. Shifting gears, he asked me to go on in and pay my respects. I still remember the super-thick shag carpet so deep you needed snowshoes to cross it.

Elvis was laid out in the parlor in proper Southern fashion: white suit and a blue tie, if I remember correctly. A long line of people waited for their turn to view him. I nearly jumped out of my skin when I heard a deep voice from nowhere singing "In the Sweet Bye and Bye." It turned out to be J. D. Summer standing behind a velvet curtain.

Elvis looked younger than I remembered. I approached the casket for a closer look. That's when I noticed that his hair had been dyed recently and a little line of black dye had rolled down his ear. Leave it to me to notice something like that. What was I going to do with this information? Was I the hair dye police? Let somebody else tell them. But then Charlie Hodges, lead guitarist and the one who always handed the King a replacement scarf when he'd tossed his to the crowd, asked me if I didn't think Elvis looked great. He proudly told me he had dyed Elvis's hair a couple of hours before. "I can see that," I told him and pointed out the problem.

I walked outside. Later I was told they stopped the whole funeral for a few minutes while they dabbed away the dye and inspected things.

The colonel was still sitting on the porch. He appeared pensive as he slowly twisted the gold ring on his finger. The ring had been given to him by a mystic named Zeta in his carny days, way before Elvis, when he was just "Tom Parker and His Dancing Chickens." Years before he had let me in on a little secret: The way he got those chickens to dance was to turn up the heat on the hot plate they were standing on. "Go pay your respects to Elvis," he said. "I've already done that," I replied. But he sent me back in again. I guess the message was that you can't pay enough respect to a fallen king. I did as the colonel said, this time promising myself not to take such a close look.

When the pallbearers carried the casket out to the hearse, there was a terrible rumble as a huge limb from a nearby oak tree broke off and crashed to the ground. Was Elvis taking literally that admonition: "Don't go gentle into that good night"? Following the hearse, a procession of white limos awaited us. There was a limousine for every group in Elvis's varied life: one for his family, one for his gal pals, one for the music moguls, and one for the colonel, manager Jerry Weintraub, RCA Records' George Parkhill, the colonel's right-hand man Tom Diskin, and me. I saw only one other actor in the assemblage, Ann-Margret. She was in a limo reserved for everybody else who didn't fit into a neat pigeonhole.

After a brief graveside service, we returned to Graceland to swap stories with Elvis's cook, the one who had made him those fried peanut butter and banana sandwiches he loved so much. Then before you knew it, I was back on the *Lisa Marie* accompanying Priscilla Presley and the real Lisa Marie, who was dressed like one of the Kennedy children, for the return trip to Los Angeles. Everyone was deep in thought and the mood was quiet.

I like to think I had paid off my marker to Elvis and the colonel in full. They had watched out for me when I needed them most, and now I had watched out for them, in a manner of speaking.

At least I thought the Vegas rescue had been when I needed them most. The payday was a lot, but it was not enough. There's no such word in Hollywood as enough, and with a beautiful model wife whose infinite alternatives to you are always in the forefront of your troubled mind, enough becomes a whole lot more. I decided to spare her the isolation of Palm Springs and move back to Beverly Hills to a rented house on Tower Road.

Now I began doing dinner theater. Not Broadway, not even New Haven or Philadelphia, but Ravenna, Warren, Dayton, and Columbus. The impresario of these productions was a "person" named John Kenley, who lived as a woman in New York but as a man here in the heartland. He liked to ride his bicycle around the theaters. My costars were personalities like Monique Van Vooren and Helmut Berger, from *The Damned,* which said it all. I'd had better audiences and better material when I was doing *Brigadoon* at Palm Beach High School. But I never felt how the mighty had fallen. It wasn't like Laurence Olivier being reduced to doing *Grease* in summer stock. But if my philosophy was that I was acting to support a lifestyle, the lifestyle I was able to support would have landed Alana and me in a little Midwestern split-level. People who had a certain image of me wanted to believe I was off in Monte Carlo when I was actually in Dayton. I didn't want to spoil their fantasies. Alana would come with me if I could get her a lead role in the show. The best thing that happened in Ohio was that Ashley was conceived there.

While I was treading the boards in the heartland suburbs, Alana was tripping the light fantastic with a very fast group of Beverly Hills wives that included Tina Sinatra; Dani Janssen (wife of *The Fugitive,* David); Ann Turkel, Scarsdale heiress and supermodel wife of Richard Harris; Joanna Pettet, still another Bond girl married to television star Alex Cord; and international playgirl Barbara Carrera. The master of ceremonies for Alana's revels was Allan Carr, the flaming caftan-clad impresario who would produce *Grease* as well as the Academy Awards shows.

I hit a low ebb when I contracted hepatitis from eating bad oysters in Clearwater, Florida, while doing *6 Rms Riv Vu.* I went down to Palm Beach and checked into Good Samaritan Hospital, where I was given a lovely room with a sun terrace. I didn't look yellow, only more deeply tanned. One Hollywood producer friend, Francis Ford Coppola's right hand Gray Frederickson, came to see me. He found me in silk pajamas lounging on my deck and said, "You never looked better." He thought he was at a spa, not a hospital. But I was sick indeed. I never had a visit from Alana, who I felt was afraid of illness. She had spent much of her life caring for her mother, so when I, Mister Suntanned Picture of Health, fell ill, it was like, "Not you, too!" Teeny and Bill did come to see me, and it marked the beginning of a rapprochement that made me feel better than anything else.

I was broke, deathly sick, and Alana was pregnant. I somehow got home to Los Angeles, where Gloria Swanson found me one of her doctors who wasn't a faith healer. Alana would make me dinner, but she didn't like sitting by my sickbed. She always had a very important party to go to. I remember dragging my jaundiced corpus out of my sickbed and sneaking over to Carr's to peer through the windows at what Alana was having to go out for.

I needed to heal fast and earn some money. I somehow survived and got a starring role in a television zombie movie with Ray Milland and Joan Blondell. The title was *The Dead Men Die,* which was the story of my life at this point. Then Ashley was born, the most beautiful child I could ever imagine. But even he couldn't save our marriage. Naturally, Alana thought I had done her wronger than she had done me. She wouldn't forgive me for leaving for still another dinner theater date in 1975 the night her mother died at Cedars-Sinai Hospital. Tina Sinatra was there with her, but I was not. Alana's grandmother had died the year before, so the loss of her mother, as badly as they had gotten along, was the coup de grâce. But even in my way off-Broadway world, the show must go on. Thus I went, and Alana would never forgive me.

Then there was the matter of Steve Mc-Queen. Even though Steve was married to

Ali MacGraw, he and Alana had already hit it off, two gorgeous country kids, I suppose, abandoned by their fathers, with alcoholic mothers, raised by other relatives, who were on their own at an early age. Steve, who was the biggest, most highly paid movie star in the world in the early seventies, began coming on to Alana, and he was pretty surly to me. One day, however, he became very nice and tried to get me to enter a motorcycle race in Elsinore, where he would be competing. How could I, Mr. Evel Knievel himself, turn him down? I may have been a faux Evel, but Steve was the real deal, having done many of his own stunts in *The Great Escape.*

I got the paranoid idea that Steve wanted to lure me up to Elsinore, where he would "accidentally" run me off the road and then have Alana all to himself. Then my stuntman friend from *Evel,* Everett Creach, called me the day of the race to warn me that it was pouring rain and that Steve was hoping I'd go down. My paranoia confirmed, I bailed out. Alana insisted there was nothing whatsoever between them. However, when we finally got divorced, very amicably at that, I frequently found Steve's favorite beer in our former conjugal refrigerator, where no beer of any kind had appeared previously on our shelves. When I found Steve's motorcycle in our garage, Sherlock Hamilton closed the case, but I'd rather have been wrong.

Before we finally split, Ann Turkel sent Alana to a self-styled hippie "shrink to the stars," Eugene Landy. Landy had begun his psychiatric career as a record producer, having discovered a shoeshine boy named George Benson and propelled him to stardom as a guitarist. He went back to school to get a psychology degree and published a book called *The Underground Dictionary,* a psychedelic Webster's. Landy was just what L.A. wanted, and his star clients included Alice Cooper, Rod Steiger, and Gig Young and his wife, who shot each other in a suicide pact. Landy would become notorious, and eventually lose his license, for becoming the full-time in-house shrink/Svengali to the wacky genius Beach Boy Brian Wilson. Landy told Alana that I "didn't hear her feelings." She took his analysis as gospel. We did try another couples therapist. She had me sit there and hold a doll called "Little Georgie" in my lap. That was the "inner me," and the therapist asked me, "What does Little Georgie want?" As I was about to bare my soul, the therapist suddenly realized that she had to run out, in the midst of our biggest crisis session, because she had an appointment to get her hair done. She left me high and dry, holding "Little Georgie."

I fell back on Christian Science principles and went to see a nutritionist on Hollywood Boulevard named Mason Rose. I was still weak from the hepatitis and needed all my strength to deal with my crumbling marriage and career. I thought we would have a discussion of orthomolecular medicine; instead we talked feelings, which were not my strong suit then. Southern men weren't supposed to have feelings, just duties. We were supposed to be strong and stalwart. Feelings were for Yankees. Rose gave me some good advice. He noted that, chivalrous Southern gent that I tried to be, I deferred too much to others. I liked to talk, he saw. Why not listen to *myself?* Get to know "me"?

I tried to reach out to Alana, but embracing her suddenly became like hugging a Frigidaire. She didn't seem to like my new vulnerability. Real men, Texas men, didn't get sick. And her party life just got to me, party man that I had been. I thought she was fiddling while Rome was burning, not taking my plight seriously. In the end, Alana moved on to greater things. I gave her half of all I had, paid up the nanny who cared for Ashley, and drove off in my yellow Rolls. Appearances still counted, no matter what.

I was terribly sad. I had really wanted

to settle down and I had chosen the least settled-down woman on the planet. I had wanted someone soft and feminine but found that underneath that blond goddess exterior was a cowboy as tough as John Wayne. What we had was less a marriage than a competition. Astrologers have told us that we were the wrong match, two hardheads. Alana was a Taurus, a raging bull; I was a Leo, perhaps not a roaring lion, but stubborn nonetheless. But somehow I think Alana reminded me of my mother: pretty, funny, and Southern to boot. I now realized if I wanted my mother, I'd better go back to the real thing.

Before I did, I crashed at the palatial estate of Bob Evans, which was like a halfway house for dispossessed husbands, a kind of Playboy Mansion for the film colony, with hot and cold running starlets. Bob was very generous. He had loved and lost a lot of beautiful women and was still smarting over the loss of Ali MacGraw to Steve McQueen, so we had plenty of horror stories to share. Alana notwithstanding, my intention was to settle down, not live it up, as would have been the case chez Bob.

Whenever I was down and depressed, I sought solace in sun and sea. I couldn't get to Acapulco, because I didn't want to be too far from Ashley. So I went to the closest version thereof, Marina del Rey, still in its swinging stewardess bachelor party incarnation. A producer friend, George Schlatter, had a boat down there, and we had breakfast together. An Alabama boy who produced the hit TV series *Rowan and Martin's Laugh-In,* George, as funny as his show, was always good to cheer you up. He restored my spirits and helped me decide to move into a Marina hotel until I got my act together. My idea was to hide out in the Marina, but the idea of hiding out in a yellow Rolls-Royce with a license plate that read GSHI — well, so much for hiding out.

I did get another movie. The title says it all: *The Happy Hooker Goes to Washington.* It was the diametric opposite of staying in the Lincoln Bedroom while dating Lynda Bird Johnson. The movie, made in 1976, was a sequel to *The Happy Hooker,* based on the best seller about the Dutch-born super-madam of Manhattan, Xaviera Hollander. In the first film, the British actress Lynn Redgrave brought a touch of class to the proceedings. For the sequel, Lynn had bowed out, replaced by Joey Heatherton, the one-time sex kitten and Rat Pack playgirl. Joey had cohosted Dean Martin's *Golddiggers* on television and was Bob Hope's sidekick on all his Vietnam USO tours. She was her generation's answer to Betty Grable, a huge pinup heartthrob for GIs.

Joey, sad to say, was the most difficult actress I ever worked with. She had sunk into cocaine and was later to the set than Marilyn Monroe at her worst. With her paranoia perhaps fueled by her drug of choice, Joey was convinced I was trying to steal all our scenes from her. I was playing her defense lawyer. As far as I was concerned, she was welcome to the scenes, and the whole movie, which had such inspired casting as the dwarf Billy Barty as a CIA agent and Ray Walston, *My Favorite Martian,* as a senator. Ray wished he had stayed on Mars.

Prankster that I could be, when pushed to the wall as I was, I decided to make Joey's worst dreams come true and steal a scene from her. We were in the back of a limo. I opened my briefcase and began flossing my teeth, then combing my hair for bad measure. Joey went crazy. She jumped out of the moving limo and nearly killed herself. That was it for two-shots. She refused to do another with me.

I thought it couldn't get worse than *Hooker,* but lightning struck twice. I got a call from a Mr. Fixit lawyer named Harry Weiss, who made his money defending moving violations and DUIs and spent it on rare antique furniture. I obviously had met him through Bill. Harry, whose trademark was his velvet fedora, had a rich client from Vegas, a Swanson food heiress, who wanted to invest in a film. In my heyday, or even less, I would have run for the Hollywood hills, but beggars couldn't be choosers. These were the days when an icon like Laurence Olivier would take big bucks from the eventually imprisoned Reverend Sun Myung Moon of the Korean cult Unification Church to star as General MacArthur in the disaster *Inchon.* Who was I to turn down a job?

But what a job! The movie was *Sextette,* starring Mae West, based on a play she had written, judging from the sex farce plot, in the Roaring Twenties when she was in her prime. The story had something to do with a peace conference where the delegates, some of whom have been married to Mae, all want to sleep with her, with riotous consequences. Now Mae was eighty-five, but in her mind time has stood still. She saw herself, and demanded that others see her, the same way Cary Grant did when she mesmerized him in *She Done Him Wrong.* What the Swanson heiress was thinking when she agreed to finance this monstrosity I can't imagine. I never met her. Maybe she was Mae's contemporary. Maybe she had sold enough chicken broth not to care.

I know what the rest of the cast was thinking, all the way to the bank. It was a stellar affair: Timothy (later James Bond) Dalton, Tony Curtis, Ringo Starr, Alice Cooper, Keith Moon, Walter Pidgeon, Dom DeLuise, even George Raft, a younger version of whom I was to play, spats and all, as Mae's gangster ex. When I met Mae for our first scene, I thought I was in Madame Tussaud's on acid. She was all of four feet tall, with platform shoes a foot high and hair a foot and a half. Here was our dialogue.

Me: "Hi baby, long time no grab."

Mae: "Vance, Vance, I thought you were dead. I was in mourning for three weeks. When I played on the piano, I only played on the black keys . . . a little to the left . . . What? . . . Cut. Cut . . . a little to the left . . ."

It sounded somehow as if it was coming out of Mae's hair. I turned in shell shock to my dresser, who said, "She's wired up," and pointed to the director. Then I realized that it was coming out of her hair. Mae was wearing an earpiece wherein her lines were being fed to her, and she just repeated them — and anything else the director said. We went back to work.

Mae called me into her dressing room to

tell me she always made love to her leading men. Then she asked me my sign. "I'm a Leo," I said.

"I'm a double thyroid," Mae riposted, as ready with a quip as she had been in her heyday forty years before. She took a glossy of herself and signed it for me. "To Vance. Sincerely, Mae West."

Mae took to me and invited me for drinks at the Ravenswood, her classic old apartment house in Hollywood. Roddy McDowall was there as well. Mae's boyfriend, a giant muscleman, literally carried her into the living room, where all the furniture was covered in plastic. At dinner in the valley we talked about the twenties and her gangster boyfriend, Owney Madden, who owned the Cotton Club in Harlem. Mae remembered every line of every song of the era, and she was great fun. There was a terrible moment when there was a gunshot boom in the restaurant, and the place went dead silent. Mae's hair band, which held her face up, had snapped with a bang, and her face collapsed. The muscleman took her out to repair the damage; she returned like a trouper and kept singing to us.

I'm glad Mae liked me, for she could be a viper. No sweet little old lady she. She was rough on Tony Curtis. One day on the set, she said, "My bodyguard's got more hair on his chest than Tony has on his head." Tony, who was wearing a toupee and was vain as a man could be, heard every word and was devastated for weeks. Ringo sat at her feet, as in awe of her as any Beatlemaniac would be of him. He had seen every one of her films as a kid in Liverpool and recited them to her chapter and verse. I got to know George Raft, who was one of Teeny's girlhood idols, as well as Regis Philbin, whose show I would later guest-host many times. So, unlike *Hooker, Sextette* was not without its redeeming values. Today, it's considered a camp classic. In Hollywood, that's why no one, up or down, can never say never.

CHAPTER THIRTEEN
THRILLA IN MANILA

Probably the only real silver lining in my split with Alana was my reunion with Teeny and Bill. I had missed them. They had made me what I was, for better or for worse, and I couldn't really turn my back on them, even if I felt they were stabbing me in it. To err is human; to forgive, divine, and I was all for divinity. I'm sure they were equally glad to have their boy back in their hearts, even though the cash cow I used to be had been milked dry. Teeny and Bill were the least provident souls on earth, and despite their antique furniture windfall, money was always an issue.

I had stayed friends with my first real flame, Betty Benson, who had in turn made and stayed friends with Teeny and Bill and kept me up to date on them. Betty continued to be married to Sam Spiegel, despite his many mistresses and his young son by one of them, but Betty always had a life of her own as well. One of her longtime swains was record mogul Morris "Mo" Levy, founder of Roulette Records and considered the godfather of rock and roll, because of his pioneering work in the field but also because of his ties to the Mafia. Bronx-born Mo, who used to own the club Birdland, was no business philistine. He wrote the doo-wop anthem "Why Do Fools Fall in Love?" or at least stole credit from singer Frankie Lymon. Like Sam Spiegel, Mo Levy, who shared Sam's taste for the high life and owned racehorses, was someone you didn't mess with.

Betty had gone to visit Teeny and Bill in Palm Beach while Mo was at the track in Hialeah. Bill and Teeny were throwing a glamorous cocktail party for Betty, with all the swells of the area invited. But when Betty arrived, Teeny was nowhere to be found. She couldn't face her guests and was locked in her room, weeping hysterically. Betty had never seen the ebullient, unflappable Teeny in such dire straits. What was wrong was that Teeny had gotten a foreclosure notice. She hadn't been able to pay her mortgage for months, and now the bank was getting tough.

Betty swung into action and tracked down Mo in Miami, or wherever he was. Big and burly and the antithesis of Teeny's soigné friends from the Everglades Club, Mo came up to Palm Beach and huddled with Betty, who told him the problem. No problem, Mo said, and handed Betty a huge wad of hundreds, $18,000 in all, enough to pay off Teeny's mortgage for months, if not years, to come. Teeny thumbed through the money, counting it in disbelief, over and over, then threw it up in the air like confetti. She rolled around in the sea of green on her bed. This was paradise. The godfather of rock had become Teeny's fairy godfather. No man, big or small, could resist the siren call of Betty Benson.

When I reunited with my family, they had gone back to their Southern roots, or at least an idealized version of them, by spending much of their time in Natchez, Mississippi. Bill had found a Napoleon III-style mansion named Glen Auburn to restore, and he did it proud, establishing it as a feature on the city's famous Garden Tour. Natchez is without question the most beautiful, best-preserved, and most evocative city of the Old South, heaven for antiques mavens like Bill. No place had more grand white-columned plantation homes with names like Dunleith and D'Evereux. It was *Gone With the Wind* that wasn't gone.

I was so entranced with Natchez that I

bought a plantation there myself, a great estate up the Mississippi north of town called Cedars. I sensed Natchez was way undervalued and got the plantation for what I would have paid for some Eisenhower-era ranch house in Encino. To me Natchez was as unique as Venice, Italy. It was only a matter of time before the world would discover it. It was also completely anti-Hollywood, which was great, though because of Ashley I would continue to keep a home in California. Furthermore, my purchase of Cedars was a vote for family solidarity. My mother would always declare, "Can't we all just live together and be happy?" Thomas Wolfe may have written you can't go home again, but I thought he was wrong. Natchez was my homecoming. I would soon buy six properties there.

How, you may wonder, could I become the Donald Trump of the Cotton Kingdom? Certainly not on *Happy Hooker* residuals. Things had changed for me. I should have shot Bob Kaufman, the screenwriter of *Hooker,* but he was so crazy and funny that I somehow knew one day he would get his brilliance on the script page. In 1977, that brilliance was confined to Leslie Bricusse's swimming pool, where Bob, who began his creative life as a stand-up comic, would pitch all his harebrained ideas. One was "Debbie Dybbuk," about a little girl who was possessed by Mel Brooks and spoke in his Brooklyn accent. Another was "How the West Was Shrunk," about a psychiatrist in the Wild West.

Then Bob came up with "Dracula Sucks." I can't even remember what his story line was, but Dracula had always amused me, and I began doing a Dracula imitation by the pool, or actually, my impersonation of Lenny Bruce doing Dracula. And that led to the idea of Dracula in contemporary New York City, coke-snorting, disco-going, gang-infested, gay-ascendant, pre-Giuliani New York City, the metropolis that had nearly gone bankrupt and that had elicited the famous newspaper headline, "Ford to City: Drop Dead." America hated New York then. The idea of a courtly European bloodsucking aristocrat tossed into this cesspool of bad manners struck me as the perfect fish-out-of-water story that all the studios said they were looking for in what was the beginning of the era of high concept.

Bob Kaufman, insane though he was, sparked to the idea immediately. He "loved" it. Of course in Hollywood, no one with any sense of reality takes such declarations of love seriously. When it came from studio executives, "I love it" was shorthand for "I hate it. Go fuck yourself!" But Bob had his own manic integrity, forged out of desperation for a deal. At the time, like most denizens of the business, he was living far beyond his means, with a Rolls-Royce and other status-symbolic attempts to "do" Beverly Hills with his wife, Robin. He would need a *Godfather* blockbuster just to pay his back debts. But as P. T. Barnum said, there's a sucker born every minute, and I had found a rich guy from Detroit to fund "How the West Was Shrunk." Bob had given me an idea to sell, so I sold it to my backer. Then I found out Bob had already sold this same idea to someone else. I needed a new idea. Enter "Dracula Sucks," from my poolside riffs. I went back to my money guy, said I had an even better idea. He agreed and gave me double the money for our development deal.

Bob had a problem, though. He couldn't get beyond his one-liners and actually write the script. Just as I had had to motivate John Milius to write the *Evel Knievel* script, I had to take a similar approach with Bob Kaufman. He was a mess, curled up under his bed, stoned on Valium. I put hundred-dollar bills on the table of his Beverly Hills Hotel suite, lining them up like roach powder. One by one, the hundreds lured him out from under the bed, and the pages started to flow. It wasn't long before we had a very funny script.

But that's all we had. The backer from Detroit had script money but not movie money. We needed more, a lot more. Enter the guy from Indianapolis. This was Mel Simon, an enormously successful shopping center developer I had met through Tina Sinatra. Fortunately, Alana and I had stayed cordial, so we didn't have to divide up our friends. Mel was an unlikely mogul, but then again, very few modern film financiers fit the cigar-chomping, polo-playing, starlet-engulfed Darryl Zanuck mode. A huge bear of a man, Mel's one stylistic idiosyncrasy was that he was an odd dresser, like a psychedelic country clubber: pink shirts, electric blue slacks, orange socks. I'm glad Teeny didn't see him then, for she might have cost me the film. When I met Mel, he was fifty, almost a billionaire, and ready to have a little fun with his money. Why else do people gamble? Mel and his wonderful wife, Bren, were coming to Hollywood the way other high rollers took their risks in Vegas.

Bob and I did a song and dance of "Dracula Sucks" for Mel, and we made him laugh, to the tune of $3.5 million, still relative chicken feed when the average movie cost $20 million to produce. But we weren't Lucas or Spielberg or even Coppola, so it looked like Mel was taking the long shot of all time. Our little film didn't exactly have star power. For a director, we hired Stan Dragoti, who was the husband of Alana's supermodel friend Cheryl Tiegs. Stan had made only one little film before, but he was a huge success in commercials and was the mastermind of the "I Love New York" campaign that helped put the strapped city on its feet.

The biggest actress we could afford was Susan Saint James, who had been costarring with Rock Hudson in the hit TV series *McMillan & Wife* and wanted a switch to the big screen. Susan was a beautiful hippie, with kids named Harmony and Sunshine, but she had superb comic timing and easily fit the part of the jaded Manhattan model that I, as Dracula, was to fall for on-screen, and I, as George Hamilton, would fall for offscreen. Susan had the rare skill of knowing when to throw a line away, while most actors hang on for dear life. We had a great give-and-take, both in the movie and in real life. My theory was that no woman could really resist an old-fashioned man in charge. I may have been a chauvinist, but I was no pig. I liked picking up checks, when that

act of chivalry was considered an anteced-
ent to sexual harassment. The way I saw it,
Drac and I weren't really that different, both
anachronisms addicted to good manners
and projecting old-world charm.

I watched a lot of old movies, to get all the
old twenties speak, "twenty-three skiddoo"
and such, for my Drac. I was very inspired
by *Death Takes a Holiday.* My idea for our film
was to have Death get the girl. That was our
biggest hurdle, and biggest innovation. Nobody wanted Dracula to be the hero. But I
did, and Mel, who pretended he was clueless
about the business, but wasn't clueless about
anything, let me do it my way. This was my
first genuine comedy, although many of my
previous films had been screamingly if inadvertently hilarious. I realized that I had been
trying to emulate Errol Flynn when I should
have been trying to channel Cary Grant.
Cary felt a lot more natural.

Every man involved with the film — Stan,
Bob, myself, the producer Joel Freeman,
who was Dore Schary's nephew — felt it
was *his* story, trying to win over an impossible woman. We thought if such widely di-
verse characters as ourselves could identify
with Dracula, there might be a lot of others
out there who would feel the same way. We
changed the title to the much more suitably

courtly *Love at First Bite,* and, when it came out in 1979, we had a smash, my first "monster" hit. The film grossed over $50 million domestically and was even bigger globally. Dracula was a household name everywhere, and now so was George Hamilton. I still wasn't a big name at Chase Manhattan, given the vagaries of Hollywood accounting, but Mel immediately signed me up to do another movie, at four times the budget. The new film would be another comic homage to an old-fashioned household name, Zorro, entitled *Zorro, the Gay Blade.* I would play both the Z-man and his long-lost gay brother. Here I would be channeling Flynn, Grant, and my brother Bill too.

But long before I could get started on *Zorro,* I had to go around the world selling *Love.* Stan couldn't go, because he was arrested at the Frankfurt Airport bringing cocaine to the Cannes Film Festival. It was for recreational purposes, but it didn't matter. Cheryl Tiegs left him, and Stan went briefly to jail, but he had a hit movie, so Hollywood forgave him.

It was amazing to me what an aphrodisiac success could be. Right after *Love* broke big, Susan Saint James and I went our separate but friendly ways (most Hollywood romances don't last longer than the shoot), and I met

Sylvia Kristel, the Dutch-born star of *Emmanuelle,* the glossy French soft-core porn film and its several sequels, all of which made fortunes. Sylvia spoke five languages fluently and was currently taking a hiatus from her English boyfriend, Ian McShane (star of today's *Deadwood*). It was love at first bite, as it were, and I invited Sylvia to join me on my promo trip to Buenos Aires the day after our first hot date. Because I had seen *Emmanuelle,* I had a pretty good preview of what that trip might entail, which was enough to make this vampire blush.

We flew down to BA on Aerolineas Argentinas, whose 747 upstairs bar was an airborne Polo Lounge. Our first stop was Bogotá, where I hit the ground running so hard and so long that I had no time at all for my sinuous consort, and even less in Buenos Aires. My public relations people were taking this tour dead seriously. I may have expected an expense account romp, but all I did were wall-to-wall interviews and ribbon cuttings. My chief minder was Enrique Herreras, a Spaniard who had previously been the manager of Julio Iglesias. Enrique, whose father was an art-collecting impresario, was as serious as an old guard Spaniard could be and as militarily disciplined as General Franco. Fun was not in his vocabulary, plus he hated

Sylvia. Naturally, Sylvia felt seduced and abandoned.

When we hit Japan, Sylvia turned the tables. Huge crowds of men turned out to see her. I had enough trouble opening opposite the new James Bond movie, *Moonraker*. Roger Moore and I had to fight it out for all the top interviews, though neither of us had any idea what we were being asked. The entire junket was lost in translation. According to Enrique, Dracula "beat" James Bond in Tokyo. As for Sylvia, she had had enough with trying to share a spotlight. Our honeymoon ended before it even could begin, and she flew back to France.

Enrique had set up a state luncheon in Manila at Malacañang Palace, so I flew on to the Philippines and checked into the newly restored Manila Hotel, which had been MacArthur's headquarters during the war. There was no time to relax. I went right to Malacañang, the arcaded Spanish colonial mansion that had also housed William Howard Taft, the American governor-general when we controlled the Philippines after the Spanish-American War. There is no other country where Americans receive such unconditional love as the Philippines. We freed them from the Spanish; we freed them from the Japanese. MacArthur said,

"I shall return," and he did. They hadn't stopped thanking us.

Having traveled the world in the sixties and seventies when the war in Vietnam made the Ugly Americans the most hated of world travelers, the welcome I received in the Philippines was a revelation. Being a movie star didn't hurt, either. Makati, the Beverly Hills section of Manila, had its own Little Hollywood, with a nascent film industry based on our own, run by the Chinese who lived in this melting pot of cultures where nothing really melted and everyone still clung to their identities.

The idea of turning Manila into a major film center was the tie that initially bound me to the first lady, Imelda Marcos. The Iron Butterfly, as her critics called her, was intent on bringing her third-world nation into the first, and she was savvy enough to understand the ambassadorial function that film could have. I can't see Queen Elizabeth screening *Love at First Bite* at Buckingham Palace, but that's what made me like Imelda from the start, her total lack of pretension and her commitment to fun. "I can give you anything but sleep," she told me early on, and she kept her word. We met at that first luncheon watching a folkloric dance recital with her Blue Ladies, a retinue of the wives of the ten most powerful men in the country. "We'd like to see your movie," decreed Imelda, who insisted on first names right off the bat. So I came back for dinner to show *Love* and met "the Dictator," as his critics called him.

For a so-called dictator, Ferdinand Marcos seemed awfully civilized. Speaking flawless, unaccented English, he roared with laughter and got every joke, jokes that may have gone over the heads of lots of Americans outside the Big Apple. Marcos was impressive. A brilliant lawyer, he had survived the Bataan Death March and become a war hero, then quickly rose to the top of the political pyramid. Imelda, an attractive blend of Spanish and Filipino blood, was very tall. She had a bachelor's degree in education and had been a beauty queen, working her way up the pageant circuit from the Rose of Tacloban to Miss Leyte to Muse of Manila, which was a kind of Miss Congeniality runner-up prize after she just missed becoming Miss Manila. By marrying Ferdinand Marcos, Imelda in effect became Mrs. Philippines. She took her show on the road, establishing diplomatic relations for her country with Red China, the Soviet Union, Libya, and Cuba. It wasn't all champagne receptions, though. In 1972, a political enemy tried to assassinate Imelda at a reception broadcast on national television, stabbing her multiple times. The assassin was shot to death on the air; Imelda got seventy-five stitches and survived.

At the palace, I was introduced to their children, Imee (little Imelda), Bong Bong (little Ferdy), Irene, and Aimee, each a paragon of local hospitality, chips off the old blocks. I saw no evidence of Imelda's alleged Marie Antoinette behavior, the thousands of shoes and minks and palace discos with Old Masters on the walls. I did hear from Fred Horowitz, Harry Winston's man in Europe, that Imelda was, with the Saudi princes and the Sultan of Brunei, Winston's top customer and the woman with the world's greatest jewelry collection. But there was no flaunting this when we met. I was treated as if I were the king, and the Marcoses were my devoted subjects.

Like all people, great and small, all the Marcoses wanted to talk about was movies. President Marcos wanted badly to make a big movie about everyone's hero, General MacArthur. When they found out that I had not only been best boyhood pals with Arthur MacArthur but also was an Arkansan like the general, the Marcoses got very excited. Imelda launched into a true story that was also a film pitch. As a little girl she had delivered a box of candy from MacArthur to a Filipino woman he had fallen in love with when he was on his first tour of duty in the Philippines, following his graduation from West point. He had then gone home to marry a Philadelphia Main Line heiress, the "right" kind of woman, but not the woman he loved. This unrequited love, Imelda explained, was the key to MacArthur's obsession with the Philippines, and why he returned, again and again. Within hours of landing with one of the greatest expeditionary forces in history, MacArthur was at this woman's door, with Imelda serving as the go-between.

What the Marcoses wanted to make was not a big war story, but an epic interracial love story, *Sayonara* crossed with *The Longest Day,* with a touch of *Madame Butterfly.* They asked me if I would help them. How could I refuse? The next day they screened *Gandhi* at the palace to show the epic scope of what they wanted to do. "Who should play the general?" the president asked me. I'm not sure if it was a loaded question, but feeling my oats with the success of *Bite,* I volunteered my own services as actor/producer. The Marcoses were thrilled, and I was thrilled that they were thrilled. They basically offered me a blank check to put the film together. I didn't see this as some Hollywood snow job but rather as another *Patton*. After all, no general had more drama in his life than MacArthur. I figured it was a golden opportunity to win an Oscar.

I told the Marcoses I had the perfect screenwriter for the project, and I went back to Hollywood to get him. John Milius, my *Evel Knievel* writer, had just hit the big time with *Apocalypse Now*. He was obsessed with war. He was a natural. The Marcoses sent me a courier with $1 million to offer him. He turned me down. Why? *Apocalypse* had been shot in the Philippines, and John, who stayed off location, had heard all the horror stories about the shoot from Coppola and company. He was terrified of the bugs, the snakes, the weather. No money was enough to overcome these fears. Some warrior. Without my dream writer, I had to put MacArthur on the back burner. While I was looking for another scribe, I came up with the idea to shoot *Zorro* in the Philippines. There was plenty of Spanish atmosphere from colonial times, and the film-hungry Marcoses would provide amazing incentives. But Mel Simon's production people, Bob Relyea and Milt Goldstein, were as chicken as John Milius was. Bob and Milt insisted on Mexico, so we shot in Cuernavaca and drank a lot of tequila.

I was intent on not letting MacArthur slip away. I was aware that Marcos himself, for all his modesty, was considered to be the richest man in all Asia, and Imelda was considered to be the most effective first lady on the planet, always doing what she set out to do. This wasn't going to be some typical Hollywood "I love it" kiss-of-death situation. The Marcoses wanted this movie, and whatever Imelda wanted, Imelda got. As part of her movie mania, she decided to establish the Manila Film Festival, to make Manila the Cannes of the Orient, showcasing the emerging Asian cinema amid the Hollywood blockbusters and European art films. Given the explosion of film in China alone, she was way ahead of her time.

I was honored to be on the guest list. The early 1982 kickoff festival was a very mixed bag, and included everyone from Peter Ustinov to Jeremy Irons to Priscilla Presley to Pia Zadora. For all her Old Masters, Imelda could never be accused of being a highbrow snob. One of the movies shown was a Filipino favorite starring the local midget star Weng Weng, called *For Your Height Only*.

No one could throw a party like Imelda. The festival was far more lavish than Cannes. She had events at all the landmarks of Manila, from the Malacañang Palace to the sixteenth-century Fort Santiago, where, bedecked in her Harry Winston finery, she presided over a medieval pageant reminiscent of both Holy Week in Seville, with floats bearing jeweled figures of baby Jesus, and Carnaval in Rio, with half-naked dancers and rocking bands. At the fort she served a dinner for two thousand, with huge Batangas buffaloes (the Kobe beef of the country) roasting on spits and Moët poured from jeroboams. For sunbathers looking for the Cannes experience, she imported millions of dollars' worth of Australian white sand to create a beach near Manila where starlets could sun topless. That was hospitality.

Terrorists threatened to blow up Imelda's newly opened palace of cinema, which was a copy of the Parthenon in Athens, and a lot of stars, like Charlton Heston and Faye Dunaway, may have been scared away, but nothing happened and they missed a great time. I was photographed dancing with Imelda, which set off endless rumors in the world tabloid press that we were having a torrid affair. Nothing could have been further from the truth. Imelda had an entourage around her at all times, with far more duties than I had on my press junket for *Bite.* If I couldn't find time for Emmanuelle, Imelda certainly couldn't find time, romantic time, for me.

Besides, that wasn't her style. She was extremely Catholic, extremely proper, and extremely loyal to her husband. She was also very innocent. She loved songs like "Feelings" and "Boogie Woogie Bugle Boy." She had cute little throw pillows everywhere, embroidered with silly sayings like "Good Girls Go to Heaven, Bad Girls Go Everywhere" and "Nouveau Riche Is Better Than No Riche at All." Imelda was an old-fashioned romantic, not a femme fatale. Like all Filipinos, her heroes were American GIs. She was afraid to sleep in the dark, always having an aide with her to keep the lights on. She also suffered from glaucoma, and because her sight was extrafragile and hence precious, she wanted to surround herself with beauty. Her idea of a truly great time was to go driving around the barrios, distributing rice to peasants. Despite her beauty queen past, she was shy and had stage fright. She was uncomfortable with the power of being first lady but rose to the occasion when it was thrust upon her.

President Marcos might not have been as loyal to Imelda as she was to him, supposedly exercising his droit du seigneur with her Blue Ladies, but this was a man's world, all Spanish macho, with a double standard that

442

Imelda lived by. Thus Imelda and I were just good friends, but I mean good, and we grew very close when we were both beset by family health problems in the early eighties. The president developed severe lupus and had to undergo dialysis, which was terribly dispiriting to this fitness addict and avid golfer who liked showing off his physique. His increasing frailty gave courage to his opponents, and political unrest mounted.

Imelda basically had to take over the government. She did it with aplomb. Once she invited me out on the Marcos yacht, where she gave a state dinner for a group of Iraqi generals, all in their green war uniforms. They were reluctant to have an American on board, but Imelda vouched for me. Caviar in oil drums was brought aboard. We ended up dancing all night with several Miss Philippines who, in a country addicted to beauty pageants, were special indeed. At the end, I gave the generals copies of *Zorro, the Gay Blade,* which they took back to Baghdad.

I had brought Bill out of retirement, like an aging, aesthetic Rocky Balboa, for the challenge of his lifetime. I had bought the Charlie Chaplin estate for a song, but Chaplin had built it for an even cheaper song, using studio set builders to construct it while they were being paid to do his films. These guys were used to building façades, not houses, and Charlie got what he paid for, which was a beautiful nothing. I renamed it Breakaway, and I had to rebuild the entire place. While Bill was living in Natchez in his Napoleonic splendor, he ended up needing money, as he always did. I thus brought Bill out to help me in what I saw as the challenge of his lifetime. The fun task I intended for him would tragically turn out to be his final commission.

Breakaway is yours, I told him; work your magic on it. But Bill was short on magic and even shorter on health. Father Time is the meanest man in town, and he was kicking the hell out of Bill. It was Teeny's aging that was aging Bill even more, even though he was barely fifty. At seventy, Teeny looked great, but the years were flying by. Bill realized that one day, and maybe one day soon, Mom might not be around to support him, not to mention my inability to do so. Faced with this anxiety, Bill basically drank himself into an early grave. He began imagining that he had far worse diseases than he did, but it was the alcohol, not the speculated cancer, that finished him. Bill would have lasted if he had just put his hand on the bottle and pushed it away, but it was the one crutch that mitigated his greatest horror, the fear of losing his mother.

I came to the Breakaway rebuilding site, where Bill was having walls knocked out and beams put in. He was sitting in the near dark, behind a great French ormolu desk in the middle of the marble hallway (about the only area not torn up) and looking the way I can only imagine Napoleon Bonaparte must have looked after his disastrous retreat from Russia. Bill seemed completely drained. Beside him sat a half-gallon jug of Popov vodka, equally drained. I didn't bother cautioning him about his drinking. I had done that countless times, to deaf ears.

Bill conceded he didn't think he could finish the task I had set for him. I had made it financially attractive, even by Bill's standards, so I knew money wasn't the problem. "I just can't do it," was his only explanation. "I don't have the energy." I didn't realize it at the time, but all the months he had been "on the beach" had taken a terrible toll. He had also fallen and badly hurt one of his "Betty Grable legs." He was in severe physical pain, but worse was the fact that his liver was being poisoned by his alcohol intake.

I went along with Bill's plan to hire his friend Jim Hanrahan, who turned out to be a very talented interior designer who breathed new life into the project. Yet it wasn't the same. Bill had always been the genius we

445

depended upon for inspiration. Not having Bill at the helm was an irreplaceable loss.

We had batteries of tests performed at Cedars-Sinai, L.A.'s "hospital to the stars." The report was far worse than we had expected. The doctor informed us that Bill's liver was severely compromised. He explained that the liver is a very forgiving organ; if not bombarded with alcohol or toxins, it can repair itself. Sadly, Bill's excessive drinking didn't allow his liver that luxury. Now Bill was dying. No matter what we did for him, it was only a matter of months before he would pass on. The doctor predicted each step in Bill's decline. The small veins in Bill's esophagus would rupture, and he would hemorrhage from the mouth. At that point, he would have to be admitted to the hospital, from which he would not emerge.

The good old Christian Scientist in me wanted to grab my Bible and *Science & Health* and put these mutterings of "mortal mind" as far behind me as possible, and that's what I did. Since the medical world could not help Bill, I decided to make his time as pleasant as I could. I rented a charming little three-bedroom home in Beverly Hills, which resembled our old house at 515 North Rodeo Drive. I set the place up to serve Bill's needs, and I remained there with only brief interruptions as work dictated. With his newfound wealth from the money I had paid him for decorating Breakaway, Bill had bought a Rolls-Royce. He told me he had never had a chance to drive it and asked if I could find a way to take him riding in what was to be his last proud possession. It was an odd request, as debilitated as he was, but I took it as a final wish and put my brain to work on how to accomplish it.

Hoisting Bill up piggyback style, something I could never have done in his full bloom of health but that was now possible because he was so thin, I carried him down one flight of stairs and out to his gleaming motorcar. He was as happy as a kid at Christmas. He let me drive, and we took a tour around Beverly Hills and its environs in Bill's high style. "That's Falcon's Lair, Valentino's old home," he'd point out. "Over there is the Harold Lloyd estate. Arthur Cameron, you know, the oil man, owned that house. He had a softball game every Sunday and John Ireland would pitch." I was receiving the benefit of Bill's rich movie magazine education as we laughed and toured and laughed some more, my treasured last moments with my wonderful and crazy half brother, half sister, surrogate father.

A few weeks after our drive, just as the

doctor had predicted, Bill collapsed, blood gushing from his mouth, and had to be rushed to the Cedars-Sinai emergency room. Following surgery to stop the hemorrhaging, he fell into a coma from which he sporadically emerged. When Bill was first admitted, Imelda Marcos called and asked to speak to the head nurse on the ward, who, like most nurses at Cedars, happened to be Filipina. The nurse nearly fainted, as if she had gotten a call from God. Suffice it to say, Bill got the superstar treatment. But even Imelda Marcos wasn't enough.

At about the same time Bill was in the ICU, Dominick Dunne's daughter, Dominique, was also admitted, having been brutally strangled by her boyfriend, a chef at the celebrity restaurant Ma Maison. We were saddened to learn that she was beyond the point of saving. Sitting in the garishly bright and unforgiving waiting room, Dominick and I tried to commiserate with each other, but words were inadequate to the task.

I eventually decided to move Bill to the Seventh-day Adventist hospital in the San Fernando Valley for two reasons. The first was Cedars-Sinai's utter resignation to the fact that Bill would die and there was nothing they could do. I have always believed in long shots. I was worried by their throw-up-your-hands approach. If you think you can't, you can't, was the way I saw it. Reason two was my discovery that a nurse was pumping warfarin, a powerful anticoagulant, into Bill's vein through an IV. I may not be a Mayo Clinic specialist, but I know you don't give a blood thinner to a patient who's been hemorrhaging. I accused them of confusing Bill's treatment with another patient's. They didn't like that much.

After a heated exchange with the hospital, I moved him to Adventist that same night. I stayed by his bed all day and slept in the maternity ward each night. His last piece of advice to me was "learn to love more." I was there when he breathed his last breath. It was serenely peaceful. Somewhere up in heaven, I was sure that Bill was standing next to Betty Grable, comparing legs. I could hear her telling Bill, "You know what, *your legs are better than mine.*" The year was 1982. The day Bill died, I learned that the Cleveland Clinic had done its first successful liver transplant. Science was a shade too late to save my brother; I had fought the good fight and lost. Relief swept over me. Anyone who hasn't been with a dying person probably won't understand this, but when you know there's no way to save someone and he's clinging to life by a thread, the end is a mercy. I wanted to walk out into the sunshine and fresh air again. I wanted to sleep in my own bed.

I had wrongly believed that Teeny had been preparing for this moment and that somehow her faith would carry her through. I did my best to cushion the blow, but there is no good way to deliver bad news. When I finished telling her, she uttered a low, mournful cry that was so pitiful it could have come only from the very depths of her soul. After a few minutes she had recovered enough to ask me to take her to the hospital. She seemed to think that there might still be some way to save Bill, maybe some heroic effort the doctors could try. I had touched his cold body. I told Mom there was nothing more anyone could do.

She immediately turned to Wayne Parks, who was Bill's decorating assistant and would do anything for Bill or Teeny. He volunteered to take her where she wanted to go. I continued to protest, but she would not hear it. How she did it, I don't know, but she made the doctors try resuscitation methods they knew wouldn't work. Teeny clung to Bill's body hour after hour after all hope, even hers, was gone. When Wayne finally brought her home again, I called her doctor to come over and give her a sedative. It look a while to work. I could see Mom was making an effort to push Bill from her mind, but time and again the memories of him came flooding back.

"I just want to die," she kept saying. "I just want to die." She finally slept for twenty-four hours and awoke groggy. After that, it was never quite the same. A process thus began that would play out over the years ahead. Since Teeny could not face the thought of losing Bill, she would not think about him at all. Every trace of Bill would have to disappear. Only complete repression would stop the pain, and over time, Mom managed to seal up, wall off, and dynamite the entrance to her memory. She had two sons now and their names were George and David.

CHAPTER FOURTEEN
THE COMPANY I KEEP

When you're going out with the most famous woman in the world, you may have achieved the impossible, but what you really want is even more impossible: to be alone. With her, that is. Nobody on earth is better company than Elizabeth Taylor, more lively, more fun, and more of a three-ring circus, despite her desperate wishes to the contrary. When I first encountered Elizabeth in her *Cleopatra* days in 1960s Rome, the paparazzi couldn't have treated her more viciously, splashing hideous close-ups of her tracheotomy scar across the news of the world. Cheesecake bathing suit photos of her making out poolside with Richard Burton may have been fair game for the reigning femme fatale, but the ghoulish press was fixated on the fatale part, exploiting beyond all canons of taste Elizabeth's fragile health and doing a rain dance for her demise. But she snapped back and showed them. She was the ultimate survivor.

When I began seeing Elizabeth, she was turning fifty-five and better than ever. The year was 1986. She had divorced Senator John Warner and shed all the weight that John Belushi had lampooned in drag on *Saturday Night Live* when he reenacted the tabloid episode of an overabundant La Taylor choking on a chicken bone. The paparazzi had never, ever let up.

For Elizabeth, looking great was the best revenge, and she had gotten down to an in-your-face va-va-voom 120 pounds. There were lots of motivations beyond Belushi. She had an international launch tour for her new perfume line, Elizabeth Taylor's Passion. She was the world's face for the war on AIDS, which had taken her dear friend Rock Hudson the year before. And Franco Zeffirelli had offered her the part of a lifetime as an opera diva in his forthcoming epic about Arturo Toscanini.

Elizabeth hadn't been in a feature film for almost a decade, and Zeffirelli, who had brilliantly directed her and Richard Burton in *The Taming of the Shrew,* had convinced her that this role could win her her third Oscar. But if she was going to play a diva, she had to look like a diva, hence the crash diet. For Elizabeth, fifty-five was going to be the new thirty-five, and I was fortunate enough to be in the right place at the right time to share the experience.

We had gotten together when a friend called me up in Los Angeles asking if I would escort Elizabeth to some charity event. I called Elizabeth to say hello and make an I'll-show-you-mine-if-you-show-me-yours proposition. I was getting an award as best-dressed man on television, or something of that ilk, at UCLA and needed a date myself. I assumed she would have zero interest in seeing me win some prize for wearing a good suit, but she surprised me. Elizabeth jumped at the chance, the kids at UCLA went wild to see her, and we were off and running for a year or so. I realized early on that if Elizabeth liked you, she would do anything for you, go anywhere, say anything. She was a "dame" in the best old sense of the world. She'd drink with you, dance with you, play cards with you, pig out with you, and it could as easily be with a bunch of truck drivers as Nobel Prize winners.

We went everywhere, starting with a visit to her ninety-year-old mother in Palm Springs, and her coming to visit mine. Then we went global, to Puerto Vallarta, where it was a little strange walking in Richard Burton's *Night of the Iguana* footsteps in the sand; to

Acapulco, where it was a little strange to walk in my own childhood footsteps from when my brothers and I had escaped there with our adventuresome mother; to Gstaad, to spend New Year's at Elizabeth's ski chalet; to Rome, to see Zeffirelli and where we had a wonderful time walking in each other's dolce vita Gucci tracks, which hadn't changed that much in the Eternal City. For all the wonderful pasta there, sweet-toothed Elizabeth's favorite dish in Rome was the crème brûlée, the very French, very decadent version from George's, off the Via Veneto, which she correctly worried could become her addictive Achilles' heel, or paunch, if she shot the Zeffirelli film.

Zeffirelli took us location scouting down the boot to Bari, where we visited the landmark baroque opera house where he planned to shoot. He sold Elizabeth hard. Streisand, MacLaine, and Dunaway, divas all, were clamoring for the part, but Elizabeth was his first choice. We flew back to New York to celebrate Elizabeth's fifty-fifth at a gala party at Tavern on the Green. All I can remember is that we were five hours late. As the American Express campaign once said, membership has its privileges.

Our endless travels took us to the Mediterranean to visit my pal Adnan Khashoggi, the billionaire Saudi arms dealer and one of the planet's all-time hosts with the most. One thing Adnan had the most of were connections. Not only was he locked in with the Saudi royal family but his sister had married Egyptian billionaire Mohammed Al Fayed, who owned Harrods, the Ritz, and everything else. Their son, and Adnan's nephew and my friend Dodi, was a film producer in L.A. (*Chariots of Fire*) who would make tragic history with Princess Diana.

Just before we flew to Marbella, the home port to Khashoggi's mega-yacht, the *Nabila,* I got an intriguing invitation from another pal, Regine, the nonpareil discotheque proprietor. Regine pretty much invented the disco, or at least the exclusive form. I had been a young regular at her first club, New Jimmy'z in Montparnasse, where there was a tiny speakeasy door-within-a-door. If Regine liked your looks, you got to party with Onassis and Callas and Princess Grace and Agnelli and Mastroianni. If she didn't, you could go around the corner to drown your sorrows in Hemingway memories at La Coupole. She was two decades ahead of Rubell and Schrager at Studio 54, plus a lot more personal and motherly, with the spaghetti suppers she would make for us to greet the dawn. In any event, Regine, who had since opened branches in Monte Carlo, Rio, and New York, was planning a nocturnal incursion on the Costa del Sol with a disco at the ultrachic Marbella Club, a country club for stars and tycoons and royalty founded by the Austrian prince Alfonso von Hohenlohe. It was almost as nice as the *Nabila,* and Regine insisted I bring Elizabeth to stay as long as we wanted.

Some luxurious terra firma didn't seem like a terrible idea. But I grilled Regine about the press. Elizabeth didn't want any paparazzi, and with good reason. Of course I knew that Regine's lifeblood was celebrity, and leaking Elizabeth's presence to the newspapers could only burnish Regine's new start-up. Regine swore on Catherine Deneuve's and Alain Delon's lives that Elizabeth was safe. "I would never betray friends," she insisted. And we were friends indeed, not photo ops. Armed with Regine's assurances, I sold Elizabeth on the holiday. We arrived and settled into a palatial suite overlooking both the blue Med and the jagged Sierra Nevadas. It was early summer and the sun was a tanner's dream. Elizabeth and I have always felt healthier with a tan. The first rays brought her out of bed and out of her clothes. She basked on the terrace wearing nothing but a Brazilian *tanga* bottom, no top, and a funny-looking flowered swimming cap.

Our first night there would feature a party with Sean Connery, a Marbella resident who was there for the golf. I knew they ate late in Spain, but it wasn't late enough for Elizabeth, who took forever getting her hair and nails done for the fete. At ten thirty she was still being beautified. By eleven thirty, Sean and his wife, Micheline, gave up the ghost. He had an early call for the links. At two A.M. we made our grand entrance, fashionably late as ever. Gypsy dancers were performing. Within an hour after arriving, the bad buzz came our way. Countess von Bismarck, I believe, was the royal with the grim tidings. Topless pictures of Elizabeth had been taken. They were going to hit all the papers the next morning. It was going to be the biggest scandal since Jackie Onassis was captured topless on Scorpios by amphibious paparazzi. This scandal was bigger, as the Junoesque Elizabeth had far more to show than the gamine Jackie. This, alas, was going to be the show of shows.

But not on Elizabeth's life. "I want those pictures!" she exclaimed. She was furious, and rightly so. I had let her down, subjected her to humiliation of the worst sort. I felt betrayed by Regine, who denied all complicity. But the buck stopped with me. A gentleman does not sell his lady friend into photographic servitude. I had to stop the presses. It was an endless night. We retired from the party and I worked the phones at the Marbella Club until dawn, calling every contact I had in Spain and in the tabloid press. Finally, my friend Enrique Herreras from *Love at First Bite* tracked down the cunning shutterbug, a fellow named Otero, who caught the first plane from Madrid and arrived at our suite at seven thirty in the morning.

Otero surrendered the roll of negatives that was going to make him rich and famous. I was about to burn it when Elizabeth, who was quietly fuming, said, "Let me see it." She unspooled the roll and held it up to the encroaching daylight. She studied it for what seemed like an eternity. I steeled myself for a torrent of abuse the likes of which had not issued from her famous lips since she starred in *Who's Afraid of Virginia Woolf?* But she didn't hit the roof at all. A sly grin crept into that beautiful face of hers. The violet eyes lit up. "I like them. Don't you? My breasts look rather good, don't you think?" She passed the roll to me.

"You look spectacular," I was forced to admit.

"What about the hat?"

"I think it works. Reverse chic."

"I hate censoring the press anyhow. Not my style. I'm a First Amendment gal."

I'm not sure how much of our English Señor Otero understood, but I've never seen anyone so relieved in my life.

The pictures came out. Elizabeth sold a lot of perfume.

But before she did, we went to hook up with Khashoggi at La Baracca, his hunting lodge above Marbella, where Elizabeth slipped on the marble floor and badly bruised her coccyx bone. A squad of doctors was summoned, who determined that Elizabeth basically had to sit immobilized for two weeks. What better recovery room than the *Nabila,* which Elizabeth had been admiring in the harbor below, with sugarplum visions of the treats the yacht's four *Michelin*-starred chefs, one French, one Italian, one Spanish, and one Moroccan, were going to prepare for her? These were pre-dot-com days, before the likes of Paul Allen and Larry Ellison decided they wanted to be kings of the sea, and the *Nabila* ruled the waves. The yacht was a floating Arabian Nights, with pools and a cinema and discos and more topless models than on the plage at high noon in Saint-Tropez. And of course those chefs. Naturally Elizabeth had pride of place. She spent the next two weeks soothing her ailing derriere in a queenly deck chair.

Eventually, we did go back to London and the Dorchester, in Adnan's private 707 with a glass floor that enabled us to see everything from the Pyrenees to the Thames far below. On the flight, Adnan's wife Lamia's private hairdresser offered to do Elizabeth's coiffure. "I like height" is Elizabeth's hair mantra. Because she is so tiny, she likes to make up for it on top. So the stylist wove some kind of seaweed into Elizabeth's do that made her look as if she had antlers. We were picked up at Heathrow by a Rolls limo that had huge doors designed to accommodate dignitaries in top hats, but Elizabeth could barely get in. On the way to the hotel, the hairdresser came with us and kept pumping it up. Way up. Eventually the damned thing got so big that Elizabeth couldn't get in or out of the Rolls. All you could see was ass and antlers. Eventually, I convinced her to cut the whole thing down, the way you would trim a hedge.

We arrived around midnight at the Dorchester, where we checked into the Oliver Messel Suite, scene of some of the most epic Taylor-Burton drag-out fights. The Burtons had smashed more furniture here than the Who's Keith Moon in his wildest demolition dreams. Still, the hotel gave her a queen's welcome. The only thing the Dorchester could not provide Elizabeth was the festive English banquet she wanted. The very stepping down on the soil of the Sceptered Isle had stirred up in Elizabeth a Pavlovian craving for roast beef and Yorkshire pudding. Despite her miracle diet, Elizabeth loved to eat. Alas, this being early-to-bed London, the hotel's kitchen had closed.

"Don't worry," Elizabeth said to me. "Just call Anton." Anton was Anton Mosimann, the Dorchester's Swiss-born head chef and the most celebrated toque in the London of the time. An essential duty of any consort of Elizabeth is to play the part of her personal concierge, which is more a gesture of chivalry than subservience. I called the kitchen, which told me that Chef Mosimann had gone home. I told Elizabeth. She was undeterred. "Call him at home." So I convinced the front desk to give me the chef's private number, and I called him.

Mosimann may have been fast asleep, but he couldn't have been more charming. Of course, he would cook for Elizabeth, he said. But he was forty-five minutes away, so it would take a bit to get to the kitchen. What did she want to eat? I'm sure he wasn't expecting to hear the request for a roast beef banquet worthy of Henry VIII and his court, but he took it like a man. At three A.M., the chef, resplendent in his white coat and towering toque blanche and his retinue of sous-chefs and footmen, whom he had surely roused from their slumbers far away, arrived at our suite with a gleaming trolley of beef complete with Yorkshire pudding and creamed horseradish, accompanied by a bottle of 1945 Lafite Rothschild. Even though Elizabeth didn't drink, she ordered the noble wine for me. Chef Mosimann had also prepared a huge bowl of crème brûlée, Elizabeth's favorite dessert. And he brought us two autographed copies of his new best-selling cookbook. Now, that was service fit for a queen. Mosimann asked us if there was anything else we might want. "Breakfast," Elizabeth chirped. But then she let him off the hook and back to his own needed dreamland. "Don't worry. I sleep late," she said with a wink.

The next morning, or probably late afternoon, I was awakened by a chiming of the suite's royal doorbell. I walked the half mile or so to open it, and staring at me were an array of the most beautiful models I had ever seen. What was this, room service for Hugh Hefner? No. It was Elizabeth's own private fashion show, arranged by her dear friend Valentino, who had sent a dozen of his finest over to model his collection for Elizabeth, so she could choose what she wanted without having to drag herself to the showroom.

Almost as scary as Elizabeth's hair were her Israeli bodyguards. Those guys meant business. I guess they were used to life during wartime and acted accordingly. When a member of the small army of paparazzi who stalked Elizabeth outside the Dorchester tried to stick his camera into the Rolls, one of the Israelis slammed the door on the photographer's hand and began dragging him along with us, until he surrendered the camera.

Sometimes, for all my chivalry, I just couldn't take the waiting around. Back in New York, we had dinner with my friend the English takeover tycoon Lord Gordon White, who, having briefly been a Hollywood agent, had never gotten over it. He'd much rather be around someone like Elizabeth than someone like Bill Gates. He had the money; he wanted the fun. After a dinner together, Gordon sent Elizabeth an amazing bouquet of white flowers. Touched, Elizabeth decided to send him a personal thank-you note. The problem was that Elizabeth was even slower at writing than doing her makeup. She had been schooled by private tutors as an MGM child star and was completely insecure about her education.

"Let's go," I urged her after a decent interval. We were already hours late for an important charity event. "I'm writing this note," Elizabeth said. "Just be a dear and wait downstairs." So wait I did, with her secretary Liz and main AMFAR assistant Roger. After an eternity, she called down, "You can come up. I'm trying to get this note right."

"It's only to Gordon," I said. "If we're going to be this late, I might as well not go."

"Don't threaten me."

"I'm outta here," I said, finally losing my patience.

"Is that a threat?" Elizabeth asked.

"It's a promise," I said, and left.

Eventually we kissed and made up, and Elizabeth never made me wait again. She was used to men catering to her, and for those men, she had no respect. But if you didn't cater to her to a certain degree, you had no chance. It was a fine line to walk, and I decided to walk it as a friend. And we will be friends for life.

But I do have a unique understanding of the Taylor psychology. Elizabeth and I did a television movie together called *Poker Alice*. Elizabeth played a lady gambler from Boston who wins a Wild West bordello in a poker game. I play her sidekick cousin and best pal and partner in crime, a platonic version of our actual relationship. The ads billed us as the King and Queen of Hearts. Tucson was anything but Rome, but Elizabeth is a total sport who can rise and fall to any occasion, be it caviar or quesadillas.

The shoot was not without its initial anxieties. The producer came up to me in a panic that Elizabeth was going to turn the movie into a small-screen *Cleopatra* budget disaster by being late to the shoot, doing endless makeup, writing notes, whatever made her late. I had an idea. I told the producer Elizabeth loves presents, little cute things that don't have to be the Hope diamond. So the first day of shooting, a Wells Fargo stagecoach arrived for Elizabeth. A handsome cowboy came out with a package. "Miss Taylor," he drawled. "We got something for you." She opened it and it was a little silver whistle. She applauded and was thrilled. The next day, the production had a Pony Express rider come for her with something else. And the next they had a bugler blowing his horn, always with a thoughtful surprise. So Elizabeth was never late, plus we got rave reviews. It's the thought that counts.

My world-famous girlfriend after Elizabeth was Danielle Steel. If no woman ha[s] ruled the screen like Elizabeth, no woman, perhaps since Jane Austen, has ruled the page like Danielle. Having sold nearly a billion copies and worth over a billion dollars, certainly no one has sold more books and has had more people see versions of these books on television. I met Danielle in 1995 when I starred in one of these movies shot in Montreal and based on her book *Vanished,* opposite Lisa Rinna, who would a decade later become my ballroom adversary in *Dancing with the Stars.* Back in my WASP-Ivy mode, and in a sleek 1930s untainted by the Depression, Lisa and I play a glamorous Manhattan couple whose child is abducted, shades of the Lindbergh kidnapping that happened at the same time.

Danielle, whom I met in the course of the film, loves history and struck me as a historical figure herself, a reincarnation of the grandes dames she writes about. Her list of husbands read like a cast of characters from her novels, all cold and controlling. Her first was the son of a Paris-Wall Street banking dynasty. Her second, on the other extreme, was a convicted rapist whom she married in a jailhouse ceremony, and the third was a heroin addict. The fourth was a Napa Valley vintner and the fifth was a Silicon Valley financial whiz. I came into her life between these two Valleys. I hope I was a peak.

How did I fit into this pantheon? I was anything but cold and controlling. I had never done time, never been a tycoon. Then again, how did I fit in between Elizabeth Taylor's Senator John Warner and Larry Fortensky? Although Danielle, who is barely five feet tall and as thin as a bird, doesn't fulfill my supposed stereotype of the tall blond supermodel, neither does Elizabeth Taylor. It goes to show that types die hard. I'm always open to suggestion, depending on what's being suggested. Our first few dinners were spent sharing our complex family histories. We had both spent a lot of childhood time in Manhattan, where Danielle was raised by her popinjay father, who gained custody of Danielle in the parents' divorce. Her father, like my mother, dressed great and gave lots of parties, on little money, though nowhere as little as we had.

When we first started dating, we had a wonderful time eating and laughing; for all her seriousness and dark past, Danielle has a great sense of humor. However, at precisely ten on certain nights, Danielle would turn into a pumpkin. No matter how much fun we were having, she would always leave me. Was there some secret lover she wasn't telling me about? Yes. His name was Smith

Corona. Danielle had more discipline as a writer than any marine drill sergeant. Every night she would go home to her old typewriter and go at it all night, fueling herself with Snickers bars. This is what best sellers are made of.

As Danielle and I got increasingly serious, I moved to San Francisco and took an apartment on Nob Hill next to the Huntington Hotel. We began a global romance as glamorous as any of the ones in Danielle's novels that "people only read about." My character, which might as well have been written by Danielle, was the international playboy/actor. I brought all my best suits, my golf clubs, and my martini shakers, and played the role to the hilt.

In San Francisco, I stood with Danielle at the pinnacle of that city's incredibly snobbish Nob Hill society, a tougher scene to crack than even Palm Beach. Danielle had broken through, thanks to her old-world style and her new-world success. The modern dot-com gold rush of nearby Silicon Valley had somehow rendered the Bay Area caste system somewhat more permeable: Wealth of a certain staggering magnitude made up for not having a forebear on the *Mayflower* or at Sutter's Mill. Danielle held court in her Pacific Heights palace that had been the home of sugar tycoon Adolph Spreckels, onetime father-in-law of Clark Gable. I enjoyed walking in Gable's footsteps and attending Danielle's exquisitely catered parties, which were worthy of not only a Hollywood king but also of Louis XIV. Because Danielle had been the object of the kidnapping ring that had broken out of a high-security pen and vowed to abduct her and her many children, she was rightfully terrified and always on red alert. She had a fully armed security team, just as a scary as Elizabeth's Israeli commandos.

We were constantly shadowed by Danielle's personal chauffeur-bodyguard, a behemoth who had previously provided similar protection for the King of Morocco. The chauffeur drove us around in a red Bentley, which Danielle insisted he park at hydrants in this hardest-to-park-in metropolis. I'm amazed that we never once got a ticket. Queens like Danielle are judgment-proof. Her best friends included fellow best seller Jackie Collins, whose fear of flying exceeds that of the airphobic Danielle. Danielle would send a deluxe private bus down to Hollywood to drive Jackie and whomever she wanted to bring up to San Francisco.

It wasn't all parties. As I noted, Danielle i the hardest-working woman in the writin business. She would stay up half the night pecking away on her old Smith Corona, snacking away on her beloved Snickers bars and smoking like a fiend, which was a very French bad habit from her school days at the Lycée Français. Once the work was done, though, we would take off to Europe, where Danielle lived large, taking whole floors at the Ritz or the Hotel du Cap whenever the spirit moved her. It was all homework for her novels.

I learned about the confluence of Danielle's art and her life on our first trip to London. I had a town house there at the time (Dracula and real estate had been good to me), and Danielle was staying at Claridge's. She wanted to go diamond shopping at Graff on Bond Street. I offered to send my car for her. "I *have* a car," she said, a Rolls she had reserved at Claridge's. You must use my car, I insisted, and I insisted I come with her as well. Your Rolls or mine? What problems! All this for Graff, which was no more than six blocks from the hotel. I must note here that whenever you date a superrich woman, the man must always pay. It's old-fashioned, but that's the way it is. You can enjoy the power of her money, but not the money itself. Otherwise, you lose all self-respect, and you'll lose her fast enough.

Unfortunately for us, my regular driver was off for the day, and there was a replacement driver, who didn't know Bond Street from Petticoat Lane. Somehow we saw the jewels and were on our way back to Belgravia for cocktails. Suddenly, in the dead center of the mad Marble Arch intersection, one of the most ruthlessly dangerous crossroads of the automotive world, up there with the murderous circle around Paris's Arc de Triomphe, the driver stalled the car and came to a complete stop. A red double-decker was hurtling toward us at full speed. I yelled at the driver, jarred him into lurching forward, and the bus missed us by inches.

When the driver opened the door for us later, the alcohol on his breath was unmistakable. The next day I sacked him and we used Danielle's driver from Claridge's. When I met her in the morning, however, instead of being rattled from our near-death experience, she had a big wad of pages. Read these, Danielle insisted. So I did, in the back of the Rolls as it snaked off to the Tate. What I read was the story of a glamorous couple on their last night together in London, a night of dancing and champagne and nightingales singing in Berkeley Square. Married to others, and their respective families in the dark about their affair, they are

472

going to say good-bye. They climb into their chauffeured Rolls, and just as they are about to savor a final kiss, the ecstasy of their forbidden romance turns into the agony of molten metal and shattering glass as the Rolls is blindsided by a speeding double-decker bus. He's near death; she survives. He goes to a London hospital; she becomes his caregiver; the families find out. Isn't it wonderful? she asked me. What could I say?

Our almost-accident became a $15 million advance and, a year or so later, Danielle's next jillion-copy best seller. By then we had broken up. I decided I was better suited to play the friend character than the husband one. Our glamorous travels were homework for her, and, as you can see, I was, too. The girl can't help it. I'm still crazy about her, and I was glad that in real life I came out unscathed, even if I didn't get a share of the royalties.

Please don't get the impression that I went out only with world-famous women. I went out only with great women, but while fame and power could be aphrodisiacs, so could a lot of other factors. Although she wanted to be famous in the worst way, Alana was a complete unknown when I met her. And no one could have been less interested in being famous than Liz Treadwell, who was my off-

and-on girlfriend for more than a decade. Liz, like Alana, had those tall blond supermodel looks that mark the stereotypical George Hamilton girl. Liz could have been a celebrated international cover girl, but she just wanted to be a country girl, with kids and dogs and horses and no makeup. Liz was the anti-Alana, hating parties and stars and glitz and flash. If I had met her first, I might have ended up a country boy myself, back to my cotton field roots.

When I did meet Liz, in the late seventies in Malibu, I was a single dad summering with my little Ashley in a beachfront cottage. Liz, who had grown up outside San Francisco, was dating the richest man in California, Donald Bren, the real estate lord who owned, among everything else, the vast Irvine Ranch in Orange County. She had just gotten back from the Philippines, where she had been doing location scouting for my future friend and director Francis Ford Coppola and his playboy producer, Gray Frederickson, who hired only the world's most beautiful women to be his assistants. Some country girl.

We met at a dinner party. This was before I became Dracula and changed my luck. Trying to compete with Donald Bren was like a ninety-seven-pound weakling taking on Mike Tyson. But of course those were the odds the Hamiltons thrived on. So I rose to the challenge, giving a dinner party and seating Liz next to me and Donald somewhere outside in the surf. I turned on all the charm I could muster. It didn't work. I got absolutely nothing except the enmity of the Mister Big of the Golden State.

But I didn't give up. All summer I took advantage of Malibu's small-town atmosphere and kept "accidentally" running into Liz at the market, on the beach, wherever, inviting her to play tennis, ride horses, go for hikes, anything. But the secret weapon was Ashley. She adored him. So I gave her my last vestige of stardom, my yellow Rolls, and asked her to take him out to the Cultured Cow, my boy's beloved yogurt emporium in the Malibu Country Mart. Ashley was so excited that he urinated all over the Rolls's exquisite creamy leather interior. Liz thought I would be horrified and blame her for ruining my car. But I laughed it off. If my son wanted to pee on my Rolls, that was his prerogative. Another time, Ashley slammed a door into a parking meter, turning each outing in the Rolls into demolition derby. Again, I thought it was cute. My lack of materialism seemed to have captured Liz's spirit. By summer's end, Mr. Bren was history.

Liz's reward was *Love at First Bite,* which enabled me to begin to entertain her in the style to which she had become accustomed, even if it didn't interest her. I loved her versatility. In jeans she could ride like the wind; in a dress she could knock the eyes out of Europe. I proudly took her to Princess Grace's Red Cross Ball in Monte Carlo and other glittering events. But Liz preferred Natchez and her role as the resident contractor/majordomo of my burgeoning real estate empire. I had bought six houses there, expecting the place to become the next Savannah or Charleston. What I didn't expect was the Southern hospitality that saw a cross burned on the lawn of the Cedars plantation and our mailbox shot to smithereens. Despite my Southern roots, I was still viewed as an outsider, a "damn Yankee." Cedars was beautiful but desolate, twenty-five miles in the Dixie wilderness outside of Natchez itself. This was Ku Klux Klan country, but it didn't scare Liz, who, in her best Annie Oakley tradition, strapped on a .45 and kept it loaded. She had a shotgun as well and knew how to use it. She thrived at Cedars building a huge fence around the plantation all by herself and raising a menagerie of chickens, goats, cows, and horses.

Eventually, the South got too hot to handle

and Natchez was too dull to be worth it. So I took Liz to a place that I knew she would love, Aspen, which was even friendlier to dogs and horses than it was to movie stars. Liz did her best to domesticate, or, actually, countrify me, but it always seemed to backfire. She organized an overnight pack trip into the Rockies with her prize mares Cajun and Buck, brought west from Natchez. It all started idyllically enough, with wine and dinner cooked over the roaring campfire, but then it started to pour endlessly, right out of Noah's Ark, and our tents leaked like the *Titanic*.

In the middle of the deluge, Liz sent me to check on the horses. They seemed fine. But the morning after, both steeds were gone, and Liz accused me of being drunk and not having checked on them, or being so drunk that I thought I had when I hadn't. We then began a slog through six miles of quicksand-ish mud. Hours later, we found the horses, just before they would have vanished forever in the wilderness. We mounted them bareback and prepared a return, but we started bickering, sort of *Two for the Trail,* and I got so frustrated that I slapped Liz's horse's ass, and the animal tossed her into the mud. That we kissed and made up afterward is testament to Liz's divine forgiveness.

And so it went. Every effort Liz made to create a normal life for us backfired, because I guess I'm just not that normal a guy. Liz may have had the strength of an ox, but she had the heart of Bambi. She was very sensitive and easily wounded. I couldn't blame her when she took up with someone else, but why oh why did it have to be Rod Stewart, before he divorced Alana? With all the blondes in the world, why did he have to keep chasing mine? As with all the women in my life, Liz and I remain close friends and she remains in Colorado. She was the one woman who was easy to keep down on the farm after she'd seen Paree.

I have also stayed incredibly close with Alana. We even had our own talk show together, *The Bickersons* meets *Regis and Kathy Lee*. What has become a great friendship is also a never-ending battle of the sexes. To wit: Alana and I were attending a wonderful party thrown by Barbra Streisand and handsome hubby, James Brolin, when I noticed what a really fine haircut Jim had. I asked him where he got it. It's the Flowbee, he said, showing me his mail-order home hair-cutting device. All you had to do was attach it to your vacuum cleaner and run it over your head. I've always had a weakness for gadgets, so I asked Jim if I could borrow it to try at home, and he agreed.

I had forgotten about the Flowbee until one night when Alana and I were supposed to go to a party. I didn't feel like going, so I begged off, claiming I wasn't well. Alana went without me, which was fine, since I was planning to try out Jim's machine. First, though, I was going to test it on our mastiff, Lolita, who wasn't too sure about the whole thing, especially when I fired up the Electrolux. I had finished trimming off one side of Lolita's coat when she began growling and baring her teeth. Maybe I'd better come back later, I decided.

A quick pass around my own head, and everything seemed to be working fine. I called Jim to tell him how happy I was. He was delighted I liked it. There's another attachment in the box, he told me, that's great for feathering your neck and trimming sideburns. Try it, he suggested. I popped on the attachment, and it too worked like a charm. My sideburns looked so great I couldn't wait to call Jim back. When I had finished, I picked up the Flowbee and decided to take one last pass around my head to be sure my hair was perfectly even. When I finally looked at my handiwork in the mirror, I had to bite my lip not to scream. I had forgotten that I'd switched attachments. Staring back at me was this horrid specter right out of medieval Europe, with hair that looked like rats had chewed on it. Far from being even all over, I had huge clumps missing. I was hideous.

But first things first. Something had to be done about Lolita. Alana loved that dog. She'd have my head, or what was left of it, if I didn't get Lolita straightened out fast. So once again I approached her with the Flowbee, but she wanted no part of it. I had no choice but to call a pet groomer. The groomer pointed out that his shop had closed at five P.M. and it was now after ten. He said it would cost a fortune for him to come out at this hour. I told him to let me worry about that. No price was too high to escape Alana's wrath.

The groomer arrived in a flash. But when he saw me and the condition of my hair, he told me never mind the dog. I was the one who needed the grooming. I followed him out to the petmobile. The age of miracles was long over, but he did his best. I ended up with a crew cut worthy of my Hackley days. I paid him $300 and got rid of him because Alana would be coming home any minute.

In less time than it took for the petmobile to pull away, I had thrown on my pajamas, grabbed the newspaper, and leaped ont the couch, all in an effort to look normal. In short order Alana came bouncing in. She sensed that something was out of place, but she didn't know what. She looked at Lolita. She looked at me. She looked back at Lolita. "What the hell have you done to our dog?" she asked accusingly. I guess I found out right then and there where I ranked on Alana's list of concerns. She hadn't even noticed the terrible buzz cut I was sporting. If push came to shove and Alana had to choose between Lolita and me, it was pretty clear whom she'd choose. I could have sworn I saw a smirk on that damned dog's face.

CHAPTER FIFTEEN
I'M STILL HERE

Fame is a many-splendored thing. I was shooting a scene at Los Angeles International Airport recently in the international arrivals building. A tiny Chinese woman stepped out of an immigration line that looked like Mao's Long March and came right up to me, rolling cameras be damned. "You George Hamilton?" she demanded.

"Yes, I am," I said proudly.

"You so old," she said.

Talk about taking the wind out of my sails. The lady held her ground and just stared at me for what seemed like an eternity, the way she might stare at Mao's embalmed body in his mausoleum in Tiananmen Square. She not only stopped traffic, she stopped the entire production. "You so old." I was un nerved and looked for assistance from on of the airport security men assigned to us. couldn't act now if I tried. The guard foun a Chinese-speaking colleague; they wer up to her and finally got her moving along, though with several parting stares.

They came back and told me what happened. The night before she flew from Beijing, the lady had seen my first film, *Crime and Punishment, USA,* made in 1959, on Chinese television. She thought I was still supposed to be eighteen. She couldn't believe how I had aged. I guess this was what Cary Grant had meant about not wanting to age on film. Quit while you still look great. James Dean never aged, nor did Marilyn Monroe. But I'll take the age, because I love being here.

Such is the magic of movies and of celebrity. You may age, but as long as you bear some shred of resemblance to your former self, people all over the world will come up to you, mostly in admiration. Your movies are an investment in yourself, not only in your posterity but in your present value. Fans from Haiti to Mozambique to Russia to Australia recognize me from my third film, my fifth, my thirtieth. You do a lot in fifty years on screen, make a lot of friends. My name is my passport, the one credit card I don't dare leave home without. It's the letter of transit that can get you out of Casablanca and into some great restaurants and hotel suites. I love that people know me. It's the greatest thrill you can imagine.

It's not all about opening doors to Ritz-Carltons and the Four Seasons. It can open gates to prisons as well. Some years ago I was doing dinner theater out in the wilds of Florida and had picked up a wild Florida beauty in the process. Driving her to my digs after the show, late at night I passed Raiford Penitentiary, in Starke, Florida. I had to stop. Raiford, which had housed such famous mass murderers as Ted Bundy and Aileen Wuornos, was the home of a jewel thief named Richard Duncan Pearson. I had once tried to do a movie about him, back in my *Evel Knievel* days, when audacious bad boys were my beat. Pearson was part of the gang of Jack Murphy, or Murf the Surf. In 1964, they had pulled off our nation's biggest jewel heist by stealing the Star of India and the DeLong ruby from New York's American Museum of Natural History. Murf had gone to Raiford on a life sentence but somehow got parole and became an evangelist. Pearson was still behind bars, and I just had to see this three-time loser once again.

My date, who thought I was mad, was terrified. The George Hamilton she expected was supposed to take her for a nightcap at the Breakers in Palm Beach, not to death row in the swamps. I wouldn't be deterred and drove up to the heavily fortified gates. Barbed wire was everywhere. Searchlights turned night into day. I pressed a call box and told them I was here to see Pearson, way out of visiting hours, but what the heck. For me the impossible was always worth trying. Suddenly a convoy of jeeps filled with machine-gun-toting guards with attack dogs roared up. My trembling date and I were ordered to put our hands over our heads and state our names and our business. As I was trying to get out "George Hamilton," a guard interrupted me. "Hey! You're Hank Williams, ain't you?"

"No, numb nuts," another guard corrected him. "That's George Hamilton. Shee-it!"

"Can you give me an autograph for my wife?" piped up a third. "She ain't gonna believe this."

"Bring 'em in," the commander ordered, and we were given Raiford's red carpet.

At about two A.M., Richard Duncan Pearson was brought in to see us. He was shaking like a leaf, more than my date. He thought they were going to execute him. The guards lavished us with coffee, doughnuts, and prison-made cigarettes, and we talked until dawn. When we finally said good-bye, I told the guards, "This is a friend. Take care of him."

"Yes, sir, Mr. Hamilton. You bet."

That is what celebrity is all about.

It's about getting into prisons. It's also about getting into the papers, into the national consciousness. It's about getting in the funny papers. I was featured in *Doonesbury,* where the George Hamilton Tanning Workshop was depicted as a Malibu institution. "George took tanning and parlayed it into a career," one of the cartoon characters said. It's also about being part of the national legend, whether it's Ryder Smith in *Where the Boys Are* or the consigliere in *The Godfather.*

As for the acting that made me the celebrity, well, let's just say it has been the means to a very wonderful end. The acting has been an adventure in itself. I wouldn't call myself a dedicated actor. I'd call myself a *scared* actor. As Evel Knievel said, "It's not fear, it's terror." That's why I work so damned hard at it, no matter how casual I might seem. And I work at it just as diligently whether I'm working for a first-time commercials director or for a master like Francis Ford Coppola. That leads to an illustration of what it's like working for a genius.

I had met Francis through my friend and his producer Gray Frederickson, a good ole boy from Oklahoma who just happened to have attended Swiss boarding schools and speaks multiple languages, and is one of the great ladies' men in a business full of them. Once I had rented Gray's Benedict Canyon home and was almost killed by a gun-wielding ex of his (or maybe one of his pals), who crashed into the house and found me in bed with a naked French model. Thinking I was Gray, she decided I had betrayed her and the wages of my sin would be death. Be careful from whom you sublet. It was a bonding experience that several years later led me to a drink at the Polo Lounge where my agent said that Gray and Francis wanted me for *Godfather III.* I thought it was a prank being pulled by Gray or the other *Godfather* producer, Al Ruddy, or maybe the joker Bob Evans. Why would they want *me* for this greatest of film sagas? And for what role? No one could tell me. But when they flew me to Rome and put me up at the Grand Hotel, I figured the joke was on them.

My first night in the Eternal City, I met up with Francis at a party given by his Oscar-winning set designer, Dean Tavoularis, and his Oscar-winning costumer, Milena Canonero. Impressed by such exalted company, I asked Francis whom I was playing. "I don't know," he told me. Talk about the blind leading the blind.

"Just come out to Cinecittà tomorrow," he said, and drank another bottle of wine. At Cinecittà, the great studio where *Ben-Hur* had been shot, Francis's first order of business was to send me to hair. My hair was quite long at the time. The female Italian hairdresser, without any preamble, shaved one side of my head. It was totally punk. This wasn't *Godfather;* it was *Road Warrior.* I was shocked. I looked like something out of Rudi Gernreich, shades of the Flowbee trauma that awaited me in later years. "I guess I have to cut the other side," she said, not really sure that she should.

"I guess you do," I said.

Now I looked like a Republican businessman from Dayton. "Francis wants your hair streaked," she now said, and within moments my head was tight as a drum and my hair looked like a psychedelic mélange of green, yellow, and white. "Your hair's very resistant," she said. I suggested she use this product known as French booster bleach to get it out. I don't know what she did, but by the time I left, my hair was orange and it was falling out in clumps. I was certain this was a Bob Evans joke and more certain I would never work again in Hollywood, this town, or any other.

Next they gave me my lines, a five-page

speech involving an Italian bank and its shareholders, although I still had no idea who I was and why I was saying it. All I knew was that it was impossible and there was no way I could remember it. I was herded into a bank meeting in a grand set that looked like the J. P. Morgan bank, full of shareholders. The older woman standing next to me was on the firing line. Francis was at the helm and ordered her to say her line, "Do devils fly with angels?" She tried, but it came out something like, "Do devils and angels hang out together?"

Francis was quite nasty to her about flubbing it, then gave her another shot, which she flubbed again. She did so for a seemingly endless series of bad takes. Then he fired her on the spot. I was next and was getting nervous about how the maestro would excoriate me and send me packing when I blew it. Finally, Francis turned to a woman who had stood next to the dismissed woman and told her to try it. She got the words right. "Too sweet," Francis scolded her. "Be mean!" And he showed her how he wanted it. "Loud and mean," he insisted.

"I can be as loud as you but I can never be as mean as you," the woman shot back. "I don't like you and I don't like what you just did to your poor mother!" the woman cried and ran off the set. I suddenly realized that Francis had fired his own mother. This was *Godfather* territory indeed. Luckily, they then shut down the set and I was off the hook.

For the next week or so I just hung around with Francis and company. I knew Rome and took him to all my favorite trattorias, cigar shops, tailors. We never talked about the film. "You're our consigliere," he told me. I thanked him for the compliment that I had steered him around so well. "Not in real life," he corrected me. "In the movie. That'll be your part."

"But what about Bob Duvall? That's his part," I said.

"It's yours now," the Godfather decreed.

Like Duvall before me, I had quite a big part. But I inadvertently made it smaller.

"You're not happy, are you?" Francis asked me one day.

"I'm having a wonderful time," I replied.

"Not you, your character! He doesn't want to be here, does he?"

I thought awhile. I told him that an attorney would want to keep his distance from his Mafia clients. "He'd rather be having a martini at the country club," I admitted.

"I think that's where he should be, too," Francis said. Not too smart on my part. I had just written myself out of the scene, and a lot of others. "But George Hamilton *loves* having spaghetti with the Mafia," I assured Francis. He knew I was good company. I knew all the right addresses, and I was good at poker, so I remained in the inner circle, which wasn't that easy. For instance, one day I ran into fellow cast member Winona Ryder, with her then boyfriend Johnny Depp. Johnny was terse as usual, but Winona seemed very down, burying her head in her arms. Later that day Francis began asking me my opinions about hairdos and makeup, what looks I liked best. What for? I queried him. For Sofia, his daughter, he said. He had just fired Winona, and Sofia would be taking over. The Godfather giveth, and the Godfather taketh away. I had witnessed both.

Another day I came into Francis's control center, his Airstream trailer, and found him completely naked, frenziedly cooking pasta. "Want some linguine?" he asked. Somehow I lost my appetite. Francis was manic and at his most confident in his genius. Then, seemingly, the lithium would kick in, and he would calm down, but his confidence in his genius would diminish as well. It was a delicate balance. I asked him what I needed to do in an upcoming scene with Al Pacino.

"Count the hairs on the back of his head," Francis instructed me. "It'll make you look interesting." The next day on the set, while counting Al's hairs, I got a call from Francis. He was directing the scene, not from the set but from the Airstream, sort of like the Wizard of Oz. He said he would prefer to make all of his films this way, by telephone and video camera, a process he very much wanted to prove and perfect. The idea was to do it all someday from the comfort of his Napa Valley estate.

Aside from finding the best place to buy custom luggage, I was indispensable to Francis in many ways offscreen, not the least of which was maintaining morale among the nonstars in the cast. One handsome extra was always moping around about wanting a speaking part that Francis never gave him. When we went to New York to shoot in Little Italy, a big black limo pulled up to the set and some visitors came out to see their friend. Leading the congregation was none other than the real Godfather, John Gotti himself, who kissed the extra on both cheeks. Apparently, he was family, connected big time. I advised Francis to give the boy a line. As usual, he listened to his consigliere's sage advice.

When the movie was done and those who

saw it began saying that my role would be the stuff of Oscars if only there were more of it, I tried to bribe Francis to edit in some of the scenes he had cut out, on my dumb advice. I offered him a Bentley Azure if I got a nomination, but Francis was too wedded to his Airstream trailer to go for the bait. It would have taken a horse's head, but that's another story. In the end, the Vatican and Freemasonry story that my character was involved in scared off the studio. This was before it entered the lexicon in *The Da Vinci Code.* Like other concepts ahead of their time, even more of me ended up on the cutting-room floor. You can catch it in the DVD version.

The acting has been my job, and the lifestyle has been my avocation, but the greatest challenges and pleasures of my life have been my two sons, nearly thirty years apart. I'm incredibly proud of Ashley, who overcame enormous early problems with drugs and addiction to emerge as a soulful man with amazing musical talent that he obviously inherited from his family, particularly from my dad, and maybe a little from my grandpa Docky, who was happiest with a banjo on his knee. I am confident that Ashley will write a major score and great songs in the years ahead. He's also the best-looking young man

I've ever seen, far handsomer than me at my best or even the Adonis that Bill was. I think about the ultimate tragedy of my friends who lost children too young, Danielle Steel, Mel Simon, so many more, and I consider myself blessed to have Ashley.

My mother always said you never get over the loss of a child. Even though she went on ten years after Bill passed away in 1985, she was never the same without him. I guess I wasn't either. Our family, like the Beatles, had a wonderful, almost musical synergy that was destroyed with the loss of our great front man. What Teeny did have was the strength that Christian Science gave her to sustain her through much of her old age. David, who lived in Palm Beach, had the major task of caring for her there, and he did a heroic job keeping the pickiest woman in the world happy.

David and his wife would do their best to help Teeny get all dressed up and take her out to the best restaurants. He'd get an orchid for her to wear, and she looked like her old glam self. She'd start out charming enough, but then she'd start asking for vodka, and when David said no, she'd whisper to a waiter or a busboy to bring her a little nip. I'd take her to a charity ball, and she'd begin asking, "Who *are* these people?"

Every party had to be in her honor. If she couldn't be the star, she wanted out. Eventually, we'd have to take her home. Such were the beginnings of her Alzheimer's.

The one place where Teeny had been secure was Blytheville, and I'd often find her in Palm Beach sitting alone, looking upward, serenely talking to Big and Docky somewhere in the cosmos. Sometimes she would call me and plaintively say, "Can't we all just live together and be one big happy family?" That was always her dream, and alas, it was never to be. I stopped trying to explain that it was in L.A. and she was in Palm Beach. When Teeny slipped on the marble floor of her apartment, we weren't sure if it was the fault of the vodka, the high heels she never would give up, or the wet floor, which she blamed. David moved her to another apartment and got a Jamaican family to move in with her. This reminded her of the old Blytheville days, and she loved holding the caretakers' children.

I found my mother's decline terribly depressing. I was used to this vibrant, loquacious beauty who could conquer the world. My mother had conquered age for the longest time. When she was in her late seventies, I received an urgent phone call from the office of a prominent Beverly Hills

495

plastic surgeon. The secretary asked me to hold for a few moments; the good doctor wanted to talk to me about my mother. I hadn't heard anything about Mom planning to have any work done. Maybe he was just calling me to introduce himself as Teeny's fifth husband. When the doctor came on the line, he told me that my mom had visited him in anticipation of having some work done. I asked him what kind of work and he informed me that she wanted to have her breasts lifted. And he went on to express his deep concerns that at her age, it was a risky proposition and he would have to recommend against it.

I heard Mom's voice in the background protesting, "I don't need my son's permission."

The doctor continued, "Although most people regard plastic surgery as a simple outpatient event, it is nonetheless surgery and involves anesthesia. I wouldn't be concerned if I were dealing with a younger person, but frankly with your mother's age and frail condition, let me put it bluntly, there's a good possibility that she could die on the operating table . . ."

I could hear the phone being ripped out of the doctor's hand as Mom commandeered the phone. "Oh, for God's sake, you're bot" such ninnies. If I want to have my breasts lifted, I should be able to. It's my decision," she protested.

"But what about the danger, Mom? You could die!" I said.

After a brief pause to think about it, she answered, "Well, if that happens, I want you to promise me one thing . . . you'll bury me topless."

Mom was being conquered by Father Time. Still, she would have her hair and makeup done until the bitter end, and there was something angelic about her in her quiet state. When I got the news she had passed away, I didn't hesitate to bring her ashes back to the only home Teeny had ever had, Blytheville. We buried her ashes in the Hubbard family plot, next to Big and Docky and Bill.

My Hubbard cousins brought out Docky's ledgers and showed us how the good doctor wrote of his own exhaustion at healing the town, and how instructions, or rather entreaties, were left by Big to a younger Teeny not to squander the principal of her inherited estate. There were records of how Uncle George Hubbard had collected Docky's long-unpaid accounts and sent the money to high-living Teeny in Beverly Hills. Now that she was in heaven, I prayed she could have everything she ever wanted, maybe even Buddy Rogers.

When Teeny was still alive and I was in my early fifties, I met Kimberly Blackford, an eye-catching beauty in her twenties who was on my yacht when I was grand marshal of the Fort Lauderdale Winter Fest Boat Parade. Kimberly slipped a drink to Teeny, who had a way of recruiting rumrunners to break my no-more-alcohol blockade. We dated intermittently for several years. In 1999, when I was heading off to the Dominican Republic to pursue my cigar business, she asked to come along. I warned her about the primitive conditions, the banged-up old aircraft we'd fly, the bugs the size of B-52s. She proved a good sport and quickly learned everything she could about the tobacco business, from cutting and rolling the cigars to planting the tobacco seeds. Speaking of seeds, I didn't know it then, but one had already been planted that was to result in a most remarkable young man, my son George Thomas Hamilton (G.T. for short).

I wish I had been the marrying kind, but wasn't. However, I agreed to make sure my son would have all he needed and expressed my eagerness to spend time with him. I hadn't forgotten my brother Bill's last word about learning to love more. G.T. is a joy I would not have missed for the world; he and Ashley are the two bright stars in my life. Mom was right; there is no love like the love you feel for your children.

I've learned a lot from my mistakes. One lesson is no more big houses. They're albatrosses, and you must take care of so many people who are taking care of you. If you lose your wallet in one room, you spend days trying to find it. Maybe when I was younger I was suffering from a sort of plantation syndrome that afflicts Southerners who grow up in the shadow of Dixie's vanished grandeur. Today I travel light and thrive on the hotel rooms I adored as a kid following my father on the road. I've also rejected the notion of having to leave a fortune to my children. Every kid I've seen inherit a fortune has been somehow hobbled by it, either squandering it on terrible things or paralyzed from doing anything for fear of losing it. I'll set aside enough for a great education that will teach them how to survive and then let the boys find their own ways. Thus being of sound mind, I want my tombstone to read, 'I Spent It All."

Right now, I'm having the time of my life. I'm here to make people happy. When people describe a contestant on *Dancing with the*

Stars as "this year's George Hamilton," I'm totally flattered. I wasn't out to be the best dancer. I was out to be the best entertainer, and in that I think I'm still succeeding. The idea of entertaining fifteen million people in one night still boggles my pretelevision mind. My "you so old" Chinese fan notwithstanding, I feel as young as I ever have, I still love chasing women, being a scamp. I'll always be a scamp.

And I'll never stop being able to laugh at myself. When I was in *Chicago* and blew out my knee, I slipped incognito into the back of the theater to see my understudy do my part. Now, my understudy, a terrific young actor named Eric Jordan Young, who reminds me of my friend Sammy Davis, didn't look anything like me. He's five seven. And he's African American. Broadway doesn't feel compelled to do the doppelganger thing anymore. But that night in the theater they had forgotten not only to put a note in the *Playbill* but also to make an announcement from the stage that Eric was replacing me. At least one woman in the packed house behind me was nonplussed. "I knew he was *dark*," she noted to her seatmate, "but I didn't think he was that *small*."

Some philosopher wrote that life to a feel

ing man was a tragedy, but to a thinking man it was a comedy. I'll never stop laughing. Don't mind if I do.

ACKNOWLEDGMENTS

Time is a thief. Sometimes it steals a detail of your life and sometimes whole stories. To help me recover much of my life's lost loot, I enlisted the help of my brother David Hamilton. David is a writer in his own right. So I asked him to go beyond just reminiscing with me and put pen to paper and actually write down these early adventures. After all, who makes a better collaborator in your life story than someone who lived it with you? With the help and indulgence of author William Stadiem, and very creative Touchstone senior editor Patricia Grader, we have used much of David's writing to tell certain parts of my story (especially my early years). It is almost impossible to capture how thoroughly funny, crazy, and outrageous my life has been, but David has gone a long way in helping me reach for it. Our family always succeeded best as a team. Even if we are a couple of teammates short, Mom and Bill

503

would be glad to know the Hamiltons are still attempting great things.

PHOTOGRAPHY CREDITS

Photographs on text pages 6 and 503: Hamilton Family Collection

Insert Pages

Photos 1–12: Hamilton Family Collection
Photos 13–15: Alana Hamilton Stewart
                Collection
Photo 16: Elizabeth Treadwell Collection
Photos 17–18: Hamilton Family Collection